GLADSTONE AND PALMERSTON

VISCOUNT PALMERSTON, 1858

THE PALMERSTON PAPERS

GLADSTONE
AND PALMERSTON

being the Correspondence of
Lord Palmerston with Mr. Gladstone
1 8 5 1 — 1 8 6 5

Edited
with an Introduction and
Commentary

by
P HILIP G UEDALLA

BOOKS FOR LIBRARIES PRESS
FREEPORT, NEW YORK

First Published 1928

Reprinted 1971

INTERNATIONAL STANDARD BOOK NUMBER:

0-8369-5812-8

LIBRARY OF CONGRESS CATALOG CARD NUMBER:

73-157351

PRINTED IN THE UNITED STATES OF AMERICA

CONTENTS

ILLUSTRATIONS

8   ILLUSTRATIONS

INTRODUCTION TO
THE PALMERSTON PAPERS

The duties of biography, however infrequently performed, are easily defined. They are, if I am not mistaken, to produce a living record of men who were themselves once living. Other forms of commemoration may be preferred—the recumbent statue and its literary equivalent, the official Life, the simple obituary notice, the panegyric, or the lampoon. Each has its merits. At least one master-piece of English biographical writing was produced as an official Life ; the lapidary inscription has, at its best, a simple dignity ; and as for the posthumous lampoon, it enjoys increasing prestige in an unchivalrous age which appears to derive unlimited enjoy-ment from gay onslaughts upon the unprotected dead. But, what-ever else they may be, they are not biography.

Its duties are at once simpler and more exacting. As it is to be a record, it must conform to the highest standards of accuracy, a test that may be applied with cruel consequences to the sprightlier pro-ducts of our time no less than to the epitaph. For accuracy connotes research, a rigorous exploration of all printed or unprinted sources of information ; and a sardonic comment or so, founded upon light-hearted acceptance of a few secondary authorities, will scarcely satisfy this arduous branch of scholarship. But bare accuracy, though it provides an indispensable foundation, is not enough. No one could mistake the Annual Register *for history or the official file that contains a soldier's* état des services *for his military biography. For accuracy itself requires that biography should attain a high degree of animation. Of the two alternatives presented by the poet Gray, the " storied urn " may satisfy a group of sorrowing relations ; but the true biographer will surely aim at the " animated bust", since he is a portrait-sculptor, not a monumental mason. His duty, in the very cause of accuracy, is to reproduce a man and not a*

9

mummy. For if the record fails to live, it is untrue to its original. He, after all, was once alive ; and his biographer's first duty is to make him live again.

One of the strangest delusions with regard to historical writing is the prevalent belief that a dull page is necessarily accurate, as though tedium were in some mysterious way a testimony of truth. Rather, I think, the contrary. For no age was quite so dull as the standard work upon it ; and that consoling fact serves to convict it of inaccuracy as a faithful evocation of the past. The yawn, which is our customary tribute, is the best evidence that one more historian has failed in his duty. Those stationary facts, that stiff procession of dead men are not the past. That was a living, shifting world that once moved up and down, laughed, whispered, nodded, set to partners, bowed, and cast its shadows in the lost sunlight of forgotten afternoons ; and if the annalist has failed to catch its movement, he is no less guilty of inaccuracy than the cruder criminal of false dates and misquotations. Error, after all, may be dull as well as picturesque ; and it is no less misleading to undramatise a living event than to dramatise the undramatic. A bad photographer may lie about his subject as much as any caricaturist ; for it is no merit in a caricature to be dull, and what is a stiff portrait but a dull caricature ? But biography must make its portraits live, this side of falsehood. The dreary treatise and the gay lampoon are both equally at fault. Indeed, the more insidious form of error lurks in a tedious travesty of the past ; since we are all naturally on our guard against the satirist, but the heavy tread of erudition always lulls our suspicions. We all believe a bore. Yet the past was not (as some bores expect us to believe) a Morgue, where dead statesmen perpetually lie in state. For they were once alive ; and biography's concern is to re-enact their lives.

Since life is neither a card-index nor a protracted obituary notice, it demands a living record. How best to write it ? There are, I fear, no more convenient rules of thumb in this than in any other art. Failures proclaim themselves, and successes leap to the eye ; but few can say how either of them came to be so. One biography may be a noble storehouse of inexpugnable facts, but its central figure somehow fails to live ; in another the figure lives, but only at the expense of fact. Yet who can tell what magic formula will serve to combine scholarship with art in their exact and due proportions ? Perhaps " the golden rule is that there is no golden rule " (as Mr. Shaw proclaimed, oblivious for a moment of the various dogmas, social and dietetic, that own his allegiance). There may be none at all. But I would hazard one, almost too obvious for statement : the writer of biography must write it. That is to say, he must, after satisfying the cruel exigencies of exact scholarship, employ the literary art, a grim requirement for the happy multitude of executors, bereaved relatives, and statesmen in retirement, who disport themselves in this agreeable field of composition. A pot of paste, some scissors, and a few mild regrets are an inadequate equipment for the biographer : he also needs a pen.

Acknowledging the fact (and richly), our own age is rather naively certain that it holds the secret of biographical writing. It loves to speak, with a faint scorn for past achievements, of biographies by ' moderns ' and ' in the modern manner ' ; and I have sometimes wondered what they are. In other literary spheres its contribution is evident to a fault. The smoking ruins of the art of poetry attest its glorious activity ; while the divagations of the novel in the direction of the consulting room (and even, in livelier instances, of the operating theatre and the County Asylum) proclaim its scientific training. But science, which has gripped history by the throat, has refrained from any similar attempt upon biography. For the late Lord Acton bequeathed no formula for our guidance in this form of composition, and that heavy hand has not yet fallen in arrest on the biographer's guilty shoulder. Indeed, the best contemporary work, if it has a fault, is perhaps a shade unscientific. Its masters, whose deftness compels our admiration, rarely admit the necessity for more than a hasty glance at the best-known published authorities upon their subject before embarking, for our pleasure, upon their gay, inimitable comments. Their documentary foundation is often absurdly slight ; and one may well fear for the future of edifices, however graceful, reared upon such slight foundations, when the harsh winds of scholarship begin to blow. It is in vain to answer that our generation has reclaimed the realm of biography for literature. For the Muse was scarcely absent when Macaulay wrote the biographical essay or Morley and Rosebery the more extended Life.

What is, then, ' the modern manner ' ? One may surmise more hopefully that it consists in a studied irreverence. Since one gifted ironist turned a mildly enquiring eye upon the Victorians, a host of writers on both sides of the Atlantic (and even beyond the English Channel and the North Sea) have regarded their ancestors with varying degrees of disrespect—some with a courteous arching of the eyebrows, others with an impertinent stare, with rudely pointed fingers, and even with ribald exclamations. But this can scarcely rank as the distinctively ' modern ' contribution to biography, since irony was not invented with the Armistice. Even our fathers did not write of their predecessors with uniform respect. After all, most of the false judgments of the Nineteenth Century proceed immediately from a fatuous desire to put the Eighteenth Century in its place. So even our own all-seeing Twentieth may be in error : at any rate, the Twenty-first will think so. Is it not dreadfully significant that Thackeray's dismissal of the Georges was dismissed a few decades later by Mr. Max Beerbohm with the comment that its style was " a trifle 1860 " in prose that is even now a trifle 1894 ? For the conscious superiority of the next generation may often yield amusing reading ; but it is rarely readable for more than twenty years. Then time moves on again ; and to the succeeding generation the ironist himself becomes ridiculous. The priest of such a cult must hold his dignity by an uncertain tenure ; he is indeed

> *The priest who slew the slayer,*
> *And shall himself be slain.*

Such suicidal irony may be (perhaps it is) the ' modern ' mode. If so, its contributions to biography can scarcely hope to be enduring. For, however exquisitely 1928 to us, we may be sure that one day they will be preposterously 1928 to others.

One must look elsewhere to find the ' modern ' contribution ; and (to this enquiring eye) it seems to consist of something far simpler. For it resides, I think, in the plain fact that biographers—and, still

*more undeniably, their readers—have at last become convinced of
the virtues of brevity. Not that these passed wholly unrecognised in
the Nineteenth Century, when the ground was fairly strewn with*
English Statesmen *or* Men of Letters *or* Queen's Prime
Ministers, *each happily disposed of in one slender volume. Morley
composed a* Burke *or two, Lord Rosebery a* Pitt, *and Froude a*
Beaconsfield, *that could compare for brevity and brilliance with
the most* staccato *roars of our young lions. The lonely masterpiece
of brief biography—Rosebery's* Lord Randolph Churchill—
*was less than two hundred pages long. But these performances were
somehow treated as exceptions, as sideshows in the great exhibition
of biography. They were usually offered with an almost apologetic
air in series, as though proximity to one another would give the
little fellows confidence. But the main attractions of the circus were
of a more heroic mould. For public taste was dominated by what
was termed 'full-length biography'; and orthodox biographical
practice seemed always to require a tribute of at least two volumes.
This sense of fitness was steadily gratified by an interminable procession of pair-horse funeral coaches, once reviewed by Lord Oxford,
himself a predestined victim, in a positive* cri du cœur—*"Gladstone, in three volumes; Beaconsfield, in six volumes; Lord Granville, in two volumes; the Duke of Devonshire, in two volumes;
Lord Clarendon, in two volumes; Lord Salisbury, in two, with the
promise of at least two more; the Duke of Argyll, in two volumes;
the Marquess of Ripon, in two volumes; Sir Charles Dilke, in two
volumes; Lord Lytton, in two volumes. . . ." Memorial piety
seemed to exact two volumes, as though there was some mystic connection between a perfect portrait and the figure '2'; and the indignant* manes *of Victorian statesmen knew no repose until the
double ritual was complete. There are still quarters where this
strange obituary mood prevails, where pious hands perform the
customary sacrifice of two (and even three) volumes. But the times
grow slightly impatient. Fiction has steadily contracted; epic gives
place to lyric verse; and even in biography faint stirrings herald a
revolution. For our own age has seen a score of Lives completed in a
single volume without endangering the adequacy of the record. And*

what is more, Lives in one volume have found readers, where the more dignified equipage of the pair-horse era found little more than a respectful raising of the hat. For there is, I think, a growing conviction that a man's true memorial is a book in which the world will read about him rather than an impressive, but unread, biography. Even executors must see that it is better, for the mere purpose of securing a favourable verdict from posterity, to be John Bright, recorded in four hundred pages, than to stagger to that chilly bar oppressed by poor Disraeli's burden of three thousand. Besides, the gain to biography itself is immeasurable, as a more shapely form of record supersedes the old haphazard cairns of miscellaneous information. A higher standard of craftsmanship prevails at once, since brevity connotes selection and arrangement. For biography has ceased to be a purely manual process, in which the contents of thirteen deed-boxes are somehow spilt into three volumes, and it becomes (as it need never have ceased to be) an ingenious blend of scholarship and literary skill.

That blend may be the ' modern ' contribution. But if the record is to be complete, the process needs to be carried a stage further. The record itself can and, I think, almost invariably should be rendered in a single volume. For there is hardly a career in human history whose facts, if mastered, cannot be stated within the limits of five hundred pages. But an active life leaves more behind than its mere facts. There is, in any given case, a vast accumulation of papers. Drawers overflow with letters ; faded tapes enclose family transactions, full of character or the indefinable flavour of a period ; despatch boxes yawn with State papers ; there may be diaries ; there will assuredly be correspondence ; and the whole detritus rolled down by a long stream of life lies waiting to be read. And much of it deserves a reading. This letter may record an isolated contact with some other figure of eminence ; that memorandum may throw light upon a diplomatic crisis of a generation later. How, then, is the biographer to accommodate this bulky cargo on board his exiguous craft ? The prevailing method of dealing with these vast deposits has been to cram them somehow into the Life. Zealous biographers, unwilling to forgo a telling letter or a vivid sidelight, insert them bodily in their suffering text. Thus proportion vanishes when one year passes in half a page, while the next (owing to some happy cache of correspondence) may fill ten pages. All balance is destroyed by these immense insertions in the labouring vessel, and one is left with an uneasy feeling that there should be a Plimsoll Line for biographers as well as for merchant seamen. For an overloaded hold may sink the ship. Even the record, raison d'être *of the whole voyage, is endangered when the master takes in more cargo than his ship can carry ; and biographers forget their foremost duty when the flow of narrative is reduced to a disheartened trickle round the bases of vast, disordered blocks of raw material.*

Half the weakness of ' full-length biography ' comes, I believe, from this misguided effort to incorporate a vast legacy of documents in the Life. For it is the attempt to give us a ' Life and Letters ' that is generally responsible for the submergence of the Life. Such a course may be possible in the case of comparatively uneventful lives or for careers which involved only a moderate amount of paper ; Sir Edmund Gosse succeeded brilliantly with Swinburne, Stanley with Dr. Arnold, and Sir George Trevelyan with Macaulay. But the method applicable (and applied by three biographers of rare gifts) to a poet, a schoolmaster with an active life of fifteen years, and a man of letters with a distinctly secondary career in politics may not be of a universal application. Least of all, to public men of the first eminence. For the same method followed with Disraeli gave us his tragic funeral procession of six lumbering pantechnicons, barely redeemed from undeserved oblivion by the incongruous spectacle of a sprightly Frenchman bringing up the rear in a neat gig ; the Victorian statesmen of Lord Oxford's litany each vanish under two volumes ; and Gladstone himself, though entrusted to a biographer of genius, is half submerged in a veritable cataract of documents. (How much more plainly the two great duellists of Victorian politics would live for us, had Morley and Monypenny each been content to paint a portrait in a single volume.) Can one emerge from any study of English biographical writing without a conviction, rooted almost to the point of dogma, that a single volume provides the ideal form of record ?

The single volume, though, is not quite enough ; since it still leaves unsolved the problem of a statesman's papers, of that vast legacy of documents which often, I have said, deserves a reading. For these, I think, there is a method, though it has scarcely found general acceptance. Having recorded his subject in a single volume, let the biographer put out his papers in extenso *; and if they run to twenty volumes, we shall not complain, since the record itself is not encumbered with this wealth of documentation. It is conceded that biography must be a distillation ; but we are all entitled to a sight of the materials from which the essence was distilled. Besides, they have a high intrinsic value quite apart from any service which they may perform by enabling us to check the biography itself. There is obviously much to entertain the student of history and the* amateur *of politics in the despatch boxes of any statesman. Even the uninstructed reader, attracted to the site by the shapely monument reared in a single volume, may desire a closer knowledge of its subject ; and that is best obtained from a perusal of his papers. Studied in this fuller form, transactions which the Life hurried across its screen will be re-enacted in slow motion ; and the familiar face is seen magnified a hundred-fold. For such documents as these may bring before us the ' close-ups ' of history.*

That method has been deliberately adopted in the case of Palmerston. His biographer has already made a record in one volume ; and it is his present purpose to supplement it with the publication of the Palmerston Papers. The mass of documents that must survive from such a career is evident, and full use has been made of them in the preparation of the Life. But it remains to publish a selection from the actual papers ; and it can scarcely be doubted that the enterprise is justified by their importance. " The life of Palmerston ", as I have already written, " was the life of England and, to a large extent, of Europe in the last sixteen years of the Eighteenth and the first sixty-five of the Nineteenth Centuries." An official career running from Wagram to the eve of Sadowa and a social life that stretched from Almack's to the widowhood of Queen Victoria drives like a mine-shaft through the strata of history ; and as one drops down through its decades, a dozen epochs become visible from new angles. The Napoleonic War seen from the War Office ; the coming of Reform viewed by a half-hearted Tory ; the age of Metternich observed by his leading adversary ; the advent of Bismarck, of Cavour, of Mr. Gladstone ; the age of post-horses ; the age of steam ; Europe in 1830, in 1848, in 1860, in . . . The long catalogue is almost endless ; and every year of it was filled with Palmerston, with busy politics, with entertaining or significant contacts. His State papers are, perhaps, sufficiently available to students in official publications and at the Record Office. But these may be supplemented with an unpublished wealth of private letters ; and there is always apt to be more information in a private note than in a dozen despatches.

For these reasons I propose to publish the Palmerston Papers, inaugurated by the present volume. They will be found, I hope, to make a contribution to national and international history as well as to the biography of a great figure and his contemporaries. The series, when complete, may contain the letters of Lord Melbourne to his brother-in-law and Foreign Secretary, in which that slightly enigmatic Prime Minister gave almost daily guidance to a restive colleague ; Lord Palmerston's own letters to Lord Clarendon in which, Prime Minister himself, he directed military operations and foreign policy through the Crimean War, the Congress of Paris, and the years that followed ; and, perhaps, the fascinating series of his lady's letters to her brother.

The present instalment contains the letters exchanged over a period of fourteen years between Lord Palmerston and Mr. Gladstone. Used sparingly by their biographers (Morley's scattered extracts fill less than a dozen pages), the series is almost wholly unpublished. In a general sense, its interest resides in one unusual feature. Our shelves abound in the correspondences of this or that eminent man with a minor personage—Disraeli's with his sister, Wellington's with Mr. Raikes—but how few exchanges are preserved between persons of equal eminence. And, in the present case, what persons. For Palmerston was never more Palmerston than when he wrote to Mr. Gladstone. Managing an

BP

awkward colleague, that wary, skilful, positive old man reveals himself in full. Genial in controversy, eloquent on national defence and the iniquity of land taxation, blandly contemptuous of Radical clap-trap, quite irresistible when Mr. Gladstone's conscience veered uneasily towards resignation, full of Napoleonic memories, and steering at eighty-one by the unchanging star of British interests— here is the whole of Palmerston, set artlessly on paper in his daily spell of letter-writing. And Mr. Gladstone? Mr. Gladstone is there as well. Not, perhaps, his deeper nature; since he considered, very properly, that his deeper nature was not quite suitable for exhibition to Lord Palmerston. That aged eye, one fears, would have been cocked in slightly irreverent enquiry at the Tractarian ardours of his colleague. But the more public Mr. Gladstone, the Gladstone of politics, is almost all there. It was a turning-point—one of the two or three—of his career. For the Liberal in him was just fluttering free from the discreeter wrappings of his Peelite chrysalis. His passion, at the moment, was for public finance; and I know of no better manual for intending Chancellors of the Exchequer than the full letters to his leader which precede and expound each Budget of the classical Gladstonian series. Not that finance was his sole topic. For one may catch significant echoes of his long journey towards democracy and of that sharp distaste for naval armaments, which was to prove fatal to him when, thirty years away, his last Cabinet gently discarded him. Every page breathes Mr. Gladstone—the conscious virtue (learned from Sir Robert) of financial rectitude; the deep conviction, followed by the clash on a point of policy; the reasoned argument maintained with an unyielding front; and then the hint, ever so slightly guarded, of resignation. Not his, perhaps, the dashing onslaught of his aged leader. For Palmerston belongs, in essence, to the cavalry of politics, and Mr. Gladstone to the infantry.

But the correspondence has a deeper interest than its mere contribution to the biography of two important and intriguing figures. For the major portion of the series dates from Lord Palmerston's second Administration, of which Mr. Gladstone was the leading member. No less than two hundred and fifty of these letters form the daily exchange of correspondence between a Prime Minister and his Chancellor of the Exchequer ; and I know of no collection in which the inner life of a Cabinet is more fully exhibited or the realities of government seen more plainly in operation. Their topics, too, are of strange interest to modern readers. The principles of sound finance expounded by a master, the race of naval armaments (this time with France) debated between the sternest of economists and the soundest of Blue Water Britons—here are two conversations of sixty years ago, which we need scarcely blush to overhear. Nor is it void of interest to find the nationalisation of railways discussed between these ancients in the year 1864 without the slightest touch of panic or undue surprise. Lighter entertainment abounds in the early history of the Albert Memorial, and the vain struggle of Gilbert Scott with Mr. Gladstone's departmental scruples about supplying guns to be melted down for bronze. And the historian will find fresh material upon the British attitude to the American Civil War, with Palmerston obviously relieved at the settlement of the Trent case and Gladstone eager for peaceful intervention in '62 and positively tracing the frontier that was to run between the two Republics of North and South with a mysteriously unnamed Southern gentleman.

If half the fascination of history resides in the opportunity to catch again the tone of voices long silent, I know of few corners where this agreeable form of eavesdropping may be more conveniently practised. And how distinct the voices are—the cheerful note of Palmerston countering his argumentative colleague with a brisk answer, Gladstone's sedate replies, and under all the talk the steady pulse of the mid-Nineteenth Century.

PHILIP GUEDALLA.

1928.

COMMENTARY

Their paths met quite late in life. The intersecting avenues of politics brought them together in middle age ; and their involuntary alliance continued, not without strain, until death ended it. Yet two such opposites were scarcely to be found in the whole garden of English public life. Their starting-points were far apart. One had commenced his journey among the urns and alleys of the Eighteenth Century, passed the fantastic summer-houses of the Regency and now, a brisk pedestrian, pursued his cheerful way across an unfamiliar landscape. But the other, a more thoughtful figure, starting a quarter of a century later in humbler regions where a stream served to turn machinery rather than to make decorous perspectives, had come by sober paths and still Oxonian waters.

They met, though. A chance agreement on a minor question was followed by irregular co-operation. The elder of the two, in momentary isolation, turned to the rather isolated group, to which the younger man belonged. A Coalition brought them into the same Cabinet, and for a year or two they subsisted on the stray contacts of Cabinet colleagues. Drifting apart, they were quite separated for a time until they came together once more, this time for six years of close and formal partnership. The partners were not always easy. For the Nineteenth Century was frequently at issue with the Eighteenth, Hawarden with Broadlands. Prime Ministers of seventy-five must often check the youthful impulses of Chancellors of the Exchequer of fifty ; and Oxford, it may be surmised, was rarely at ease with Almack's. Yet they worked on, as strange a pair as the winds and waves of politics have ever brought together.

23

I

The older man was Palmerston. Older, that is, as years are reckoned, by twenty-five ; and a quarter of a century may often separate two men quite as effectually as an ocean. But older, in the more significant arithmetic by which one age is parted from another, by a whole century. For his junior was born in the full-throated dawn of the Nineteenth Century. What a presage it was to be born in 1809. The Queen was still unborn ; but Darwin and Alfred Tennyson started on their course that year. Choirs invisible chanted the opening bars of a fresh cantata ; and the world was warned for a new birth of time. There was no knowing what 1809 might lead to.

But if it was significant of Mr. Gladstone to be born in 1809, to be born in Liverpool was quite conclusive. It is impossible to think of any figure of the Eighteenth Century being born in Liverpool ; for that age was far too urbane to recruit its characters from such a source. Cathedral towns, the countryside, London, the universities, even (in rare and not wholly satisfactory instances) Scotland—all had been drawn upon to fill the eighteenth-century stage. But scarcely Liverpool. That was an altogether novel source of supply. An infant born in Liverpool was plainly called to play its part in a new world. For the event might form a precedent ; and, if followed, there was no knowing what Liverpool might lead to.

So Liverpool and 1809, in powerful conjunction, marked the nativity of Mr. Gladstone. But Palmerston was born a century away. The chairmen lounged outside his father's house in Park Street, Westminster ; and in the failing light of October, 1784, London lay all around it—Charles Fox's, Sir Joshua's, Dr. Johnson's London, where Garrick played and Mr. Walpole wrote his letters. His enshrinement in the age was something more than a mere accident of chronology.

Palm.
463

For the Palmerstons lived at the very heart of the Eighteenth Century. They breathed its thin, exhilarating air, revolving elegantly in a modish world of polite accomplish- **Palm.** ments. Had not a Colonel John Burgoyne composed a verse **22** or two in honour of the Viscount's first marriage ? Did not his bride's untimely grave wear a stanza of his own composition ? He rhymed at Bath, sat to Sir Joshua, and walked with Mr. Wilkes. His talk buzzed in the ears of Mr. **Palm.** Walpole ; his travels were approved by Mr. Gibbon ; and he **25** stood by one evening to watch them tease the little Burney about an *anonyma* called *Evelina*. Surely the son of such a father was a child of the Eighteenth Century itself.

Indeed, he seemed to be. The very year that he was born **Palm.** the awful sponsorship of Samuel Johnson had imposed his **27** father on The Club. The age informed his birthplace too. For he was born in a new house beside the grille of Queen Square, where sceptred Anne presided and, decorously housed, Westminster electors shook hands over the imperfect durability of young Mr. Pitt's " mince-pie administration ". The same age informed his childhood, when he was brought down—" a fine, eager, lively, good-humoured boy "—to his mother's dressing-room and shown off to callers, or when Charles Fox and Sheridan dined downstairs, or Mrs. Crewe, heroine and reigning toast of the Whig buff and blue, invaded them and carried his parents off to a water-party. For the Eighteenth Century grinned down at him in stone from every door in Queen Square ; it lurked among the artificial mountains of their garden at Sheen ; and where else could it reside than behind the solemn porticoes of Broadlands ? Each of his homes was full of it. So were his holidays when, every refinement of the age presiding, they posted all the way to Italy and studied the antique. The age enfolded him ; and when he climbed the hill to Harrow, Harrow (it may be presumed) was not more than usual in advance of its age. So Harry Temple, as he grew, was framed in his Eighteenth Century.

Not that he drank more deeply at its springs than any of his fellows. For, once born, it was not easy to escape that rich initiation. It waited for its children in every turn of thought, of speech, of decoration ; and they bore the mark of it—more plainly, indeed, than the children of almost any other age. The mould was quite complete ; and it has left the products that emerged from it quite unmistakable. For one may sometimes misdate a Puritan by a century or so ; romantics are often interchangeable between Victoria and Elizabeth ; but eighteenth-century work ? One never errs with that. For that has a finish that excludes all possibility of error. It was so final, too. No age, I think, since that of Rome was ever half so final. (Small wonder, then, that Mr. Gibbon envied the Antonines, one age of perfect certainty gazing at another with respect across the intervening seas of doubt.) Surely Providence had always intended chairs to be made exactly so, spoons to be shaped thus, pictures painted precisely as Sir Joshua said, books written on Dr. Johnson's principles, and fugues composed as the polite world knew that a fugue should run. Mankind appeared to have reached a sort of equilibrium. That is, the better sort of mankind, which owned a small sufficiency of land and a town house in France or England. The human race, of course, contained uncharted multitudes besides. There were all the crowds that filled the streets, the clods that laboured in the fields, the lazy mobs of Spain and Italy, to say nothing of the un- numbered serfs of Muscovy, the uncouth Germans, and the opinionated Americans far below the western horizon. But the polite world, it was well known, lay within a few days' drive of Paris and London ; and within that exquisitely ordered plot the Eighteenth Century reigned. The reign was almost universal—over art, philosophy, religion, letters, manners, domestic comforts, and the proper conduct of an ode. It was at once a style, a code of manners, and a point of view. And to right-minded persons there seemed to be no more reason why the reign should ever end than that of

George III ; or if it did, it would, at most, be followed by
another exactly like it. For it would always be the Eighteenth Century.

Palmerston was born into that stationary world and pro-
gressed in it with moderate decorum. Harrow taught him a
classical quotation or so, recognised to form an indispensable equipment for public life. From Edinburgh he im- Palm.
bibed the more nutritious element of Adam Smith's political 43
economy imparted (with philosophical additions) by Professor Dugald Stewart. And at Cambridge, a young Viscount now, he learned with a delicious thrill the proximity
of great affairs. For great affairs lay tolerably near to any
Viscount of nineteen ; and he could awe his sisters with
knowing information about one of Fox's intimates and Mr. Palm.
Canning's foolishness and the right way to foil the egre- 46
gious Buonaparte in his tents at Boulogne. His tutor favour-
ing the notion, he even indulged in an electoral flutter, Palm.
fighting the University seat at Cambridge left vacant by the 51
death of Mr. Pitt. But Parliament denied her youthful suitor
and continued to reject his addresses, until a kindly pro-
prietor returned him for a rotten borough. He was a place-
man too ; for a thoughtful guardian prevailed upon a Palm.
nobleman of his acquaintance to accommodate his ward 53
with a seat at the Board of Admiralty. So, member for
a town with no electors and functionary with no work, he
entered public life ; and what entry could well have been
more eighteenth-century ?

No less of its age, his actual initiation in public affairs
breathed the very air of Frederic and Catherine. For his Palm.
instructor was that old Lord Malmesbury who, redolent of 48
ancient missions to Potsdam and St. Petersburgh, abounded
now in diplomatic wisdom for the guidance of Pitt and
Dundas and was not averse to instructing a young ward at
Park Place in the finesse by which a vanished generation
had maintained the poised elegance of the Balance of
Power. Formed by Malmesbury and Adam Smith, Lord

Palmerston approached the age of office. For he was twenty-
Palm. five, a Harrovian, and reputably connected. So Mr. Spencer
59 Perceval asked him to be his Chancellor of the Exchequer.
But Palmerston, with a rare modesty, declined, preferring
to be his Secretary at War instead. There was a war on hand
Palm. of course. But the humbler office struck him as " one better
60 suited to a beginner ". He declined the Cabinet as well. For
the young gentleman was strangely aware of his limitations.
But the War Office drew him ; and one autumn day in 1809
he climbed the staircase at the Horse Guards.
Glad.   That winter a less favoured infant was born at Liverpool.
I. 7 What influences brooded above 62 Rodney Street it is less
easy to enquire. But that they were not the grinning masks of
Westminster or the nymphs and fauns of Broadlands or
Sheen's suburban dryads is all too evident. No babble of
the town came here, no Sheridan appeared to dine, no Fox,
no Mrs. Crewe ; but other corn-merchants with a sober
appetite for conversation with John Gladstone on the
price of best Danzig, slightly evangelical neighbours, and
(on several unforgettable occasions) Mr. Canning. The
eighteenth-century mould was broken now. Here, plainly,
was an avenue that led into a new age ; and while Palmerston was busy at Almack's or the War Office, the young
novice walked sedately down it. Liverpool handed him to
Eton, Eton to Christ Church ; and the majestic processes of
English education formed him while Lord Palmerston,
modish and industrious by turns, pursued his cheerful
way.

    Their paths, so widely separated at their starting-points,
diverged still further ; and there seemed no reason why they
should ever meet. One had been sent to Harrow ; the other
was despatched to Eton. One went to Cambridge ; so, by a
natural inference, the other went to Oxford. True, both of
them were Tories ; and at the start there was even a faint
convergence in the direction of their Toryism. For Mr. Canning's was the slightly erratic star of both their compasses.

Was he not the divinity of Liverpool ? Had not an infant
Gladstone at the age of two been taken down into the Glad.
dining-room and mounted on a chair to pronounce the very I. 10
first and by far the shortest of all his speeches (consisting of
the three words " Ladies and gentlemen ") in Mr. Canning's honour ? The brisk young Viscount at the War Office
was turning Canningite as well. For his views on Irish toler- Palm.
ation, though his own, were shared by Mr. Canning ; and 111
when the Canningite banner passed to the leaner hand of
Huskisson, Palmerston found a welcome echo of the fiscal Palm.
opinions once learnt at Edinburgh from Dugald Stewart.   117
   But they never met as Canningites. For while Mr. Canning waxed and waned, the small Etonian was parsing Glad.
Juvenal and rowing with Arthur Hallam ; and in the un- I. 40
easy summer of 1828, when the Duke dismissed them and Palm.
the little group dissolved, the youth from Liverpool was 125
reading hard for Oxford. Oxford transformed him ; for he
grew up to be Oxford, as someone said, on the surface, but Glad.
Liverpool below. That was the queer blend of North and I. 192
South in Gladstone, which once led a critic to describe him Glad.
as an ardent Italian in the custody of a Scotsman. But Pal- I. 18
merston, disdaining such extremes, was always English—
the poised English of the Midlands. Did not the Temples
come from Warwickshire ? His qualities were soberly
applied to administering the army, settling War Office
claims, moving his Estimates, and learning foreign affairs
from information thoughtfully supplied by Madame Lieven
through their pretty friend Emily Cowper, whilst a dark
schoolboy construed the classics or surveyed the world from
Oxford. Oxford inclined him to the Church ; and their Glad.
diverging paths diverged still further. For Palmerston was I. 81
at no moment inclined to holy orders. And even in politics
their minds parted company, since the elder Canningite
veered towards Reform, while the sterner undergraduate
was steadfast in the ancient faith and alarmed the Union
with a terrific homily three-quarters of an hour long on the

Glad. iniquities of Grey and his Whig colleagues. But Palmerston,
I. 74 alas ! was now a Whig.

Their two paths quite separated now. When the dark
young Tory won his first election in 1833, he saw across the
House of Commons a trim Foreign Secretary of forty-eight,
heard the cheerful renegade expound the dreary complications of the Belgian question from a Whig Treasury Bench,
Palm. and shared the indignation of Mr. Mackworth Praed against
169 the Canningite, who once

> could sit
> By Londonderry's side,
> And laugh with Peel at Canning's wit,
> And hint to Hume he lied ;
> Henceforth I run a different race,
> Another soil I plough,
> And though I still have pay and place,
> I'm not a Tory now.

Glad. But Mr. Gladstone was a Tory. His Toryism was quite un-
I. 104 doubted. Even his maiden speech displayed the dangers of
a too precipitate liberation of West Indian slaves. Lord
Palm. Palmerston might " wish that the word ' Protection ' was
178 erased from every commercial dictionary ", or ask brightly
" what could be so absurd as to require a man to subscribe
Palm. to the thirty-nine articles before you will allow him to cure
185 you of a fever ". But young Mr. Gladstone was stout for the
Corn Laws, coercion in Ireland, and the maintenance of
religious tests in Parliament and universities. Small wonder,
then, that when the Tories came in, Sir Robert kept a trifle
for his promising young friend and proposed him for a
Lordship of the Treasury, speedily exchanged for the better
post of Under-secretary for the Colonies. Peel won him. For
Glad. the unbending man had said, " Well, God bless you,
I. 122 wherever you are ". He had expected something colder ;
and Peel replaced Canning as the divinity of his political
worship. That year his busy conscience had its first uneasy

contact with the harsh syllogisms of office. For there was a
scheme in the pigeon-holes of the Colonial Department to
provide West Indian negroes with religious instruction ;
and the devoted Churchman was tormented by a fear that
it might prove to be the wrong variety. But the supreme
sacrifice of resignation was not required of him. For the
Whigs were too quick for them, and they were all out
again in 1835.

The two streams resumed their accustomed courses—
Gladstone's in Opposition and Palmerston's in the agreeable turmoil of the Foreign Office. He was past fifty now,
and Peel's young recruit was twenty-six and ageing fast.
For while Palmerston's life was divided between despatches
and Lady Cowper, Gladstone was deep in the society of
Dr. Pusey, Wordsworth, Henry Hallam, Rogers, Peel, and
the most improving company that life could offer in the
last years of William IV. Even Carlyle, buried deep in
Chelsea, heard of " a certain W. Gladstone, an Oxford
crack scholar, tory M.P., and devout churchman of great
talent and hope ", slightly defaced by " Coleridge shovel
hattism ". He saw the Duke and liked him, heard Chalmers
preach and disapproved, studied the Church and wrote a
book about it. The years—the early, troubled years when
Queen Victoria was young and Melbourne shrugged ·an
indulgent shoulder at the spirit of the age—were gliding by.
Lord Palmerston was drafting stiff despatches, thinking of
marriage, marrying his Emily, honeymooning at Broadlands, and, back in London for the first of Lady Palmerston's
parties, drafted indomitably on until the Whigs went out
again in '41. But while Palmerston enjoyed his leisure (and
Punch portrayed him as " Cupid out of Place "), Gladstone
at thirty-three was deep in melancholy reflections—" I
now approach the *mezzo del cammin* ; my years glide
away ". (That was a sentiment of which Palmerston was
never capable, even at eighty.) " It is time to look forward
to the close, and I do look forward. My life . . . has two

Glad.
I. 125

Glad.
I. 176

Palm.
242
Glad.
I. 182

prospective objects, for which I hope the performance of my present public duties may, if not qualify, yet extrinsically enable me. One, the adjustment of certain relations of the church to the state. . . . The second is, unfolding the catholic system within her to some establishment of machinery looking both towards the higher life, and towards the external warfare against ignorance and depravity." How could they ever meet ?

Palm.   Once, indeed, in 1840 they met in debate, when Mr.
220 Gladstone expended all his moral indignation on the China war, and Palmerston with unruffled blandness " put it to any man opposite whether he could say with a grave face that he honestly believed the motive of the Chinese Government to have been the promotion of the growth of moral habits ". But Mr. Gladstone rarely experienced difficulty, now or hereafter, in voicing his opinions with a grave face. His growth continued. With the Tories back in office, he
Glad. was Peel's Vice-President of the Board of Trade, " set " (as
I. 244 he ruefully complained) " to govern packages ". But packages, under the stern impulsion of Mr. Cobden and the Anti-Corn Law League, were rapidly becoming the main
Glad. concern of English politics. Gladstone had conjectured
I. 239 rightly that " Cobden will be a worrying man on corn " ; and corn worried older heads than the Vice-President of the Board of Trade. But whilst his leaders fought a slow rearguard action with their fiscal doubts, his mental processes
Glad. were surer ; and by the end of 1841 he was " far gone " in
I. 250 the Cobdenite direction—as far, indeed, as Palmerston, who had denounced Protection for ten years. But a coincidence of fiscal views made no bridge yet between Whig and Tory Free Trader. For other matters kept them apart. Foreign affairs were now entrusted to the gentler grasp of
Palm. Aberdeen ; and Palmerston was rarely tender with his mild
242 successor, " thinks Lord Ashburton a rascal, Sir R. P. ditto :
Palm. Lord Aberdeen ditto : ditto : " and denounced the pacific
247 beauties of the American treaty as " the Ashburton

capitulation." But Gladstone viewed Lord Aberdeen with positive devotion. Besides, he soon became his colleague in the Cabinet, when Peel raised the promising apprentice to be President of the Board of Trade. Their embarrassments continued, as ministers balanced precariously between their party allegiance to Protection and the growing weight of their Free Trade opinions. Gladstone's ingenuity of statement was never more severely tried : one naughty hearer said that his arguments were all in favour of Free Trade, but his parentheses for Protection. The break came at last, when the driving rain of 1845 destroyed the Irish crop and, with it, all that remained of Peel's fiscal orthodoxy. But before it came, Gladstone was released from his official agonies. His conscience, stirred by an increase of the public grant for Catholic education in Ireland, came to the rescue ; and he resigned upon Maynooth before Peel split his party, leaving the world a little puzzled and Disraeli comfortably certain that he had ended his career. But he was still a faithful Tory ; and before the year was out, Peel reconstructed a ministry to repeal the Corn Laws and brought back Gladstone as Colonial Secretary.

    He was a Peelite now ; and when the hunt was over in the " sad, fierce session " of 1846 and the Tory squires had driven their own faithless leaders out of office, he sat on the front Opposition bench with Peel and Graham (in embarrassing proximity to the triumphant mutineers, Disraeli and Lord George Bentinck), ready to disapprove of anything Whig ministers might do. It was a strange fate. For Peel's ex-ministers were a quarterdeck without a crew, a little staff of generals that deserved high command more obviously than any other group in politics and were left almost without a single follower. Liverpool was quite submerged in Oxford now. Indeed, in 1847 he was elected for the University itself and less inclined than ever to become a Whig. Palmerston was back at the Foreign Office, a cheerful contrast to the " irreparable losses " mourned by the royal pair

Glad. I. 264

Glad. I. 272-4

Glad. I. 279

Palm. 265

C P

Palm. at Windsor. Aberdeen's half-hearted sketch of an *Entente*
273 *Cordiale* vanished in the *imbroglio* of the Spanish-Marriages ;
Palm. the policy, which Palmerston had once described as
244 putting " our foreign affairs . . . upon a sliding scale, as well
as the corn duties ", was only heard in Opposition ; and
Aberdeen's faint outcries in the House of Lords were cheer-
Palm. fully dismissed as " antiquated imbecility ". So it was
295 hardly to be expected that the favourite disciple of Lord
Aberdeen and Peel would be drawn to Palmerston.

Indeed, he was not. What had the demure Oxonian of
forty in common with the expansive minister of sixty-five ?
Both were industrious ; Palmerston's alarming tale of 29,000
despatches for the year 1848 compares favourably with
Gladstone's customary fourteen hours a day when in office.
But how different were the fruits of their industry. For
while Palmerston loved (like Carteret) to "knock the heads
of the Kings of Europe together and jumble out something
that might be of service to this country ", Gladstone was
busy with a tariff or the nice poise of Church and State. One
pen was all point, the other all reservations ; one loved to
qualify a statement, the other emphatically did not ; and
what livelier contrast can be imagined than a Palmerston
despatch beside a length of Gladstonian dialectic ? Even
the older man's consummate skill of fence failed to command the junior's admiration, though in after years he paid
a belated (and, perhaps, a slightly envious) compliment
to his " happy faculty of making his words exactly fit
Talks. his meaning ". But even that was praise of the village
50 quarterstaff conferred by a master of the rapier ; and the
Palm. gay, slashing speeches " full of sarcasm, jokes. and clap-
293 traps, the whole eminently successful ", which roused the
bile of Mr. Greville, were not to Mr. Gladstone's taste. His
broader qualities—the sober skill which brought Europe
through the flying sparks of 1848 without a general con-
flagration, the swift turn that faced a world transformed,
a world of revolutions and resurgent nations, of Lamartine

and Mazzini, with the same point that had once fenced with
Metternich and Talleyrand, the unchanging constancy
which could announce that " we have no eternal allies, and   Palm.
we have no perpetual enemies. Our interests are eternal and   281
perpetual, and those interests it is our duty to follow "—
these were gifts that made no appeal to Aberdeen's disciple.
For the guiding principle of Lord Aberdeen's diplomacy
was invariably to do what Lord Palmerston would not
dream of doing ; and it almost seemed in later years that
the principle of Mr. Gladstone's was to do what Lord
Palmerston would not have done. Trained in that cautious
school, the younger man was apt to overlook the merit of
the achievement in the risks by which it was surrounded.
For he was sadly disinclined to agree with *Endymion's* praise
that Palmerston was " never better than when the gale ran   End.
high "—or that, if he was, it was in the least praiseworthy   III. 166
to be so. And there is poetic justice in the fact that Disraeli's
attempt to be Palmerstonian in 1878 found its severest
critic in Mr. Gladstone.

But though he disapproved, he could not quite withhold   Palm.
his admiration. One summer night in 1850, after a censure   306–9
by the Lords, Palmerston spoke in his own defence. The
Queen, the Prince, the *Times*, and half the Cabinet were
hostile, to say nothing of a lively Opposition. Even his
friends were doubtful, since the battleground provided by the
preposterous Pacifico was scarcely favourable to manœuvre.
For it seemed more than a shade excessive to blockade the
port of Athens and seize Greek shipping in order to enforce
the questionable claims of a not less questionable British
subject. But Palmerston was equal to his brief, surveyed the
claims, stated the inalienable right of British subjects to protection, and then warming to his case reviewed his conduct
of European policy for the past twenty years, returning in
his last sentences to the opening theme, restated in the
tremendous invocation, " *Civis Romanus sum* ". He spoke
(entirely without notes) from a little before ten till nearly

half-past two. The House was dazzled. Even Mr. Gladstone, speaking on a later evening, expressed their admiration of a minister of sixty-five who "from the dusk of one day to the dawn of the next . . . defended his policy before a crowded House of Commons in that gigantic intellectual and physical

Glad. effort ". Not that he approved. For Palmerston's Greek
I. 370 policy was gravely denounced on moral principles, and he found time for a scornful comment on the Foreign Secretary "like some gallant knight at a tournament of old, pricking forth into the lists, armed at all points, confiding in his sinews and his skill, challenging all comers for the sake of honour, and having no other duty than to lay as many as possible of his adversaries sprawling in the dust". That had never been Lord Aberdeen's way ; neither was it Mr. Gladstone's.

Two days later Peel fell from his horse ; and in two more he died. The sudden, tragic happening seemed full of consequences for all except the man it happened to. For his career had ended four years earlier, on the summer night in 1846 when the flushed squires trooped back from the division-lobby—" the Manners, the Somersets, the Ben-

Bent. tincks, the Lowthers, and the Lennoxes " (in Mr. Disraeli's
299 gleeful catalogue) . . . " Sir Charles Burrell, Sir William Jolliffe, Sir Charles Knightly, Sir John Trollope, Sir Edward Kerrison, Sir John Tyrrell . . . and the Duncombes, the Liddells, and the Yorkes . . . the stout heart of Mr. Buck . . . the pleasant presence of Walter Long "—and whooped him out of office with a view-halloo. But though his death was almost void of significance for him, it was full of consequence for others. For it left the Peelites leaderless, a little widowed group, devoted (like the Canningites before them) to a posthumous loyalty. There is always something a

Palm. shade irritating about the friends of deceased statesmen.
134 " Their airs," as I have noted of an earlier instance, " their weeds, their sadly shaken heads begin to pall ; and soon a hasty world resents their dutiful reference of all questions to the unforgotten words of a single oracle." But, irritating

or not, the Peelites were a political force of rare significance.
For they had gifts. Half the talent in English politics was
concentrated in the tiny group of Peel's bereaved lieuten-
ants. It was in vain for Disraeli to ask with his familiar End.
sneer a generation later, " Would that band of self-admir- III. 342
ing geniuses, who had upset every cabinet with whom they
were ever connected, return on the shoulders of the people,
as they always dreamed, though they were always the
persons of whom the people never seemed to think ? " Of
course they were self-conscious, and it almost seemed as if
the hall-mark of a Peelite was to be more than a little
priggish. But they were gifted. Only the accident of their
bereavement deprived them of direction for their gifts.
They had no reasonable hopes of obtaining office as a
unit ; for without Peel they were too few. The Tory squires
had turned their backs upon them, and Disraeli stood at
the gates of the Tory Eden with the flaming sword of his
invective. So that way was closed to them. Besides, their
fiscal views were far from Tory now. Their Tory associations gone, nothing remained for these Tories, who had
lost half their Toryism and all their Tory friends, but soli-
tude and a slow drift towards the Whigs. The Whigs would
need their gifts. Not that their gifts were popular. The mild
sagacity of Aberdeen, the competence of Graham, even
the brighter flame of Gladstone and Sidney Herbert, all
seemed a little pale beside the fine flamboyancy of Bright and
Cobden, the fire that still burnt at intervals in John Russell,
Palmerston's inimitable manliness, or the icy virulence of
Disraeli. It was no passport to popularity to be a Peelite. But
then the little group was never anxious to make converts : for,
their numbers fixed once for all at their bereavement, it is
scarcely open to a band of widows to make posthumous additions to their strength. The castaways seemed soberly content
upon their desert island and made no signals of distress. They
had their principles ; they had their gifts ; still more, perhaps,
they had their consciences. And Mr. Gladstone was a Peelite.

II

Marooned among the lonely mariners who had once sailed with Peel, there seemed to be less chance than ever for Mr. Gladstone of a voyage with Palmerston. For that cheerful officer walked the Whig quarterdeck, wholly indifferent to Tory castaways. Yet the next year was scarcely out before they had a friendly encounter. Home politics failed to unite them, and foreign affairs seemed scarcely to provide a likely basis of agreement. But a common interest in one foreign country brought them together. Both men had strong Italian sympathies. Had not the small Harry Temple travelled in Italy, nearly sixty years before, in the year of the French Terror ? Besides, if he loathed anything, it was a despot ; and Italy had always been the chosen playground of every despotism disliked by Palmerston. There were the Austrians, to start with ; and he disliked their strutting white-coats as much as any refugee in Leicester Square. For Austria meant always Metternich ; and Metternich was almost always wrong. Palmerston had once informed the House of Commons that " Providence Palm. meant mankind to be divided into separate nations. . . . 282 There is no case on the globe where this intention is more marked than that of the Italians and the Germans, kept apart by the Alps, and as unlike in every thing as two races can be. Austria has never possessed Italy as part of her Empire, but has always held it as a conquered territory. There has been no mixture of races. The only Austrians have been the troops and the civil officers. She has governed it as you govern a garrison town, and her rule has always been hateful. We do not wish to threaten ; Palm. but . . ." There was the Pope as well—" His Emptyness 312 the Pope ", as he once described him—and the atrocious *Bomba*. So Palmerston was nothing if not sound upon Italian freedom. To Gladstone Italy meant something deeper than a tempting row of tyrannical Aunt Sallies. He had travelled in Italy as well, when his first book was in the press ; he had even made love in Italy ; for his declaration to Miss Glynne was appropriately staged in the Colosseum. But Italy held more for him than any personal associations. For Rome was in Italy—Rome, where he had listened to endless Italian sermons and heard mass with Manning. They sometimes said he was a Jesuit ; and he regarded Rome with almost mystic awe.

But Rome was not his goal that autumn, when he went abroad for a daughter's eyesight. They went to Naples, *Glad.* where he enjoyed the unpleasing spectacle of King *Bomba's* I. 389– prisons. He saw Poerio on trial as well and heard him sen- 402 tenced to twenty-four years in irons ; he listened to Lacaita, and emerged with an awkward certainty that " the negation of God erected into a system of government " ruled in the Kingdom of Naples. It was still more distressing to learn from Poerio himself that " the present government of Naples rely on the English conservative party ". Conservative himself, he resolved to destroy this scandalous reliance. Lord Aberdeen must hear of it ; he must tell Aberdeen ; and that ripe intelligence would surely find a way to end these horrors. A friend who met him at the station on his return to England found that he could talk of nothing else. Lord Aberdeen was soon acquainted of the facts, and showed himself " kind, just, moderate, humane ", and almost intolerably discreet. Nothing embarrassing should be said in public—Mr. Gladstone might, perhaps, prepare a statement of the case for him. Then the sagacious man composed a letter to Vienna. His old friend Prince Schwarzenberg was asked to act, deliberated for eight weeks, and replied a little tartly that, as a special favour, Mr. Gladstone's views should be conveyed to *Bomba*. It was in February, 1851, that Gladstone had returned ; he saw Aberdeen in March, wrote him at length in April ; and in

July, his patience quite exhausted, he published the letter as a pamphlet. In fact, he published two. Lord Aberdeen was slightly shocked ; Prince Schwarzenberg .was deeply pained ; an Englishman in Paris was blackballed for an exclusive club because he bore the revolutionary name of Gladstone ; and Gladstone himself was overwhelmed with explosions of Italian gratitude. Palmerston was frankly pleased. Gladstone had seen him in the spring and assured

Ash. him that " the Neapolitan is a *Governo infernale*, and that,
I. 257 as a gentleman and a Christian, he feels it his duty to make known what he has seen of its proceedings ". Lord Palmerston had reached the same conclusion years before ; but when his visitor added the frank confession that he had been wrong in his attacks on Palmerston's Italian policy, he was distinctly gratified. Evidence from such a quarter was of the highest value ; and when the pamphlet came

Palm. out, a gleeful Foreign Office transmitted copies to every
318 Court in Europe. He paid a public compliment to Gladstone in the House of Commons. Indeed, he could afford to ; for the rueful Aberdeen confessed that its appearance had given Palmerston a score. When the Neapolitans attempted to reply to Mr. Gladstone's charges, Palmerston

Ash. trounced their rejoinder as " a tissue of bare assertion and
I. 258 reckless denial, mixed up with coarse ribaldry and commonplace abuse of public men and political parties ". A Note of his to Naples presently administered a ringing

Ash. broadside, mildly described by a courtly Neapolitan to his
I. 262 sovereign as " *uno delli solite impertinenze di Lord Palmerston* " ; and "that three-decker Palmerston" (as Canning had once called him) went gaily, all sails set, to the support of Mr.

1 Gladstone. Their first exchange of letters concerned the Neapolitan reply, Gladstone addressing his " dear Lord " a little stiffly and remaining faithfully his Lordship's ; while Palmerston, with less reserve, addressed his answer

2 to " Dear Gladstone ".

So Italy served to break the ice between them. Not that

Gladstone had turned Palmerstonian by sudden conversion.
For he could still assure Lord Aberdeen that he " need
not be afraid, I think, of Mazzinism from me, still less
of Kossuthism, which means the other *plus* imposture,
Lord Palmerston, and his nationalities ". But sympathy
with men who suffer for a cause may often turn to
sympathy with the cause itself ; and Italy (like Ireland)
was one of the subjects on which wisdom came only by
degrees to Mr. Gladstone. At present it had merely served
to bring him within hail of Palmerston. But they came
closer soon.

Within a month of his first note to Gladstone, Palmerston
was out of office, dismissed by a felicitous combination of Palm.
the French *coup d'état*, the Queen, the Prince, Lord Nor- 320-7
manby, his brother Phipps, and an unusual access of resolution on the part of John Russell. He was not pleased to go ;
for Palmerston was fond of office. Besides, his situation was
very far from easy. He had a following outside the House
of Commons. But politics in 1851 were conducted in the
House rather than on the platform ; and in the House he
was a trifle lonely. For, parted from the Whigs, he was in
no sense a Tory. John Russell, in an estimate of his ad- Palm.
herents, put them at ten ; and now, perhaps, he turned a 331
friendlier eye towards the lonely Peelites on their rock.
Free Traders like himself, they were neither Whig nor
Tory ; and when the Tories came back to office (and Palmerston refused to join them for the single reason that he
opposed " not the principle, but . . . the expediency of the Palm.
imposition of any duty, under any circumstances, upon 336
foreign corn "), he concerted some of his Parliamentary
plans in Opposition with Mr. Gladstone.   **3, 4 & 5**

That autumn they came closer still. Peelites and Palmerston together devised the formula with which a decent
Parliamentary burial was given to Protection. Gladstone Glad.
and Sidney Herbert conferred with him at Carlton Gar- I. 433
dens ; there was a brisk exchange of notes ; and contact was **6 & 7**

definitely established. Then the Tories fell ; and England passed to the milder rule of Lord Aberdeen and that Coalition under which " the country was governed for two years

End. by all its ablest men, who, by the end of that term, had suc-
III. ceeded, by their coalesced genius, in reducing that country
322-3 to a state of desolation and despair ". It was a blend of Whigs and Peelites, with Gladstone as Chancellor of the Exchequer and Lord Palmerston somewhat incongruously housed at the Home Office. They corresponded now as colleagues ; and quite soon their quality began to appear. They had their first brush on taxation, when Mr. Gladstone scandalised the new Home Secretary by proposing to extend the depredations of legacy duty to real property itself. Lord Palmerston was shocked. The squire of Broadlands was ex-

9 cusably a trifle sensitive to land taxation ; and he gravely asked to be supplied with information on " the amount of

10 Confiscation " in a stated case. He even worked out an

11 elaborate statement shewing the burdens on landowners. The Chancellor (as Chancellors are apt to) disputed his

13 figures ; and the battle was fairly joined, with Gladstone courteously regretting that " our Arithmetic does not harmonise better " and Palmerston, quite unconsoled by the contemplated end of the Income Tax in 1860, responding

14 stoutly that " an Impost which confiscates for four years more than a third of a Man's Income must be acknowledged to be a great Individual oppression ". (The sunshine of a vanished day dwells happily on their discussion.) But they had other topics, when Mr. Gladstone in support of an application by the Canon of Ely encountered Palmerston's invincible objections to intra-mural burial. For the new

22 Home Secretary had become ardent upon public health and had " thought it right to discontinue everywhere the barbarous Practice of depositing human Bodies under the Floor of Buildings frequented by human Multitudes. . . . People might as well want to bury Dead Bodies in the Cellars of their Houses, or under their Libraries, as in Churches ".

Another branch of social reform was no less sturdily approached :

"The Beer Shops licensed to have the Beer drunk on **16** the Premises are a Pest to the Community. They are Haunts of Thieves and Schools for Prostitutes. . . . That Beer should be sold like anything Else, to be taken away by the Purchaser to be consumed at Home is most reasonable and the more People are enabled so to supply the labouring Classes the better, but the words 'licensed to be drunk on the Premises' are by the common People interpreted as applicable to the Customers as well as to the Liquor, and well do they avail themselves of the License."

That was good Palmerston, and perhaps good sense as well ; for his design had been to abolish beershops by permitting **Palm.** shopkeepers to " sell beer like oil and vinegar and treacle, **346** to be carried home and drunk with wives and children ". Ashley, his son-in-law, had taught him a good deal about such things. But the rough-and-ready temperance was, one feels, Palmerston's own ; though it is a shade distressing to find him suggesting in the same week, *à propos* of the new **15** War Department land at Aldershot, that Government should turn an honest penny " by letting off Bits at the out-skirts for Public Houses, Booths, &c."

But larger topics soon absorbed them. For the good inten-tions of Lord Aberdeen were leading down an inevitable incline to the Crimean War. With such affairs in prospect, Home Office questions failed to absorb Lord Palmerston. When the Queen asked him about labour troubles in the North of England, he replied absently, " No, Madam, I **Palm.** have heard nothing ; but it seems certain that the Turks **348** have crossed the Danube " ; and it is a shade significant to find the Turkish ambassador in correspondence with the **18 & 19** Home Secretary on matters of war finance far removed from

Palm. the province of the Home Department. For ten exciting
353-5 days in December, 1853, he was out of office, resigning on
a singularly untimely recrudescence of John Russell's passion for Reform Bills and returning in unruffled triumph
over the body of Reform. During this episode his Peelite
Glad. colleague was strangely uneasy ; Gladstone paid him a pro-
I. 490 tracted call and frankly confessed to Aberdeen that he " had
had wishes that Palmerston were back again on account of
the Eastern question ". Here was a strange confession for
Peel's favourite disciple. But Palmerston's view of the war
had won him ; and when the course of operations was dis-
21 cussed in Cabinet, Gladstone wrote strongly in the Palmerstonian sense that " the Black Sea is the true centre of the
war and Sebastopol the true centre of the Black Sea ". So far,
indeed, was he persuaded of the soundness of his view that he
was unwilling to submit it for confirmation by the soldiers—
" Reference no doubt must be made to the judgment of the
generals : but had I the power I would confine that reference
as much as possible to the sufficiency of force, and restrain
them as much as possible from weighing (except with a
view to any immediate and urgent necessity) the importance of this object ". There, through the unexpected lips
of Mr. Gladstone, speaks the civilian minister in time
of war.

He entered into Palmerston's designs, informing him with
glee unusual in a Chancellor of the Exchequer that " the
Admiralty have just written to us for sanction to a very large
Expenditure (not voted by Parliament) upon Floating
Batteries and Gun Boats with a view to an attack upon
Cronstadt in the spring. . . . Of course we gladly agree to it ".
But as the war dragged on and the cruel winter of 1854 shut
down upon the trenches before Sebastopol, the Coalition
entered on the last and most painful stage in the lives of Coali-
tions. For it began to crack ; and the cracks, as usual, came
from inside. Indeed, a high proportion of them came from
John Russell, with whom resignation was becoming almost

a mannerism. He resigned on all occasions and for the oddest reasons—once because Palmerston was not promoted Palm.
to the combined offices of Secretary at and for War, and 365
very nearly once again upon a point (said to affect his per- Glad.
sonal honour) relating to the removal of an official from the I. 520
Woods and Forests. He resigned again in the last week of
January, 1855. This time he chose a more substantial
reason. For Mr. Roebuck had proposed an enquiry into the
conduct of the war ; Lord John concurred in the proposal ;
but as his colleagues, who not unnaturally failed to relish being
made the subject-matter of an enquiry, were of the contrary
opinion, he resigned and (to everyone's surprise) maintained
his resignation. The debate on Mr. Roebuck's motion would
be critical ; and it is significant of their increasing friendliness 24
that Lord Palmerston was anxious to put Gladstone up to
deal with certain awkward personal aspects of the case. Glad- 25
stone was willing ; but the Cabinet decided otherwise. The Glad.
debate came on, and the Government was badly beaten.   I. 523

With the Coalition ended, Gladstone and Palmerston
might naturally have been expected to return to their respective tents—Palmerston to the Whig fold and Gladstone
to the lonely fastnesses of Peelite isolation. But for a time
they somehow failed to separate. When Derby tried to form Palm.
a ministry and invited Palmerston to join, that wary elder 366
made the surprising stipulation that Gladstone and Sidney
Herbert should be included. Then he declined, and Gladstone declined as well. Indeed, their answers were concerted. A note survives, which shews the two men in 26
consultation ; and Gladstone's diary records two talks with Glad.
Palmerston. The next stage was reached, when Russell I. 525–7
made his attempt and called on Mr. Gladstone, " his hat Glad.
shaking in his hand ". That was scarcely the touch by I. 530
which Governments are formed in time of war ; and Russell
also was found wanting. Then, all more palatable alternatives having failed, the Queen sent for Palmerston ; and
Palmerston agreed to try.

27   A brisk note informed Mr. Gladstone that he was " one
of the first Persons with whom I wish to communicate ",
and he was soon invited to become Lord Palmerston's
Glad. Chancellor of the Exchequer ; the persuasive man " dwelt
I. 533–6 on the satisfactory nature of my relations with the Liberal
party ". Here was a grave predicament. For it appeared
to the distracted Peelite that he was invited to rejoin " the
Aberdeen cabinet without Lord Aberdeen " ; and this,
indeed, was precisely what Lord Palmerston asked of him.
Followed a wearing interval of runnings to and fro, of
anxious consultations, and of painful letter-writing. Sidney
Herbert was inclined to join, and Aberdeen himself gave
a surprising blessing to the notion. But Gladstone, with
28 infinite compunction, refused. His refusal was composed
with extreme labour, and his hesitations breathe in the
numerous erasures of the draft. In its final form, it hinted
at a fear that Palmerston might possibly not make the most
of every chance of peace. But the decisive factor was the
omission of Aberdeen—" I must freely own that I regard
the presence of Lord Aberdeen as having been all along,
with reference to these absorbing questions, a vital element
in the Cabinet, at least for those who, like me, find in him
on the whole the nearest representation of their leanings
with respect to peace, and of their opinions with respect to
29 the Turkish Empire ". Palmerston replied—first shortly
and on the next day at length. Gladstone's " apprehen-
30 sions, that at some time or other, some Question or other
may arise upon which for want of the aid to be derived
from the Counsel of Lord Aberdeen and Lord John Russell
you may be at a loss for a sufficiently guiding Clue to a right
Decision " or that the Cabinet might one day take a course
of which he would disapprove were briskly dismissed as excessive modesty on the part of Gladstone and—admirable
summary of Gladstonian dialectic—" the Shadow of a
future Shade ". The peaceful nature of his own intentions
was stated in a deeper tone :

My dear Ld P.

After very anxious consideration I have now to give you an answer... [illegible crossed-out text] ...add that agreeable to my wishes & feelings.

You propose to form a Cabinet of which I understand from you that Ld John Russell as matters now stand will not in a meantime, and to which Ld Aberdeen adhering as not adverse to Palmy.

There are many considerations which on ordinary occasions would govern my conduct, but which I [crossed out] now bring myself to regard as secondary. For example I confess myself doubtful as to the full efficiency of such a Cabinet as you could form with one concurrence [crossed out], and I am also very doubtful as to the prospects of Parliamentary support.

I grant however that at this moment all other questions are absorbed in those questions which relate to the war: will the war be prosecuted with vigour...

[several lines of crossed-out and interlined text at bottom]
...opportunity be seized for bringing it to...

for the restoration of peace amidst ~~dangers~~ all the ~~doubts~~ difficulties ~~& intricacies~~ & ~~intricacies~~ these besetting difficulties that must ~~perhaps~~ be probably ~~which~~ attach to the processes ~~by which~~ task?

~~it was~~ is ~~to be attained~~?

As to the first question I feel no doubt — ~~As to the second~~ ~~can we~~ ~~with not fear~~ but I pass on to the other.

~~Enghte the doubt~~ here I ~~have to~~ observe that if Lord Aberdeen is ~~into~~ to quit the office of Prime Minister, ~~under the vote of the House~~ he will be excluded from it on account of leanings & sympathies with respect to ~~Palestine~~, and of opinions with respect to ~~maintenance~~ the State in ~~the~~ Turkey, in which I share.

The answer to the question however is really to be sought not in ~~a formal~~ the words Yes or No but, in the ~~composition~~ entirely materials of the Cabinet by which ~~it~~ is to be the subject handled. As it stood under In the Cabinet ~~of~~ Lord Aberdeen there was every security that the great

...would be presented to us with
all the advantages *discussion of thereby the*
of accomplished ministers of foreign policy, all
alike attached to the principles of
British freedom, ... always regarding
the ~~application~~ of them from the same
point of view ... giving the ... ...
... a combined result as ... could
fairly represent the relation ...
due to the several elements of each
case as it arose.

I must frankly own that I regard the
presence of Lord A... as having been all along
with reference to these absorbing questions
a vital element in his Cabinet, at least for those
who like me ~~there~~ find in
him on the whole the ... ...
representation of their leanings with
respect to peace &c. their opinions

with respect to the Turkish Empire.

You will perceive that I am now speaking not of any personal matter, but of that composition of the Cabinet as a whole which is the only good foundation of the full confidence necessary to justify the act of entering into it.

Under these circ[umstances] I am afraid I could not have a reasonable expectation of giving you in the Cabinet that full & undivided support wh you wd justly expect from yr Colleagues, and I therefore feel that I ought not to be among them.

I remain my dear Ld P

Yours sincerely

" . . . you misjudge me. If by a Stroke of the wand I could effect in the Map of the World the Changes which I wish I am quite sure that I could make arrangements far more conducive than some of the present ones to the Peace of Nations, to the Progress of Civilization to the Happiness & Welfare of Mankind but I am not so destitute of Common Sense, as not to be able to compare Ends with Means, and to see that the former must be given up when the latter are wanting ! And when the Means to be brought to bear for the attainment of any Ends consist in the Blood & Treasure of a Great Nation, those who are answerable to that Nation for the Expenditure of that Blood & Treasure must well weigh the value of the objects which they pursue, and must remember that if they should forget the just Proportion between Ends & Means the good sense of the People whose affairs they manage will soon step in to correct their Errors, and to call them to a severe account for the Evils of which they would have been the Cause."

Statesmen in time of war have written worse than that. Slightly reassured, Mr. Gladstone entered upon a second day of conferences. He was still averse from joining ; and so were Graham and Sidney Herbert. But Aberdeen applied the final salve to their uneasy consciences, strongly advised their joining, and propelled them gently into the arms of Palmerston. " Lord Aberdeen," asked Mr. Gladstone, " when we have joined the Palmerston cabinet, you standing aloof from it, will you rise in your place in the House of Lords and say that you give that cabinet your confidence with regard to the question of war and peace ? " And Aberdeen replied, " I will express my hope that it will do right, but not my confidence, which is a different thing ". The strange dialogue left them completely satisfied ; and they joined Palmerston with easy minds. Gladstone composed a second letter no less laboriously than the first, informing Palmerston **31** that he was willing to recognise Lord Aberdeen's "confidence in the Cabinet as equivalent to his presence" and adding thankfully that " Lord Aberdeen will be in a condition to make such declarations on the subject that fills all our thoughts, as to remove any bar to my entrance into your Cabinet with the feelings and intentions I could desire, if you continue to wish it ". The junction was complete, and late the same night he was advising Palmerston as to a **32** minor Government appointment.

The voyage, alas ! was brief. It lasted just a fortnight. Then the Peelite consciences were troubled once again, Glad. and (at their own request) they walked the plank. For I.537-9 Palmerston, opposed at first to Mr. Roebuck's proposed enquiry, was now inclined to grant it. Gladstone demurred ; the Prince was painfully reminded of the Committee of Public Safety ; and the Queen hoped loudly that authority would not be permitted to pass into the hands of those " who are the least fit to govern ". Mr. Gladstone argued tenaciously that such powers should not be delegated to an irresponsible committee, that every minister but one had opposed it on its first appearance, that the House, if it insisted, had manifestly no confidence in them, and that, in fine, they had best resign. But Palmerston was never less inclined to resignation. Enquiry or no enquiry, he proposed to remain Prime Minister and to win the war. Called at seventy to govern England in a crisis, he had little taste for technicalities about a committee ; and ministers who felt otherwise about it must please themselves. They did. After endless agonies of argument Graham, Gladstone, and Sidney Herbert all resigned ; and Palmerston was left to find new tenants for the Admiralty, Treasury, and Colonial Office. Their countrymen were strikingly unmoved by this apparent desertion in face of the enemy ; and *Punch*, rarely sympathetic to intellectual refinements, depicted them as a trio of domestic servants informing their employer that " Really, sir, this ' *inquiry* ' is so very

My dear Lord Palmerston

I thank you very much
for your letter of this morning: and
I have availed myself of Lord
Aberdeen's ~~kindness~~ offer to converse
with you. I have { heard from / seen } him
since his visit.

In my letter of yesterday I said that
I regarded Lord Aberdeen's presence
in his Cabinet as having been all
along a vital element with respect
to the question of war & peace. ~~I was~~
~~then and~~ I now am ~~said~~ as I was then

willing to recognise his confidence in
the Cabinet as equivalent to his presence.
I write frankly without fear of offending
you, although you speak of mistrust, a
word which does not truly describe my
feelings. Individual temperaments &
leanings must differ more or less: nay
it is from such ~~differences~~ distractions within due
as they have been in the last Cabinet
bounds, afford the best security for wise
counsels. My statements with respect to
you ~~are~~ I hope you will rather infer from
what has passed between us on various
occasions, ~~partly~~ & among ~~them~~ one
about twelve months ago. But I hope ~~I may~~
It is I but
enough for me to say
justly say that I could not either consistently or consistently express myself
with whom I have acted all my life, in
from Lord Aberdeen, with regard to the
he ... by the
question of war & peace. I have ~~now~~ the

happiness however of finding that Lord
Abn will be in a condition to make such
declarations on this ~~word~~ as to remove any
(subject that fills all our thoughts)

been by any expressed into your Cabinet
~~with the feelings conditions I could desire~~
if you continue to wish it.

In adding ~~I that~~ two conditions. I know
that if you seek me, you seek me with a
view to the ~~continuance~~ of our financial
policy in the same spirit in which it has
hitherto ~~may~~ been ~~conducted~~. But I ought
add
to ~~observe~~ that my constituency ~~if in some
respects~~ peculiar. & I think they ~~might not un~~ justly
as matter of honour
expect of me that if the policy of any Govt to
might
which I ~~belonged~~ were not marked by a friendly
friendly
spirit towards the Church of England (by which
boldly any favour to
I do not mean the ~~permission~~ of encroachment
either on civil or on religious rights) I should
resign my seat into their hands

'*inconvenient*' that we should like to leave at once ",
beneath the stern rubric " Mr. Bull wants to know ' the
reason why ' ". And that Palmerston himself was equally
resigned to their departure appears from his wife's cheerful statement that Gladstone's successor at the Treasury
was " thought to be much more satisfactory than Glad- Palm.
stone's sophistry and eloquence and long-winded orations ". 374
So, for a time, they parted.

DP

III

The next chapter in their relations opened more than
four years later. But what changes in the interval. By 1859
Lord Palmerston—the Palmerston of 1855—had vanished
in a more stable figure. That had been a war-time expedient ; but this was a national institution, whose stability
compared favourably with that of the Bank of England and
the Nelson Monument. His sudden rise to power was almost
accidental, due mainly to his countrymen's irresistible
tendency in time of war to exclaim " Wanted, a man ",
and to the evident unmanliness of everyone but Palmerston. He played that part to perfection ; and the spirited
old man brought his country through the black winter of
1855. He showed besides an ample measure of administrative vigour, creditable in a former colleague of Lord Liverpool who had once sent drafts to Wellington in the Peninsula. But he had more to show than a war-record. Few
statesmen have survived a war-time apotheosis. But
Palmerston was lucky. There was a striking lack of competition in public life. His older rivals were either dis-
credited like Lord John and Aberdeen, or unreliable like
Derby ; while the younger men were untried Tories like
Disraeli, or Peelites and consequently unaccountable. The
dismal course of the Crimean War had thrown up no
popularities to rival his ; for, with the best intentions, it
was not easy to make a national hero of General Simpson.
Besides, the world was still disturbed. There was still need
of Palmerston, with the Mutiny on hand and trouble in
China, to say nothing of a French Emperor who combined the incalculable with the certain menace of his name.

So Palmerston survived, ruling Victorian England
with something approaching monarchy, and kept his court
Palm. at Cambridge House. It was years now since Lord John
303 had confided to a grateful sovereign that he was " too old

to do much in the future ". Since then this hopeful diagnosis Palm.
had been repeated at frequent intervals. Derby had told 366
her that " his day was gone by", and Disraeli favoured a
noble correspondent with his conclusive verdict on " an
old painted pantaloon, very deaf, very blind, and with Palm.
false teeth, which would fall out of his mouth while speak- 372
ing, if he did not hesitate and halt so in his talk ". Yet,
strange to say, his countrymen infinitely preferred him to all
comers. Even the Queen was quite anxious now, when his Palm.
majority was threatened. Indeed, a momentary threat 393
succeeded. But the General Election of 1857 repaired his
losses, and Palmerston reigned on.

Gladstone was changed as well. Not that the lonely
figure of 1855 was less lonely now. If anything, he was more
solitary than ever ; and his reflections in the political
Thebaid appeared to lead to little except unfavourable
verdicts on Lord Palmerston. That sprightly figure became
increasingly distasteful to Mr. Gladstone. Had not Lord
Palmerston supplanted his venerated Aberdeen ? Worse
still, he had failed to see the Peelites' point about the
Roebuck enquiry and then flamboyantly proceeded to win
the war. To Mr. Gladstone's fancy, Palmerston began to
embody all that was worst in public life. There was a distressing lack of principles about his rough-and-ready
judgments ; he never searched the fundamentals ; and,
worst of all, he was lamentably popular. For nothing
annoys an anchorite like popularity. Released from their
official alliance, Mr. Gladstone reverted to strong hostility,
assailed the Government, was positively found in association with the anti-patriotic Radicals of the peace party,
and even assured a constituent that the end must be utter
" confusion if it is not stopped by the failure of Lord Glad.
Palmerston's physical force, the only way of stopping it I. 567
which I could view with regret, for I admire the pluck with
which he fights against the infirmities of age, though in
political and moral courage I have never seen a minister so

deficient ". So it is not surprising to find him writing in
Glad. 1857 that " I can neither give the most qualified adhesion
I. 566 to the ministry of Lord Palmerston, nor follow the liberal
party in the abandonment of the very principles and
pledges which were original and principal bonds of union
with it ". Not that he found the Tories any more con-
genial ; for where Disraeli led, it was not easy for Gladstone to follow. So for a while he balanced uncomfortably
between his strong distastes.

Distastes, indeed, almost appeared to have more force
with him than positive inclinations. For they deflected him
from either side of politics. A distaste for pure Toryism
kept him a Peelite still ; but a distaste for Palmerston
postponed his arrival at the natural destination of the
Peelites in the Liberal Party. It helped him, though, to
form an association of great value for his ultimate hegira to
the Liberal Mecca. For his anti-Palmerstonian bias brought
him in contact with the Radicals ; and when he thundered
against the China war, he found himself in the company of
Mr. Cobden. A distaste for Palmerston assembled the
oddest bed-fellows in Opposition, and strange combination of Gladstone, Cobden, and Disraeli drove him to the
dissolution of 1857. Indeed, the watchful Shaftesbury
darkly attributed Gladstone's involuntary manœuvres
to his Church opinions—" To my own influence over
Palm. future Ecclesiastical appointments (should Palmerston
391 continue in power), I forsee the termination. They will say
that my advice led him to the nomination of the several
clergymen, that this exasperated Gladstone, and gave rise
to the effort and the coalition ". The conjecture was a
trifle wild ; but, from whatever cause, Gladstone in 1857
was strongly anti-Palmerstonian.

In the same mood a few months later he helped an odd
assortment of Tories, Radicals, and Peelites to defeat the
invincible Prime Minister. The Conspiracy to Murder Bill
had represented Palmerston's courteous acquiescence in

French objections to Parisian assassinations conducted with
bombs made in England. The bombs had failed. But
though Orsini missed the Emperor, he brought down
Palmerston. For a rebellious House of Commons, that had
learnt indifference to the feelings of foreign despots in
Palmerston's own school, gave him a fatal dose of his own
medicine. Gladstone himself assumed the master's tone and   Palm.
loftily asserted the right of " discussing questions of English   400
law upon English grounds and English considerations " ;
and the Government went down before his onslaught, the
executioner writing austerely in his journal, " Palmerston
has resigned. He is down. I must now cease to denounce   Glad.
him".   I. 576

   A fresh problem faced him. Should he turn Tory again ?
Lord Derby, who was now Prime Minister, made him a   Glad.
formal offer of the fatted calf ; but he regretfully declined.   I. 577–8
His new friends, the Radicals, were quite anxious, though ;
and Mr. Bright assured him that he had " many friends   Glad.
there, and some who would grieve much to see you leave   I. 579
them ". Was the erratic ship to find an anchorage at last on
that side of the stream ? The Tories scarcely thought so.
For their approaches were renewed a few weeks later, with
a large-minded offer by Disraeli to waive his own leadership in favour of the Peelite veteran, Graham. But it all
came to nothing ; and Mr. Gladstone still swung free from
any party moorings on the broad stream of politics. Nothing
indeed, seemed certain in his future, except that it would
not be Palmerston. Someone conjectured that " personal
dislike and distrust of Palmerston is the one absorbing   Glad.
feeling with him " ; his attitude was even diagnosed as   I. 581
" violent personal prejudice " ; and he confessed himself
that " on the whole perhaps I differed more from Lord   Glad.
Palmerston than from almost any one, and this was more   I. 585
on account of his temper and views of public conduct, than
of any political opinions ". But politicians' ships often
arrive at unexpected ports.

In 1858 Mr. Gladstone seemed at the most distant point
of his protracted and rather tortuous Odyssey. It even
brought him to Ithaca itself, where he presided over the
Ionian Islands in a happy blend of Homer and constitutional principles and listened to gratifying cheers of
" ζήτω ὁ φιλέλλην Γλάδστων ". But he was home again in
the first weeks of the next year ; and the party landscape
in 1859 was remarkably absorbing. For with the Tories in
a manifest decline, the old problem still persisted—what
was to happen to the Peelites? Graham and Aberdeen were
now past active politics ; but Sidney Herbert seemed to
have years before him, and Gladstone was not quite fifty.

Glad.   He still voted with the Tories but was heard to say sharp
I. 623 things about their foreign policy. He was full of foreign
        affairs now ; " foreign politics ", as a friend wrote,
Glad.   " seemed to have the chief place in his mind ". Perhaps
I. 624 the Ionian mission had changed his interests. Besides, his
        old Neapolitan opinions were stronger now ; Panizzi and
Manin had taught him the full lesson of Italian freedom,
and he had dined with Cavour on his way home from
Corfu. So his distaste for Palmerston began to vanish in a
larger sympathy with his Italian leanings. For a pupil of
Manin could scarcely sympathise with the Austrian bias of
Lord Malmesbury and the Tories. He voted with them,
though, in the last division. But when Palmerston returned
in triumph, he promptly became his Chancellor of the
Exchequer. Herbert was there as well ; and the much-
travelled Peelites had cast anchor at last in the calm waters
of a Palmerston Administration.

The change was odd. Oddest of all, the thoughtful Peelite
almost seemed to have entered the Liberal Party from the
Glad.   Radical wing, was " exceedingly sorry to find that Cobden
I. 626 does not take office " and " very glad we have Gibson ".
For his personal connections were all among the peace men
of the extreme left, strange relic of his anti-Palmerstonian
wanderings. Oxford began to show unpleasant symptoms

of repudiating her favourite son, since sudden changes are
inimical to ancient universities. But it all seemed so simple
to Mr. Gladstone. He was supremely tired of playing
Ishmael. It had dawned on him that he was positively
"mischievous in an isolated position, outside the regular party
organization of parliament ". Besides, he was profoundly Glad.
conscious that " in finance there was still much useful I. 628
work to be done ". There was Reform as well. But foreign
affairs were the deciding factor. With France and Austria at
war in Italy, " the overwhelming interest and weight of the
Italian question, and of our foreign policy in connection
with it, joined to my entire distrust of the former government in relation to it, led me to decide without one
moment's hesitation ". So Italy resolved his doubts. He
could write of his " real and close harmony with the new
premier, and the new foreign secretary " ; and soon a
nervous colleague was complaining of "Johnny and Pam like Palm.
twins, too much united on foreign affairs, for with Gladstone 410–1
as their ally they are inclined to meddle too much in
Italian affairs ". He was with Palmerston once more ; and
Italy, which had first brought them together in 1851,
united the strange pair again in 1859.

Their official correspondence opened briskly, with
Palmerston expatiating on the military virtues of a 37
Gibraltar cable and cheerfully devising fresh forms of
martyrdom for Mr. Gilbert Scott and his designs for the 39
new Foreign Office. Grave news from China startled them
that autumn ; and he outlined the alternative lines of 41
operation in an appreciation that would have done credit
to any General Staff :

" We cannot I think avoid avenging so unprovoked
and faithless an outrage. There seem to be three Things
which might be done.
Firstly an attack and occupation of Pekin. . . . But
this could not be done before the Spring.

Secondly we might take possession of Chusan and hold it till the Chinese did what we wanted, or we might make it a Place of Rendezvous for any Force intended to enter the North of China but this alone would be a feeble proceeding.

Thirdly we might blockade China' by Cutting off Communication by the Grand Canal, either by establishing ourselves at the Yang tse Kiang at the Point where the Canal cuts it, or by taking possession of Tien sing. . . ."

Quick thinking for a Prime Minister of seventy-five.

His concerns were no less martial, when he wrote to Mr. Gladstone on coast defences and naval construction. The Chancellor was inclined to be a trifle sceptical about " those maritime castles which we call line of battle ships and which seem to be constructed on the principle precisely opposite to that of all land fortifications, and to aim at presenting as large a surface as possible to the destroying fire of an enemy ". But Palmerston responded stoutly " in Favor of having as many of them as needed to over match those which could be brought against us. I take it the Command of the Ocean will still be with the Power that can fit out the strongest Fleet of Line of Battle ships. Smaller vessels may be useful as auxiliaries in the narrow seas or to defend Coasts and Colonies, but the heavy Battery of a First or Second Rate will always be too much for smaller vessels ". He still had his doubts about iron plates ; so, for the matter of that, had half the partners in *Messrs. Sibley, Rhead, and Sibley.* But, to a man who had seen Trafalgar, the principles of sea-power were plain enough.

Later in the year more peaceful matters claimed them. Cobden had seen a Frenchman, who proposed an Anglo-French Commercial Treaty. He mooted it to Mr. Gladstone and, with Cabinet approval, went off to Paris with semi-official authority to sound the French. Palmerston, an older Free Trader than any of them, read his reports with

9 Piccadilly
29 Nov. 1869

My dear Gladstone

With Reference to
what you say in your
letter of the 25 there are
good opinions both ways
as to size of Battts this
but I own I think the
Balance of argument
strongly in favor of having
as many of them as needed
to over match those which

would be brought against us. I take it the Command of the Ocean will still be with the Power that can fit out the Strongest Fleet of Line of Battle Ships. Smaller Vessels may be useful as auxiliaries in the narrow Seas or to defend Coasts & Colonies, but the heavy Battery of a First or Second Rate will always be too much for smaller vessels

2 Rather Iron plated
ships with Steel tack
That as improved science
will bring to bear against
them remains to be seen
but even then it will be
some time before they
can be completed in
sufficient numbers by any
Power to constitute the
main arm of naval
warfare

Yrs Sincerely
Palmerston

No. 29

Ld Palmerston

interest ; and Bright's malicious hint that " he did all he   Palm.
dared to make the Treaty miscarry " seems, in the light of   418
his hopeful little notes to Gladstone, to have been quite   **51 & 54**
unfounded. They were in the fullest sympathy now,
with the Chancellor thanking his aged leader, " as one   **53**
of the public, for your excellent speeches at Romsey ",
and Lady Palmerston reciprocating by " spouting as   Glad.
she read by candle-light " a speech of their Chancellor's   II. 19
on Italy. For Italy still made a bond between them ;
and the Prince Consort's hesitations on Italian policy   **55**
were vigorously dispelled by some hours of Mr. Gladstone's
dialectic.

   As 1860 opened, the great Budget was in full preparation.
The strain wore him a little thin, and a passing illness
involved postponements. But the Prime Minister was kindness itself, found it " better to give you Law till Friday ",   **58**
and adjourned the awkward question of coast defences   **60**
which had threatened Gladstone's peace of mind. Then,
aided by " a great stock of egg and wine ", the momentous   Glad.
speech was safely delivered ; and Palmerston sent generous   II. 27
congratulations, hoping that his colleague was " none the
worse for that Triumph on Friday for which the Govern-   **63**
ment is much the better ". But their skies soon darkened.
For the Lords rejected the proposed repeal of the Paper   Palm.
Duties. Palmerston was not inconsolable ; he had disliked   419
the scheme, had gone, indeed, so far as to inform the Queen
that if the Lords rejected it, " they would perform a good
public service ". The service, good or bad, had been performed ; and while the Prime Minister doubted the
wisdom " of starting at the present moment a nice Question
of Functions and Privileges between the two Houses of
Parliament ", Mr. Gladstone wrote a resounding minute in   **86**
favour of " the principle, that the Lords are not to tax the
people without their consent ". For the apt pupil had learnt
his Radical lesson all too well. (Small wonder that he took
his name off the Carlton Club that year.) But Palmerston,

103 less ardent, sent him little notes on the extreme advisability of avoiding a revival of " the Question between the two Glad. Houses ", and even whispered to John Russell as he rose II. 33 to speak, " You won't pitch into the Lords ". For now their paths had met, had even crossed, and Gladstone's positively seemed to run a little further to the left.

Coast defences still menaced their harmony, with the 93 Prime Minister writing firm minutes on the strategy of invasion and even Herbert at the War Office taking a most un-Peelite tone. They corresponded amicably on Church appointments ; and Mr. Gladstone expressed his views on Oxford matters, with the judicious caution that Professor 115 Jowett " has been the subject of controversy in the University and his opinions are highly distasteful to the great majority ". But armaments were the real menace. Palmerston Palm. had gaily informed the Queen that " however great the 420 loss to the Government by the retirement of Mr. Gladstone, it would be better to lose Mr. Gladstone than to run the risk of losing Portsmouth or Plymouth ". A hint of increased 117 naval expenditure stung Mr. Gladstone to a fully reasoned memorandum, refusing bluntly to decide on a break-neck entry in the race of naval armaments with France " between Monday and Wednesday afternoons ". The Prime Minister 118 replied a little drily that " no doubt a full Exchequer is a good Foundation for National Defence but if the superstructure is wanting, the Foundation would be of small avail and if the French had the Command of the Sea they would soon find means to make a full Exchequer empty ". The new friend of Mr. Cobden could hardly be expected to concur in such reasoning—still less in its highly Palmerstonian conclusion :

> " The anger of a Power no stronger than ourselves may be borne, with Regret if you will but without alarm. The anger of a Power greatly and decidedly stronger must cause apprehension, and is likely to lead to disaster or

This letter was with
held on previous
then the prospect
wanted in this Mr.
was not likely to go
forward
WEGladstone

11 Carlton H. Terrace
Feb. 26. 1861

My dear Lord Palmerston

Your Memorandum of yesterday, and
the accompanying circumstances, I think require
from me in answer more than remarks upon the
particular proposal.

You have a right to expect the services of a Chancellor of the Exchequer with whom you can take
counsel upon all measures of finance, whether military or other, in their beginnings

Not merely reasons affecting myself, but a sense
of what is due to you, make me feel the unseemliness of my renewing during the present Session
a series of struggles such as were those of last year

upon the Fortifications, the Paper Duty, and the Question of Taxing Bills.

By what is due to you I mean what is due not only to your station, and to the credit of your Government, but to the kindness and consideration with which you have treated not on many occasions.

The most natural sequel to what I have said would be at once to place my resignation in your hands

But one strong public motive, over and above many which are personal, disinclines me to any such step at the present juncture. I earnestly desire, and I feel it to be a duty unless it is crossed by some other duty yet more imperative, to render any account of the measures of last year; which; whether they were good or bad, were in their bulk sufficient to stamp a character on the Session This account can only be rendered in full by means of the Budget, which, in proposing measures for the future, will also wind up the past and will [illegible] offer to objectors the legitimate occasion for asking the judgment of Parliament.

Any such question must be disposed of shortly after Easter; and I desire to be in at the death, even though it should be my own. But in at the death I cannot be, if our plan of Naval Expenditure for the year is to be abandoned within a fortnight after its announcement: and in that case it would be better that you should at once commit my duties to other hands, than that a struggle such as

those to which I have referred should begin
in the Cabinet of tomorrow.

I remain

Sincerely yours

W. E. Gladstone

My Memorandum in the Cabinet box will
explain to our colleagues what I have to say in relation to the
immediate question: This letter of course is
for you as Head of the Government

Humiliation ; and no People are more prone than the French to make arrogant abuse of predominant Power."

On the receipt of this Gladstone played for a moment with the idea of resignation. Indeed, he composed a carefully contingent letter of farewell. But he kept it on his desk for two days ; and in the interval the projected naval increase was shelved. So it was never sent. Nothing, perhaps, is more remarkable than the absence from their correspondence of unequivocal resignations by Mr. Gladstone. For his resignations have become almost legendary ; irreverent myths describe the Prime Minister's chimney smoking with his frequent holocausts of Mr. Gladstone's resignations. But few, if any, of them survive ; and we are scarcely entitled to assume that they all perished in the study fireplaces of Broadlands and Cambridge House, since no drafts of them remain at Hawarden.

Their struggles on finance continued. But they struggled inside the same Cabinet ; and it sometimes struck Gladstone that " we are not Mr. Burke's famous mosaic, but we are Glad. a mosaic in solution, that is to say, a kaleidoscope ". He II. 37 could see now that the old man was guided by two motives, " an intense love of Constitutional freedom everywhere Talks. and . . . a profound hatred of negro slavery "—and to these 128 his new-born Liberalism responded freely. But in a talk between them Palmerston confessed to a third ambition, which evoked less enthusiasm from Mr. Gladstone—" to put Glad. England in a state of defence. In short, it appears that he II. 45 now sees, as he considers, the opportunity of obtaining a long-cherished object ; and it is not unnatural that he should repel any proposal which should defraud him of a glory, in and by absolving him from a duty ". A slightly rueful confession followed—" I am now sure that Lord Palmerston entertained this purpose when he formed the government ; but had I been in the slightest degree aware of it, I should certainly, but very reluctantly, have abstained from joining it, and helped, as I could, from another bench, its Italian purposes ".

Glad. Still, he had joined it now ; and he was not sorry. Better,
II. 140 perhaps, to be a lonely Chancellor fighting Estimates " at the dagger's point " than a still lonelier voice in Opposition.
Things were brisk enough in 1861, with the Prime Minister
125 blandly declining " to make the Fate of my administration depend upon the Decision which Parliament may come to upon your Proposal " about the Paper Duties, a stand-up
136-40 fight upon a trifling Bill about the new Law Courts (in which Palmerston, after a surprising claim that the First Lord of the Treasury was constitutionally entitled to the leading voice on finance, managed a soft answer that turned away a resignation), and a stern enunciation of naval policy. Lord Palmerston abounded in technical considerations—how ships cased with iron had an immense advantage ; how the French in 1862 would have seventeen of these destructive engines to Great Britain's fifteen or sixteen ; how the French armoured ships were sensibly constructed, while the British (as was only to be expected from a Tory Admiralty) were all wrong ; how, therefore, even parity of numbers would conceal a real inequality of fighting strength ; how the best thing to do was to build hard—the whole concluding with his familiar argument " that Peace and Good understanding between England & France are a great Security for the Peace of Europe as well as for the welfare of England and France and that Peace and Good understanding between England & France are most likely to be permanent when France has no Naval Superiority over England "—hard reading for Mr. Cobden's pupil.

But Mr. Cobden and the friends of peace had graver things to think of in the closing weeks of 1861. For the calm waters of British policy were invaded by the alarming backwash of the American Civil War. At first the official mind was not greatly interested ; and Palmerston expressed

a correct conviction that " our best and true policy seems Palm.
to be to go on as we have begun, and to keep quite clear of the 427
conflict between North and South ". Some day, of course, the
war would end. But that seemed a distant prospect, vaguely
explored in a minute of the Prime Minister's : " It is in the
highest Degree likely that the North will not be able to Palm.
subdue the South, and it is no doubt certain that if the 428
Southern Union is established as an independent state, it
would afford a valuable and extensive market for British
manufactures. But the operations of the war have as yet
been too indecisive to warrant an acknowledgement of the
Southern Union ". That was the easy tone of 1861, though
Palmerston occasionally dropped in at the Confederate
office off Pall Mall and Mr. Adams gloomily foresaw the
worst from Mansfield Street. The worst nearly happened on
the winter day that London heard the news about the
Trent. For a Northern cruiser had stopped that British
mail-steamer on the high seas and removed two Southern
passengers. If Palmerston desired a war, here was his
chance. Indeed, he had a word about it with Judge Mann, Put.
of Georgia, in Suffolk Street, Pall Mall. But though no war 210.
ensued, at least one sturdy Federal is still convinced of
Palmerston's malignity and tells how a warlike Premier Linc.
suppressed the lawyers' peaceable opinion, drafted a stern des- 88
patch to Washington, and threatened to resign because Prince Put.
Albert changed the draft, whilst an indignant London mob 205–11
broke palace windows. The truth is less friendly to romance,
but more creditable to Palmerston. For he brought the
lawyers to the decisive meeting of the Cabinet and positively
invited more of them than custom required ; for a note sur- **153**
vives in which Gladstone was asked by the Prime Minister to
bring his friend Phillimore, the international lawyer. Prime
Ministers who mean to have their way at all costs rarely
invite an unnecessary wealth of legal advice. He suppressed
no opinion, since the lawyers were quite clear that the Ad.
Northern captain was gravely in error. He drafted no I. 212

Russ. despatch, since the despatch was drafted by John Russell.
II. 346 The despatch itself was " softened " by the Cabinet ; and
Glad. further amendments by the Prince Consort were received
II. 74 by Palmerston without demur. For an unfriendly colleague
Palm. testifies that he " thought them excellent," and the Queen
430 herself alluded subsequently to his entire concurrence.
Moreover, to complete the dissipation of the Northern
legend, Palmerston did not threaten to resign, and no
angry mob broke windows " in the wing of Buckingham
Palace then occupied by the Prince," for the simple reason
that the Prince Consort was then sinking into death at
Windsor, and mobs, however angry, do not waste stones
on empty palaces.

The *Trent* affair gave Palmerston a *casus belli*. But he
did not take it, because he did not want one. Cobden,
Palm. indeed, suspected as much—" I do not believe in war.
431 Palmerston likes to drive the wheel close to the edge, and
show how dexterously he can avoid falling over the preci-
pice. . . . He and his colleagues knew there could be no
war ". A genuine relief breathes in his confidential note to
155 Gladstone after the incident was over—" You will have
seen that the Trent affair is satisfactorily settled and that
the Prisoners are given up. But *uno avulso non deficit alter*.
Not indeed *aureus* : but I hope it will not be *ferreus*." That
was not the tone of a man just disappointed of a chance
of war.

Their American reflections took a different tone late in
Russ. 1862. Russell had always favoured a joint Anglo-French pro-
II. 344 posal to the disrupted States, and Gladstone's mind moved
further in the same direction. Mrs. Gladstone learned
from her husband in the summer that the Prime Minister
Glad. had " come exactly to my mind about some early repre-
II. 75 sentation of a friendly kind to America, if we can get
France and Russia to join ". But Palmerston, more cautious,
Palm. was still waiting " to know that their separate Independence
437 is a Truth and a Fact before we declare it to be " ; and that

would be settled by the war-news. Gladstone was more impulsive and actually favoured his leader with a memorandum on the frontier-line between the two Republics. It **183** followed an exciting conversation with " a Southern Gentleman, whose name I need not put on paper", and dealt in satisfying detail with " the question always represented on the Federal side as physically and socially incapable of solution, for political purposes, the Question I mean of the *Border* between the Northern and Southern Republics, presuming there will be only two, of which he does not feel quite sure". The autumn found intervention coming nearer, with the Confederates closing in on Washington and the Prime Minister writing to ask John Russell " if this should **Russ.** happen, would it not be time for us to consider whether in **II. 349** such a state of things England and France might not address the contending parties and recommend an arrangement upon the basis of separation ? " Russell concurred and was in favour of an immediate proposal to the French, followed by a joint Anglo-French approach to Russia. But Palmerston was rather inclined to wait on military events— " If the Federals sustain a great defeat, they may be at once **Russ.** ready for mediation. . . . If on the other hand, they should **II. 350** have the best of it, we may wait awhile and see what may follow ". At this stage he wrote to Gladstone, informing him of the proposal –Gladstone, he knew, " would be inclined **185** to approve such a Course " ; something might happen in October or even earlier. Meanwhile, he had seen that Gladstone was going north to make a speech and trusted that his eloquent colleague would " not be too sympathising with the Tax Payer, nor tell the Country that they are paying too much Taxation have too large Establishments, and ought to agitate to bring the House of Commons and the Government to more economical ways and Habits. These Topics suit best Cobden and Bright and their Followers ". Mr. Gladstone received the news of intervention with frank delight. The Southern victories, he felt, were themselves a **186**

danger to ultimate peace ; since the demarcation of a frontier on the lines of his earlier memorandum might be
endangered by an undue rise in Southern spirits. Besides,
Lancashire itself, if left much longer, might prejudice the
chance of British interference—" The population of Lancashire have borne their sufferings with a fortitude and
patience exceeding all example, and almost all belief. But
if in any *one* of the great towns, resignation should, even for
a single day, give place to excitement, and an outbreak
should occur, our position in the face of America, and our
influence for good might be seriously affected : we might
then seem to be interfering, with loss of dignity on the
ground of our immediate interests, and rather in the
attitude of parties than as representing the general interests
of humanity and peace". His desire for peace was genuine
enough, and even for peace at the expense of British
Glad. interests ; since he believed sincerely that " were the Union
II. 92 split, the North, no longer checked by the jealousies of
slave-power, would seek a partial compensation for its loss
in annexing, or trying to annex, British North America".

With such thoughts in his mind Mr. Gladstone went to
Glad. Newcastle and told a wildly cheering crowd that " there
II. 79 is no doubt that Jefferson Davis and other leaders of the
South have made an army ; they are making, it appears, a
navy ; and they have made what is more than either, they
have made a nation". His fatal eloquence had outrun the
Cabinet, and there was a hail of disputatious memoranda.
188 Gladstone's contained a reasoned argument founded on
the assumption that " we wish the war to end, and that we
see no early probability of its ending if left to itself". A
joint Anglo-Franco-Russian mediation, he argued, would
have immense moral authority :

> " The nineteenth century has many boasts, some
> fictitious and some real. Among the most real, and also
> among the noblest of its distinctions, as I think, has been

the gradual and sensible growth of what may be rudely called an international opinion, which carries in the main the authority of the mass of nations, and, whenever it is brought to bear, powerfully influences the conduct of each nation in particular ; acting in a manner more or less analogous to that in which public opinion, as we commonly term it, acts upon the institutions and policy of a well-ordered country."

Should not some such moral force dictate to the Americans that " this horrible war ought to cease " ? The time was ripe for intervention, since the war had manifestly reached a deadlock. Besides, an outbreak in suffering Lancashire might at any moment prevent Great Britain from intervening with dignity at a later stage. There was another reason, too :

" The people of England are being rapidly drawn into Southern sympathies. It is one thing to anticipate an issue of the war favourable in the main to the Southern view : it is quite another to sympathize with men whose cause is, as I think, seriously tainted by its connection with slavery. Yet the sight of a minority, heroically struggling against the effort of a much larger number to place them in a political connection that they abhor, probably with a withdrawal or limitation of their rights as freemen, has an irresistible tendency to arouse active sympathies in England on behalf of the weaker side, even apart from the disgraceful circumstances which have attended the forcible re-establishment of the Northern rule, particularly in New Orleans.

" The more these positive Southern sympathies increase, the less shall we be able to maintain a friendly and impartial aspect in any proceeding that may be taken."

The case was strong for intervention in a war which, " being
Ep

the most gigantic . . . has also perhaps become the most purposeless of all great civil wars that have ever been waged ". He even invoked the cause of negro emancipation, reasoning that " the longer interference is delayed, the less favourable will be our position, and the less clear our title, for urging on the Government of the Southern Confederacy the just claims of the slave ".

It was a rousing broadside with which Mr. Gladstone followed his Foreign Secretary into action. But the Cabinet was obdurate, though at the outset he had felt that " both Lords Palmerston and Russell are *right* ". They flagged, though ; " Lord Russell rather turned tail. He gave way without resolutely fighting out his battle ". And, as for Palmerston, he was now " very much inclined to change the opinion on which I wrote to you when the Confederates seemed to be carrying all before them, and I am very much come back to our original view of the matter, that we must continue merely to be lookers-on till the war shall have taken a more decided turn". So Mr. Gladstone's Newcastle declaration was left in the air ; and more than thirty years later he repented of it in almost an excess of sack-cloth. The wary Premier had waited, as he always meant to, for the war-news ; and the rolling gun-fire of Antietam checked the great *démarche*.

They corresponded upon other matters. There were still armaments ; and he could never bring his Chancellor to see that " we have on the other side of the Channel a People who, say what they may, hate us as a nation from the Bottom of their Hearts ", to say nothing of their " able, active, wary, counselkeeping, but ever planning sovereign". They could never "forget or forgive Aboukir, Trafalgar, the Peninsula, Waterloo and St. Helena ". Lord Palmerston could not forget them either ; and his policy in 1862 continued to be deeply coloured by Napoleonic memories. He asked his colleague almost sharply whether the whole mass of national opinion had been wrong, " and have Bright and

Glad.
II. 85

Palm.
433

Glad.
II. 81

164

Cobden and yourself been right ? " And Gladstone
answered stiffly that " in all good humour, I prefer not **166**
being classed with Mr. Bright or even Mr. Cobden ". But
the Prime Minister quizzically made his point by forward-
ing a Radical leaflet, which appeared to couple Gladstone
with Cobden in opposition to " Palmerstonianism ", and **173**
adding helpfully that the Chancellor might " not have
seen how your Name is taken in vain by People with whom
I conceive you do not sympathise ".

A graver matter engaged them, as official minds began
to wrestle with the problem of a memorial to the late Prince
Consort. At first, Wolsey's Chapel at Windsor was to be **162**
re-decorated for the purpose ; and there was talk of a new
National Gallery in Burlington Gardens, to be called " the **171**
Albert Gallery " and adorned with a statue of the Prince.
Then their preoccupations shifted to the Kensington site, and
Mr. Gladstone recorded his conviction that " the ground
belonging to the Commissioners at Kensington is the true **197**
place for an effective Memorial to the Prince Consort. On
that ground it will tell its own story and tell it well : no one
would have occasion to ask ' why is it here '. The Prince
on that ground would be like Wren in St. Paul's." Not
quite, though. Happily perhaps for Wren, he built St. Paul's
himself : the Prince's monument was left to others.
Mr. Gilbert Scott, that paladin of the Gothic Revival with
whom Lord Palmerston had already had painful passages Palm.
on the subject of the new Foreign Office, conceived the bold 414
design of " a kind of ciborium to protect a statue of the Scott.
Prince. . . . These shrines were models of imaginary build- 225
ings, such as had never in reality been erected ". Quite
undeterred, the gallant architect proposed to erect one ; **205**
and ministers were presently assailed with vast demands
for old guns to be melted down in order to translate his
leaping fancy into bronze. But Mr. Gladstone was severe :
the guns could not be given up without a Vote. Scott **206**
pleaded hard. The Prime Minister had already cautioned

205 him " that he is bound in Honor as a Gentleman not to run the Queen into any Expence for the Memorial beyond the amount of the Subscriptions and the vote " ; and he re-

219 mained acidly convinced that the architect was " an incorrigible Encroacher and thinks of nothing but what he calls his own Fame as an architect ". Gladstone was equally

220 unsympathetic—" I would not give 1/- to Mr. Scott, after the warning he has had, on his ground of his fame "—and though the battle for the Russian guns raged quite as fiercely as though Woolwich Arsenal had been the breach at the Redan, they were never captured. For " the four Great Groups at the outer angles of the steps ", for which the architect demanded thirty-four tons of bronze, were executed in marble. Such are the tribulations of an artist fallen among politicians.

The Civil War continued to recur in their correspondence. There is no reference to the strange avatar of *Number 290*, better known to Northern shipping as *Alabama*. But

209 Mr. Cobden warned the Cabinet that " *the neutrality code is henceforth, so far as we may require its benefits, a dead letter*. It will only be felt when we become belligerents what a suicidal game we have been playing. But there is a far graver question involved in the iron-clad vessels of war now being built for the Confederate government. Without exception every American I see says if they go to sea and commence hostilities against the Federals, we shall have war at once ". They never went to sea. The anecdote of the Laird rams, which was rehearsed at length to Gladstone, is eminently

212 creditable to Palmerston's good sense. Their parentage, as he confessed, was " curious and intricate ". Built to Confederate orders, they had been transferred to a questionable Frenchman and reassigned to the Egyptians, who rejected them ; and the unlovely vessels lay at Liverpool. But their purpose was sufficiently evident from the fact that they were " iron plated and furnished with projecting Beaks to act as Rams ". So, while Russell detained them with a cheerful

disregard of law, Palmerston advised the Admiralty to buy Russ.
them and at the same time asked the Turks to make an offer II. 359
in case they were unsuitable for the British Navy. The
method, it must be confessed, was highly informal. But respect for formalities might have let the rams slip away to
sea ; and Palmerston's judicious purchase effected more
than all Mr. Cobden's protests.

Not that he bore the slightest malice. He had once told
Cobden himself that personalities never ought to be remem- Cob.
bered for three months ; and when a pension was proposed II. 230
for Cobden, he cheerfully concurred—

" Gladstone mentioned to me more than a year ago **221**
the wish of Cobden's friends that a Parliamentary Pension
might be obtained for him, as he was very poor, having
sadly mismanaged his own affairs, just as he would, if he
could, the affairs of the nation. Gladstone felt at that time
that it was too soon to make any such proposal, because
the fruits of the French Treaty were not then ripe ; and
I therefore offered Cobden his choice of being made a
Privy Councillor or a Baronet. But in the true spirit of a
Republican Radical he refused any Honour that was to
come from that hated Being, a Sovereign. I daresay he
would gladly accept a House of Commons Pension, and
I for my part should have no objection to propose it to
Parliament, if the Cabinet should think fit. Cobden had
certainly great merit in the conception of the Treaty, and
in working it out. . . . The Proposal certainly could not
with any justice be represented as springing from Party
Favour, for with the exception of Bright and Disraeli we
have not a bitterer enemy than Cobden on any bench in
the House of Commons."

The matter rested there ; and Cobden continued to fill
England with the dreadful tale of Palmerstonian profligacy.
He even favoured Mr. Gladstone with two lengthy protests

Cob.
II. 460 against expenditure on armaments and, in particular, on the defence of Canada. The letters reached the Prime Minister, who responded with an acid minute :

216 " These Letters of Mr. Cobden's are like his Speeches Illustrations of the Saying that shallow Streams run with the most violence and the most Noise. The Letters are full of Inconsistencies Contradictions and Forgetfulness of Facts. He compares the British Navy with the Federal one, forgetting that England on his own admission ought to have a Navy superior to that of any other naval Power in Consequence of her smaller Condition and her beyond sea Possessions, whereas the United States are purely Continental with no Possessions beyond Sea. . . . He is always railing at the aristocracy and alleging that our Institutions are maintained for and exclusively filled by them. This is very snobbish, and fitter for a Shop apprentice in a Back Alley in the City, than for a Man engaged in public Life and with a Knowledge of the practical working of our Constitution. What was the aristocratical parentage of Clyde, of Lyndhurst, of Campbell, of Thompson, of Longley, of Peel ? "

Plainly the two could never hope to agree. But precisely a week later Mr. Gladstone wrote, by desire of the Prime Minister, to offer Cobden the Chairmanship of the Board of Audit. The offer was refused. But offer and refusal were equally honourable to both parties.

Cob.
II. 464

Gladstone's activities in 1863 were not confined to the Estimates and the Albert Memorial. For he learned something of a graver obstacle with which his subsequent career was to be confronted. That year he went for the first time **210** to do what Palmerston cheerfully described as " Suit & Service at Balmoral ". The royal mourning was at its **211** deepest ; and his stay was scarcely enlivened by a slight

carriage accident to the Queen. Her views were freely expressed. On the Laird rams " she did not appear to lean
towards over-conciliation of the Federal Government ".
But on Schleswig-Holstein she was full of a notion " that
gross injustice is done to the people especially of Schleswig
in altering the terms of their succession and their relation
to Denmark and to Holstein against their will or without
their consent ". A letter to his wife put it more candidly,
recording the Queen's " immense interest in Germany, her   Glad.
recollections of the Prince's sentiments being in that, as in II. 97
other matters, a barometer to govern her sympathies and
affections ". She was " intensely interested " in the prob-   Glad.
lem, " because the Prince thought it a great case of justice II. 102
on the side rather opposite to that of Lord Palmerston and
the government policy. She spoke about this with intense
earnestness, and said she considered it a legacy from him ".
Here was an awkward obstacle looming dimly in front of
Mr. Gladstone. For it was scarcely to be hoped that all
his policies would invariably conform to the posthumous
desires of the Prince Consort.

A livelier obstacle loomed in his path early in 1864 ; and
this time it was Lord Palmerston himself. The occasion was
Reform ; and the Prime Minister's affection for that pro-
gressive cause was distinctly qualified. His distaste was
natural, perhaps. One revolution, after all, is enough for
a lifetime. He had been nearly fifty when the Reform Bill
of 1832 transformed the world, and it was not easy for him
to contemplate another. Besides, John Russell was the
eternal zealot of Reform ; and Palmerston could hardly be
expected to share the worst of Johnny's weaknesses. So
when a private member's Reform Bill came on, Mr. Gladstone got a cautious little note of warning from Cambridge
House, hoping that " in what you may say upon Baines's   **226**
Bill you will not commit yourself and the Government as
to any particular amount of Borough Franchise. . . . No
Doubt many working men are as fit to vote as many of the

Ten Pounders, but if we open the Door to the Class the Number who may come in may be excessive and may swamp the Classes above them . . . and then these working men are unfortunately under the Control of Trades Unions, which unions are directed by a small Number of directing Agitators ". The judicious warning reached Mr. Gladstone on the Treasury Bench ; and, with a somewhat liberal interpretation of his instructions, he informed a startled House

Glad. that " every man who is not presumably incapacitated by
II. 126 some consideration of personal unfitness or of political danger, is morally entitled to come within the pale of the constitution ". This said, he wrote hopefully to the Prime

227 Minister, trusting that " others will give you a better account of any impression left by what I said than myself. . . . I hope I did not commit the Government to anything : nor myself to a particular form of franchise ". The hope was sadly disappointed. For his aged leader informed him after

228 reading his speech on the next morning that " there is little in it that I can agree with, and much from which I differ ". He added almost bitterly that it was " more like the Sort of Speech with which Bright would have introduced the Reform Bill which he would like to propose, than the Sort of Speech which might have been expected from the Treasury Bench in the present State of Things. Your Speech may win Lancashire for you, though that is doubtful but I fear it will tend to lose England for you. It is to be regretted that you should, as you stated, have taken the opportunity of your receiving a Deputation of working men, to exhort them to set on Foot an Agitation for Parliamentary Reform—The Function of a Government is to calm

229 rather than to excite Agitation ". Mr. Gladstone answered at length, emphasizing the qualifications with which his statement had been hedged, and denying roundly that he had ever incited working men to agitate. The Prime Minister responded curtly with a cutting from the *Times*, in which he

230 had thoughtfully " marked . . . that Part of your Speech to

which I alluded as an Exhortation to the working men to
agitate for Parliamentary Reform ". But Mr. Gladstone **231**
failed to " see in the passage marked anything in the nature
of an exhortation ". Such metaphysics were too fine for
Palmerston, who answered that " it is quite true that you **232**
did not use words directly exhorting them to agitate, but
what you said seems to me to have no other meaning ".
Slightly chastened, Mr. Gladstone informed another correspondent that he had " unwarily, it seems, set the Thames Glad.
on fire ". But, with a pardonable pride in the conflagra- II. 130
tion, he proposed to perpetuate it by reissuing the speech
in pamphlet form. Lord Palmerston endeavoured to dis- **233**
suade him ; but Gladstone was firm and emphasized the
value of a correct text of his speech in view of " the tendency **234**
of all reporters, especially in the case of a speaker difficult
to follow, to omit qualifications, which are sometimes in
themselves material and which always affect the general
colour of a speech ". The Prime Minister consented almost **235**
sulkily, and the argument was over.

Not that their harmony was clouded by this brisk debate.
A faithful secretary once noted sadly " how they misunder- Glad.
stood one another, and how evidently each mistrusted the II. 51
other, though perfectly cordial and most friendly in their
mutual intercourse ". So when the Tories threatened a vote
of censure over Schleswig-Holstein, Palmerston could still
inform his Chancellor in a friendly note that " we shall **239**
want a great Gun to follow Disraeli. Would you be ready
to follow him ? " He briefed him loyally, referred him to
the appropriate Blue Book, and cautioned him that " it **240**
would be well not to be too hard upon the Danes. It is true **241**
that they were wrong in the Beginning and have been wrong
in the End, but they have been most unjustly used by the
Germans and the sympathies in the majority of the House
and in the Nation are Danish ".

Their customary debates upon expenditure continued.
The ball, as usual, was opened by the Chancellor ; and the **245**

Prime Minister replied in " a pamphlet letter ". Small wonder that, with such opportunities of seeing Lord Palmerston's handwriting, it remained in Mr. Gladstone's memory as one of the two perfect things that he had known. This time that firm caligraphy insisted that " any Body who looks carefully at the Signs of the Times must see that there are at present two strong Feelings in the National Mind, the one a Disinclination to organic Changes in our representative System ; the other a steady Determination that the Country shall be placed and kept in an efficient Condition of Defence ". If so, the national mind was a striking replica of Palmerston's ; and their correspondence on the subject

closed with a bold assertion of the fact—" You say that you think that it has been my personal Popularity, and not the Conviction or Desire of the Nation that has kept up the Estimates at their present Amount. In this it appears to me that you misplace Cause and Effect. This British Nation is not one that would be disposed to unnecessary Burthens out of Regard for any individual Man ; and if I have in any Degree been fortunate enough to have obtained some share of the Good will and Confidence of my Fellow-Countrymen, it has been because I have rightly understood the Feelings and Opinions of the Nation, and because they think that I have, as far as any Scope of Action of Mine was concerned, endeavoured to maintain the Dignity and to uphold the Interests of the Country abroad, and to provide for its security at Home. You may depend upon it that any Degree of Popularity that is worth having can be obtained only by such means and of that Popularity I sincerely wish you the most ample share ".

For once, the Prime Minister was almost crushing.
Meanwhile, he pressed his case for military and naval expenditure. " Gentlemen's Houses are better and more extensively provided than was formerly the case. Tenant Farmers are not disposed to live in the Houses which were held good enough for their Predecessors ; and the Labourers

have had provided for them Habitations which would have satisfied the Smock Frock Farmer of former Times." So why not a corresponding increase of outlay on military establishments? A modern warship cost £270,000 where Nelson's Admiralty could build a first-rate for £1,000 a gun. Then there were Armstrong cannon; and the new Enfield rifle cost far more than Brown Bess, to say nothing of the coming need to replace it with a breech-loader. The needs of the services were almost lovingly enumerated; and it is not surprising that when the letter came, the Chancellor recorded " a dark prospect ". Glad. II. 139

Once their attention strayed to an unusual topic, when Mr. Gladstone hinted at " the purchase of the Railways by the State, with a view not to State Management but to a large reduction of charges and an *approach* to uniformity in the rates ". The Prime Minister was far from shocked, pricked up an aged ear, and asked for details. He was particularly anxious to learn " how would you deal with Railways to be henceforward made; for we may be pretty sure that we have not yet come to a *Ne plus Ultra* in the Construction of Railways ". Such an enquiry was eminently creditable to a man born forty years before the first railway. Gladstone replied in hopeful detail with a project that bears a striking resemblance to the proposals of his Liberal successors with regard to coal-mines. For the railways were " to be worked by Commercial firms or companies as lessees from the State, in conveniently divided groups, and probably to be superintended, as far as the State is concerned, by a Board or Department having a qualified independence of the Executive Government ". But Palmerston found the addition of two or three hundred million to the National Debt a shade alarming; and, composing his features into the stern expression of an economist, he denounced the scheme with a fair show of reason as " on the first Blush a wild and more than doubtful Project ", whilst even Mr. Gladstone found it " a vast and staggering one ". 244 249 250, 253 254 255

The years slipped by ; and their customary occupations
Glad. brought them together into 1865. The fight on the Estimates
II. 140 was " almost as rough as any of the roughest times ", though
Gladstone finally acknowledged that " the concessions
256 made, inadequate as I think them, were made in a spirit of
conciliation. . . . I therefore, although reluctantly, agree to
the Navy Estimate ". Palmerston expressed enlightened
257 views in favour of the reduction of indirect taxation rather
than of the Income Tax—" The Taxes on Tea, Sugar,
Coffee Beer & Spirits take away a far larger Proportion of
the Spendable Means of the Poorer Classes than of the
Richer Classes ". Not that their prospect was one of unin-
terrupted harmony, since his restive colleague proposed to
express an individual view upon the Irish Church. The
262 Prime Minister was firm upon the obligation of ministers
Glad. to refrain from such private excursions. But Mr. Gladstone
II. 142 had his way. Indeed, in the closing stage of their relations
he generally did. For fifty-five has frequently the best of the
argument with eighty. Besides, Palmerston felt an instinc-
Palm. tive certainty that " Gladstone will soon have it all his own
453 way ; and whenever he gets my place, we shall have
strange doings ". He did his best to keep him in the seat at
Oxford, though, and even made a timely Oxford Bishop
271-4 during the General Election when it was by rights the turn
of Cambridge. But then he always had a high opinion of the
restraining influence of Oxford on Mr. Gladstone. Had he
Palm. not said of him, " He is a dangerous man ; keep him in
455 Oxford, and he is partially muzzled ; but send him elsewhere, and he will run wild " ? Oxford dismissed him ; and
soon South Lancashire electors heard a deep voice inform
Glad. the Free Trade Hall, " At last, my friends, I am come
II. 146 among you, and I am come among you ' unmuzzled ' ".
There would be strange doings now ; and when Palmerston
277 congratulated him on his victory in Lancashire, he added
almost ruefully that " many Friends would have preferred
seeing you still for Oxford ".

MR. GLADSTONE, 1865

They still corresponded steadily on the small change of official business. Some revolutionary had shocked Mr. Gladstone and his advisers with a proposal to grant a half- **278** holiday on Saturdays to the Civil Service. But Palmerston was more sympathetic :

"These Reports are just what might have been ex- **279** pected ; no Employers of Labour like to give up any Portion however small of the Time of those who work under them. . . . This was the Line taken by Master Manufacturers against the Ten Hours Bill. If men were mere Machines which would regularly do a given Quantity of Work in a given Time like a Steam Engine such Calculations would be unanswerably decisive, but in considering such Matters we ought to bear in Mind that men are moral and intellectual agents, and that the work performed by them in a given Time depends much on the cheerfulness & good will with which it is done, and that both Cheerfulness & Goodwill very much depend upon the Belief that those who superintend and direct have some Sympathy for the Employed, and a Desire to lighten their work as far as can be done, without Injury to Interests concerned."

For Palmerston had learnt much of his Liberalism from Shaftesbury.

A smaller question faced them, when they considered a minor vacancy at the Admiralty. Goschen was thought of, **281** though Palmerston surmised that " he is largely engaged in commercial Pursuits which he would not give up for office, unless it were an office of some prominent political character ", while Mr. Gladstone had heard " young Trevelyan **282** very highly spoken of ". They were still writing hard in the first week of October ; and a note of October 7 informed **283-4** the Chancellor that Palmerston did " not foresee any Reason for calling the Cabinet together till the 10th of

November ". There was much else that he did not foresee—
a sudden chill, a week of illness, and the end. So Mr.
Gladstone was left to compose his lament, in a letter to
Panizzi, with its strange hint of Landseer and the haunting
thought of Italy :

Glad.   " *Ei fu !* Death has indeed laid low the most towering
II. 151-2 antlers in all the forest. No man in England will more
sincerely mourn Lord Palmerston than you. Your warm
heart, your long and close friendship with him, and your
sense of all he had said and done for Italy, all so bound
you to him that you will deeply feel this loss ; as for
myself I am stunned. . . . Tomorrow all England will be
ringing of it, and the world will echo England."

For Italy, which had first brought them together and kept
them close to one another, was present at their parting ;
and the strange partnership was over.

REFERENCES

(Numerals refer to letters or documents printed in the Correspondence.)

Ad.   GREAT BRITAIN AND THE AMERICAN CIVIL WAR.
E. D. Adams. 2 vols. 1925.

Ash.   LIFE OF VISCOUNT PALMERSTON, 1846–1865.
Evelyn Ashley. 2 vols. 1876.

Bent.   LORD GEORGE BENTINCK : A POLITICAL BIOGRAPHY.
B. Disraeli. 1852.

Cob.   LIFE OF RICHARD COBDEN.
John Morley. 2 vols. 1881.

End.   ENDYMION.
Earl of Beaconsfield. 3 vols. 1880.

Glad.   LIFE OF WILLIAM EWART GLADSTONE.
John Morley. 3 vols. 1903.

Linc.   ABRAHAM LINCOLN.
G. H. Putnam. 1909.

Palm. PALMERSTON.
Philip Guedalla. 1926.

Put.   MEMORIES OF MY YOUTH.
G. H. Putnam. 1914.

Russ.   LIFE OF LORD JOHN RUSSELL.
Spencer Walpole. 2 vols. 1889.

Scott. PERSONAL AND PROFESSIONAL RECOLLECTIONS.
G. G. Scott. 1874.

Talks. TALKS WITH MR. GLADSTONE.
Lionel A. Tollemache. 1898.

CORRESPONDENCE

1   *Gladstone   to   Palmerston*

Fasque,
Fettercairn,
Oct. 25. 1851

My dear Lord

Will you excuse my asking of you the favour to give directions that a copy of the Neapolitan Reply to my letters to Lord Aberdeen[1] may be sent me from Naples through the Foreign Office in the original Italian? as I have no prospect of being able to procure it within any limited time. The Neapolitan Government have not thought fit to send it me. I have written to Prince Castelcicala[2] for it but have had no reply. Mr. Murray my publisher cannot find a bookseller's parcel to come for some time, and I do not think anything would be allowed to come to me by the post. To excuse the trouble I am giving I have gone through this process of exhaustion. Unless I hear to the contrary I shall conclude you are kind enough to comply.

I have forwarded to your Lordship a letter and memoir from Signor Ricciardi which has been unfortunately delayed from being sent in a parcel. I may perhaps spare you a few minutes by saying that the memoir is chiefly historical and that the part immediately bearing on the present and future commences about three pages from the end

I remain my dear Lord
Faithfully yours
W. E. GLADSTONE

[1] *Two Letters to the Earl of Aberdeen on the State Prosecutions of the Neapolitan Government.* By the Right Hon. W. E. Gladstone. 1851.
[2] Neapolitan Ambassador.

2   *Palmerston to Gladstone*

C[arlton] G[ardens] 17 Nov. 1851

DEAR GLADSTONE

I have to apologize for not having answered your Letter, but I sent you the Neapolitan Pamphlet, (answer It cannot be called)[1] & I hope it reached you.

3   *Palmerston to Gladstone*

C[arlton] G[ardens] 9 May 1852

I missed my opportunity yesterday Evening of saying that I shall be obliged to leave the House of Commons early Tomorrow, to go to the Concert at the Palace ; so that I may be unable to stay out the Debate.

I am rather inclined to think that a good Many independent Men would be rather disposed to let the Bill [2] which is announced for Tomorrow, come in ; and to deal with it according to its Merits, instead of resisting its Introduction. I have no very strong opinion one way or the other ; but I should rather have been disposed to let the Bill be brought in, if the announced Arrangement should appear to be as good as any other, which in other possible Circumstances might be offered to Parliament.

The objection no doubt is, that the discussions which are sure to arise in the Progress of such a Bill, would tend to prolong the Session, but other Matters will keep us sitting till towards the End of June or Beginning of July, and if this Measure was still undetermined at that time it would probably be thrown over to be Food for the next Parliament

If the Government is beat on this question by a Combination between one set of Men who object only to the Time

---

[1] Palmerston described it elsewhere as " only a tissue of bare assertion and reckless denial, mixed up with coarse ribaldry and commonplace abuse of public men and political parties ". *Ash.* I. 258.

[2] A Bill for Assignments of Seats in lieu of St. Albans and Sudbury.

chosen for the Measure, and another set of Men who object
to the Measure because it does not Sufficiently increase the
strength of the Manufacturing or Metropolitan Representation the verdict will in general opinion be taken as having
been given on the last of these Counts, and any future
Proposal will be expected to be framed in accordance with
what will be assumed to have been the Decision of the
H^e. of C^{ns}.

Would there be any advantage in this ?

Might it not be urged that a Measure which is not in
itself objectionable (always assuming, what remains to be
seen, namely that the proposed arrangement is such a one)
ought not to be peremptorily rejected on the score of want
of Time to consider it, when there is a Probability that
nearly Two Months are before us for that Purpose ?

4   *Gladstone to Palmerston*

6 C[arlton] G[ardens] May 9, 52.

An opinion wh. I expressed in the first debate after the
accession of the present Ministry to power respecting the
measure wh. is to be proposed to-morrow left me no
option, when the intention of Gov^t. was announced, except
either to object or to be prepared with reasons for an
altered view : and if the objection was to be taken not on
the merits but on the score of time and circumstances it
appeared as if it cd. only be urged with full force and
propriety on the introduction of the Bill.

Any difficulty arising out of my former declaration
would of course affect no one but myself. From a few words
however wh. you used on Friday I gathered (perhaps
prompted by my wish) that you approved of the course I
meant to take and I am sincerely sorry if I misunder-
stood you.

Still it seems to me that there is a principle involved in that understanding with the Govt. wh. confines them to a particular order of measures, and that if this measure sh^d. be allowed to proceed that understanding cannot be successfully indicated on future occasions wh. might arise.

On one point however I think I may remark the apprehension you entertain of a confusion in the public mind between resistance founded on time and resistance on the merits : for after considering the question it appears to me that the proper motion for me to make will be not a simple negative but either the previous question or to pass to the order of the day.

5   *Palmerston to Gladstone*

C[arlton] G[ardens] 10 May 1852

Your Notion of moving the orders of the Day is certainly a good one ; such a Motion would be more in Keeping with your Grounds of objection than a simple Negative.[1]

6   *Palmerston to Gladstone*

C[arlton G[ardens] 21 Nov. 1852

I send you a Copy which I wish to have back again, of a note which I wrote to Charles Villiers this Morning.

What should you think of such an amendment[2] as is

---

[1] This course was followed, and the Government suffered a defeat, Gladstone moving his amendment and Palmerston voting with the majority.

[2] Villiers' motion was as follows :—

" That it is the opinion of this House, that the improved condition of the Country, and particularly of the Industrious Classes, is mainly the result of recent Commercial Legislation, and especially of the Act of 1846, which established the free admission of Foreign Corn, and that that Act was a wise, just, and beneficial measure.

" That it is the opinion of this House, that the maintenance and further extension of the policy of Free Trade, as opposed to that of Protection, will best enable the property and industry of the Nation to bear the burthens to which they are exposed, and will most contribute to the general prosperity, welfare, and contentment of the people.

" That this House is ready to take into its consideration any measures consistent with the principles of these Resolutions which may be laid before it by Her Majesty's Ministers."

sketched on the accompanying Paper as a Middle Term
between the Resolution of Villiers and the amendment of
Disraeli [1]? It is compiled from the Queen's Speech and the
Resolution & amendment.

7   *Gladstone to Palmerston*

6 C[arlton] G[ardens]
Nov. 21, 52.

I heartily concur in the general view with wh. you have
written to Mr. Villiers : and I feel very strongly the discreditable and disparaging position in which the H. of
Commons is likely to place itself on Tuesday by its mode
of handling the last act of a great controversy.

Your draft [1] I think meets such objections as can be
reasonably taken to Mr. Disraeli's amendment and I sh[d].
sincerely rejoice to see it adopted : or if it sh[d]. be objected
that in its general structure it is too near that amendment,
then some such equivalent form of words as Herbert sent
you to-day.

He and I with Goulburn have let Villiers know that we
shall vote with him as against the Gov[t]. amendment if

---

[1] Disraeli moved to substitute the following words :—

" That this House acknowledges, with satisfaction, that the Cheapness of Provisions, occasioned by Recent Legislation, has mainly contributed to Improve the
Condition and Increase the Comforts of the Working Classes ; and that Unrestricted
Competition having been adopted, after due deliberation, as the Principle of our
Commercial System, this House is of Opinion that it is the Duty of the Government
unreservedly to adhere to that Policy in those Measures of Financial and Administrative Reform which, under the Circumstances of the Country, they may deem it
their duty to introduce."

[2] Palmerston's amendment, which was carried, was to make the motion run as
follows :—

" That it is the Opinion of this House that the improved condition of the Country,
and especially of the Industrious Classes, is mainly the result of Recent Legislation,
which has established the Principle of Unrestricted Competition, has abolished
Taxes imposed for the Purposes of Protection, and has thereby diminished the Cost
and increased the Abundance of the Principal Articles of the Food of the People."

no accommodation is brought about ; which alternative however we have strongly urged.

Whether we are free to support a middle issue in preference to either is a question on which I could not give a positive answer without consulting them.

8   *Palmerston to Gladstone*

C[arlton] G[ardens] 14 March
1853

Can you help St. Germans [1] & the Paddies in this Matter ?
The Expence would probably not be large, and Irish Gratitude would no doubt last at least a Fortnight.

9   *Palmerston to Gladstone*

C[arlton] G[ardens] 22 Ap 1853

Would you have the Goodness to send me your proposed Scale of the Succession Tax on land shewing the Minimum and Maximum and the conditions of Relationship which are to govern the Scale ? Could you also as an Example state what would be the amount of Confiscation which according to the Scale would fall upon a young Man who at an age when his Life might be valued at 40 yrs. Purchase might succeed by Inheritance or Will to a Landed Estate the Taxable Income of which might be Two Thousand a year ?

I should like also to know what are the charges which are to be deducted from the gross Income to arrive at the Taxable Income and Capital, and over how many years the Payments are to be spread.

[1] Earl of St. Germans, Lord-Lieutenant of Ireland.

10 *Palmerston to Gladstone*

C[arlton] G[ardens]10 May 1853

I Send you a Calculation of the Effect of a Ten per Cent Tax on Inherited Land, to show to what degree it would become Confiscation and I do not think it is a good answer to say that the Inheritor on whom 10 pr C^t would be levied would be a Person who did not expect his Succession. In the first Place that is assuming as a general Case that which may be only the Exception, secondly it cannot be a sound fiscal Principle to measure Imposts by what is assumed to have been hoping in a Mans Mind, instead of taxing him according to his Capacity to pay, and lastly the Property of a Man so succeeding is not less his own, and is not more the Property of the State than is the Property of a Man succeeding in the most direct Manner.

(Enclosure)

Charges on a landed Estate which are periodically occurring & which are to be paid out of Income

———

Tithe Composition
Church Rates
Poor Rates
County Rates
House Tax
Assessed Taxes
Land Tax
Insurance
Chief Rents
Repairs of Mansion & outbuildings
Wages of Servants to take Care of House
Maintenance of Garden
Pensions to old Servants and worn out Labourers
Repairs of Homesteads outbuildings & Cottages on Farms

Allowances to Tenants for bad seasons & other Casualties
Local Subscriptions & charities
Agency, collection of Rents Payment of local Charges &
    Keeping accounts
    (This is generally 5 pr. C. on amount collected.)
The aggregate amount of these outgoings may be safely
taken at one Third of the Gross Income

		£
Suppose Gross Income		5000
deduct mortgages &c.		2000—
Taxable Income	—	3000
Suppose Succeeding owners Life		
worth 16 yrs Purchase		£
his Taxable Capital would be	—	48000
The amount payable out of		
this at 10 pr. Ct.	—	4800
If this is to be paid in 4 years		
The annual Payment would be	—	1200
add outgoings as above ⅓ of 5000 =		1600
Total payments to be made	—	2800
Net Income	—	3000
remains for owner for Four		
Years, annually	—	200

11   *Gladstone to Palmerston*

Downing Street.

May 10, 53.

    The calculation you have sent me, irrespective of the fact
that it tries a general rule by a case which would not happen once in one thousand times, is not accurate in its basis ;
because a great number of the items which you have com-
prised in the income that is to bear the tax would be deducted from it, and set aside from the computation.

Others of them, such as wages of servants to take care of a house and local subscriptions to Charities, certainly would not be deducted, and ought I think to be considered as *bona fide* parts of Income.

If the gross Income were £5,000, the Mortgages £2000, the deductions probably £800, I should state the case thus :—

Income £2200
  Value of Life (much more than the average value on succession) 16 years   £35200.
  Amount of Tax   ..   ..   ..   £3520.
  If payable in 4 years (the time given would be nearly 5 from the demise),
      Annual Payment   ..   ..   £880.
  Income Remaining ..   ..   ..   £1320.

Now this case would be almost the very severest that in any case could occur : and it would occur to a stranger acceding to a property of which he would have had usually no expectancy. I do not think this shows the law as a very harsh one.

The real question however is, will you retain the present scale with 10 per Cent for strangers or will you reduce it, at the same time raising the Tax on direct successions to make up the deficiency in revenue. That for my own part I should be disposed to regard as a more harsh and certainly a far less politic proceeding.

12   *Gladstone to Palmerston*

Private.   Downing St.
                     May 11. 53.

I write a line to correct a partial error in my statement— sixteen years purchase is *not* so rare a valuation for a life as I had thought. The very highest of all, a life of four years, passes eighteen. I have not yet got a complete Table.

13   *Gladstone to Palmerston*

Private.   Downing St.
                                                  May 11. 53.

I am sorry our Arithmetic does not harmonise better.—
I never said the cases in which the high rate of 10 per Cent
would attach were only one in a thousand—even as to
rateable property I imagine they would be more numerous
than this : and as to personalty very much more
numerous : what I said was that the case supposed by
you would probably not occur once in a thousand times :
that is to say the case where the 10 per Cent Duty was
conjoined with a life worth the very high rate of 16 years
purchase.—I can only give a conjectural estimate : but *if*
the 10 per Cent succession to land happens once in fifty
times, and *if* a life reaches 16 years purchase at the period
of succession once in 20 times, then the two conditions would
obviously coincide once in 1000 times.—The suppositions
I have put seem to me reasonable as to land :—not as to
personalty.

I have not yet learned the amount now levied by the
ten per cent rate off personalty i.e. (speaking roughly)
under the present Legacy Duty. But I believe it is *large* :
and I do not see that you recommend the alternative
of raising the tax on the direct successions which
would I apprehend strike land two or three times more
heavily.

Your objection that the proportion of Income taken is
too large might be met, if it were really for the interest of
landed proprietors that it should be so met, by a provision
for prolonging the time for payment, with some subsidiary
regulations, over a greater number of years than four where
the quota annually falling due exceeded a certain proportion of the income : but the case must be very rare, and I
am doubtful 1. whether it be worth the odium of a new
distinction between land and personalty—2. as to the policy

of encouraging landed proprietors to load the future in order to escape present effort and sacrifice.

There is no doubt that a strong support especially from the Radical quarter might be had for a change in the scale of consanguinity which would relieve the remote at the expence of the direct successions. I should not wonder if it were to be suggested in the House : for my own part I am indisposed to such a change on equitable grounds, and I likewise see plainly that as between land and other kinds of property it would tend materially to augment the relative burden of the former.

You have stated to me the uncommon case : let me now state in return the ordinary one.

From the general course of things, and much more by the aid of our system of entails and settlements, it happens that the great bulk of successions to *land* will be liable to the lowest rate of duty.

I take first the case of succession to a life interest only : and start from your figures—

Gross Income	£5,000	
Mortgages	£2,000	
Remain	£3,000	

Deductions (as by me)
16 per cent on Gross (they would sometimes be more) £800
Taxable Income £2,200
Average value of Life on Succession, say 12 years
Taxable Capital £26,400
Tax payable in 8 half yearly instalments £264
or per annum £66
Leaving to the possessor £2,134
and being a tax on his annual Income of 3 *per cent.*
or the same as the Income Tax (plus a small fraction) : which will have begun to diminish before one single landed Estate will have paid up its full Legacy Duty—and which

by means of the Legacy Duty Parliament will, if so minded, be *enabled* for the first time since 1845 to dispense with in 1860.

In my humble but sincere opinion, differentiation of the Income Tax is the true mother of confiscation to the land : and the new Legacy Duty, so far from introducing it, will be the present and I hope the permanent means of averting that fearful risk.

My chief fear is lest, as in the case of the ninepence Income Tax, this letter, were it spoken, should be held to prove too much—if you like it however, I think this correspondence as it brings out views of the subject from distinct points, may be circulated among our Colleagues—with or without further additions to it, as you may wish.

I have only to add the case would in some points of view be yet more striking were I to take the case of a person succeeding to the absolute possession.

14   *Palmerston to Gladstone*

C[arlton] G[ardens] 12 May 1853

I received your Letter of yesterday, but surely an Impost which confiscates for four years more than a Third of a Man's Income must be acknowledged to be a great Individual oppression the just Basis of Taxation being generality and not individuality,—and if as you say the Cases in which the high Rates would attach are so rare as not to be more than one in a Thousand the Gain to the Revenue can bear no Proportion to the Hardship inflicted on the picked out Individuals. But your high Rates above 5 pr. Cent. apply to many Degrees of Relationship through which Landed Estates are not unfrequently inherited, and you will be involving in much Embarrassment and in temporary Poverty many of the Gentry of the Country besides giving encouragement to the Feeling that the Government is influenced by Sentiments of Hostility to the Landed Interests.

15   *Palmerston to Gladstone*

C[arlton] G[ardens] 13 Oct 1853

These are the Papers about Aldershot, You will see at a Glance by the Railway Map in which I have marked by a Cross the situation of the Ground how centrical and commanding the Position is with Reference to the Facility of sending Troops in Time of War to London or to any Part of the South Coast and with a view to national Defence the Power of assembling a small army there would be of more value than a Fortification costing many Times as much as the ground would do.

In Time of Peace its value would be great as affording the means of Training both Regulars & Militia ; and if at any Time we should change our mind which is not likely, it would always sell for about the same sum we might have given for it. In the mean while Income might be made of it, by letting it out for Pasture when not wanted for Troops, and by letting off Bits at the outskirts for Public Houses Booths &ᶜ . . .

16   *Palmerston to Gladstone*

C[arlton] G[ardens] 20 Oct 1853

The Beer Shops licensed to have the Beer drunk on the Premises, are a Pest to the Community. They are Haunts of Thieves and Schools for Prostitutes. They demoralize the lower Classes. I wish you would turn your mind to consider Whether this Evil could not be abated.

That Beer should be sold like anything Else, to be taken away by the Purchaser to be consumed at Home is most reasonable and the more People are enabled so to supply the labouring Classes the better, but the words " licensed to be drunk on the Premises " are by the common People interpreted as applicable to the Customers as well as to the Liquor, and well do they avail themselves of the License.

17   *Palmerston to Gladstone*

C[arlton] G[ardens] 20 Dec[r]
1853

FitzRoy has sent me your Letter of yesterday to him. Pray thank Aberdeen for his message, and assure him that it never could for a moment enter into my Thoughts to suppose that he could have any Connection with the Propagation of Falsehoods.[1]

18   *Palmerston to Gladstone*

C[arlton] G[ardens] 10 Feby. 1854.

I have received the inclosed today from Namick Pasha[2] What is your opinion as to the arrangement proposed by Goldsmith & Palmer ?

(Enclosure)

longs salle[3]
fevrier 10 1854

EXCELLENCE

Le baron de goldsmid a été hiere chez moi ma laissés ses projet d'emprunts le contenu du qu'elle má desapointe, je lá presente si inclus,

votre devoué
NAMIK

---

[1] Probably as to Palmerston's resignation.   [2] Turkish Ambassador.
[3] This note in peculiar French was evidently written in the Treasury.

WHAT EVERYBODY THINKS

YOUNG PALMERSTON (a sharp, clever boy). "Oh, crikey! What a Scotch mull of a
Prime Minister!"
(That may be, but it is not Pretty to say so).—*Punch.*

19   *Gladstone to Palmerston*

D[owning] St. Feb. 10. 54

Of course I have nothing to do with the question as to the verification of powers : but I send you a printed formula with a Memorandum at the foot from which it will be seen that the proposal to H.E. Namik Pacha very nearly corresponds with the process used by the Treasury in raising loans for the West Indies under the Act 11 & 12 Vict.—which loans have the Imperial Guarantee.

I do not know whether you meant to ask my opinion as to the commission that Messrs. Palmer & Goldsmid propose to charge : nor am I in a condition to give one : but I think the Governor & Deputy Govr of the B. of England would be the persons best qualified to advise on that subject & to them if you should wish it I will apply

20   *Gladstone to Palmerston*

Downing Street

4 May 1854

I think the Tiverton petitioners do not quite apprehend the spirit and effect of the Clauses of the Oxford Bill, For even if the limit of 100 Boys be retained, in the form of Exhibitions the same or even a more effective stimulus might still be made available for the encouragement of the School, than it now receives through the medium of Scholarships and Fellowships felt by the College to operate very injuriously to itself.

21   *Gladstone to Palmerston*

June 22/54

I cannot doubt that for us the Black Sea is the true centre of the war and Sebastopol the true centre of the Black Sea. I incline to believe that as far as danger to the westward

G**p**

of the Black Sea is concerned, we now may leave it with tolerable safety to Omer Pacha and to Austria aided by natural impediments.

On the other hand I do not venture to hope that the shame of dismantling Sebastopol and surrendering the fleet by her own act could be endured by Russia under any circumstances which we are entitled to contemplate as likely to accompany the conclusion of a peace.

Among secondary advantages the Sebastopol enterprise presents this material one, that our great defect and difficulty, as also those of France, are in the arm of cavalry ; while the great needs for Sebastopol are in infantry artillery and fleets which we can better supply.

Some given armament by land, be it 70,000, be it 80,000, be it what it may, will with the proper appurtenances suffice to enable England and France to attempt Sebastopol without absolutely losing their hold upon other points—Varna for example—which it may be necessary to retain.

I must agree with the Duke of Newcastle that it is better to postpone an attempt on Sebastopol than to make it with an insufficient force : but I think it scarcely too much to say that all efforts made & all attention bestowed in other quarters will be *wasted* until France and England have brought their force available for Sebastopol up to the point of sufficiency.

It appears to me that the odds are greatly against us if, whether voluntarily or of necessity, we postpone this effort to a future year.

Reference no doubt must be made to the judgment of the generals : but had I the power I would confine that reference as much as possible to the point of the sufficiency of force, and restrain them as much as possible from weighing (except with a view to any immediate and urgent necessity) the importance of this object as compared with others, which we may without presumption regard as being with respect to all general grounds nearly a settled point.

22   *Palmerston to Gladstone*

Broadlands

1 Oct. 1854

I am very sorry that I cannot comply with the wishes of the Canon of Ely that Permission should be given to continue Burials within and under the Cathedral. I have thought it right to discontinue everywhere the barbarous Practise of depositing human Bodies under the Floor of Buildings frequented by human Multitudes and I could not make Ely Cathedral an Exception to the general Rule.

People might as well want to bury Dead Bodies in the Cellars of their Homes, or under their Libraries, as in Churches.

In almost all of these Cases the real Question is one of Fees, & though I am sorry to interfere with Ecclesiastical Emoluments which are far from being generally too great yet Regard to Rules of Health must supersede pecuniary Considerations.

23   *Gladstone to Palmerston*

[Quoted, *Ash.* II. 68]

Private.   Hawarden N. W.

4 October 1854

I am sorry you can do nothing for my friend the Canon ; and when we meet I may perhaps try to move you, but I do not write to trouble you on that subject now : my purpose is to offer you a congratulation which I feel to be especially due to you upon the great events which are taking place in the Crimea. Much as we must all rejoice on public grounds at these signal successes, and thankful as the whole nation may justly feel to a higher Power, yet in looking back upon the instruments through which such results have come about I for one cannot help repeating to you, which I hope you will forgive, the thanks I offered at

an earlier period, for the manner in which you urged—
when we were amidst many temptations to far more
embarrassing and less effective proceedings—the duty of
concentrating our strokes upon the true heart and centre
of the war at Sebastopol.

You will be glad to know that the Admiralty have just
written to us for sanction to a very large Expenditure (not
voted by Parliament) upon Floating Batteries and Gun
Boats with a view to an attack upon Cronstadt in the
Spring—should the Emperor of Russia not before that
period have recovered his senses as one would fondly hope
he may do. Of course we gladly agree to it.

24   *Palmerston to Gladstone*

Piccadilly 25 Jany 1855

I understood Lord Aberdeen to say at the Cabinet this
afternoon that John Russell will Tomorrow in the Explanation [1] which he intends to make read the Correspondence
which passed in December between him and L^d. Aberdeen
about the Change which he wanted to effect in the War
Department. Now if John Russell goes into that matter I
think you should be prepared to make any observations
which his Statement may call for. It would scarcely be possible for me who was the subject of that Correspondence [2]
and not a Party to it, to take a prominent Part in any
Discussion which may arise out of it.

25   *Gladstone to Palmerston*

Downing St. Jan. 26/55.

The office you propose to me for to-night is a difficult
one, and more so than it need otherwise have been on

[1] Of his resignation.

[2] Russell had proposed that Palmerston should become Secretary of State for War.

account of Lord John's broil with me about Kennedy.[1] I incline after reflection to think I am not the man for it. But whatever is thought best I will do.

Lord Aberdeen tells me you wrote an admirable letter to Lord John on the step he has taken. Would you mind letting me—or the person whoever it may be that is to comment on Lord John's statement in case of need—see that letter ? It would be a great help.

26 *Gladstone to Palmerston*

Thanks for the opportunity of perusing the answer you sent to Ld. D.[2] I will take my chance of finding you during the day.

D. St. F. 1. 55.

I answered last night in the sense which I mentioned to you.

27 *Palmerston to Gladstone*

4 Feby 1855

Lord John having failed in making a Government the Queen has desired me to endeavour to form one and as you are one of the first Persons with whom I wish to communicate on this matter I will call upon you this Evening a little before Ten.

28 *Gladstone to Palmerston*

Downing Street,
Feb. 5. 1855.

After very anxious consideration I have now to give you an answer : the answer, let me add, least agreeable to my wishes and personal feelings.

[1] Russell had nearly resigned over a dispute with Gladstone relating to the dismissal of an officer from the Department of Woods and Forests. *Glad*. I. 520.

[2] Derby had asked Palmerston and Gladstone to join him in a Government ; both declined. *Glad*. I. 526–7.

You propose to form a Cabinet, of which I understand from you that Lord John Russell, as matters now stand, will not be a member, and to which Lord Aberdeen likewise is not about to belong.

There are many considerations which on ordinary occasions would govern my conduct, but which I could now bring myself to regard as secondary.

I grant, indeed, that at this moment all other questions are absorbed in those which relate to the present War. Will the war be prosecuted with vigour ? Will the formation of the new Government have a salutary effect, or otherwise, abroad ? Lastly, and most of all, will every opportunity be sought, and husbanded to the utmost, for the restoration of peace, amidst all the doubts, intricacies, and daily shifting difficulties, that must too probably attach to the task ?

As to the first question I feel no doubt.

As to the second I am not without fears : but I pass on to the third.

And here I must observe that, if Lord Aberdeen is to quit the office of First Minister under the late vote of the House of Commons, he will be excluded from it on account of leanings and sympathies with respect to peace, and of opinions with respect to the State and institutions of Turkey, in which I share.

The answer to the question, however, is really to be sought not in the words Yes or No, but entirely in the materials of the Cabinet, by which the subject is to be handled.

In the Cabinet as it stood under Lord Aberdeen, there was every security that these great affairs would be presented to us with all the advantage, which the discussion of them by the most powerful and accomplished masters of foreign policy, not always regarding them from precisely the same point of view, yet all alike attached to the principles of British freedom, could secure.

1855

PALMERSTON

SEEING THE OLD YEAR OUT   AND THE NEW YEAR IN

This state of the Government went far to insure such a result to our deliberations as would fairly represent the relative weight due to the several elements of each case as it arose.

I must freely own that I regard the presence of Lord Aberdeen as having been all along, with reference to these absorbing questions, a vital element in his Cabinet, at least for those who, like me, find in him on the whole the nearest representation of their leanings with respect to peace, and of their opinions with respect to the Turkish Empire.—You will perceive that I am now speaking not of any personal matter, but of that great public question, the composition of the Cabinet as a whole, which is the only solid foundation of the full confidence necessary to justify the act of entering into it.

Under these circumstances I am afraid I could not have a reasonable expectation of giving you in the Cabinet that full and unreserved support which you would justly require from your Colleagues ; and I therefore feel that I ought not to be among them.

29   *Palmerston to Gladstone*

Piccadilly 5 Feby

1855

I have received your Letter with the greatest Regret. Your Decision being taken it is useless to advert to Passages in your Letter in regard to which I cannot subscribe to your opinions, and with respect to which I might have much to say ; but I think it right to explain that you seem to have misinterpreted what I said to you yesterday evening about Lord John Russell.

It was not in my Power to say that he would or would not belong to the Government I am endeavouring to form, and I had in Fact had no Communication with him since I had received at six oclock yesterday afternoon the Queen's Authority to endeavour to form an administration.

30   *Palmerston to Gladstone*

[Partly printed, *Ash.* II. 79–80]

Piccadilly 6 Feby 1855

I was too much engaged when I received your Letter yesterday afternoon to be able to send you any other answer than an acknowledgement, but as I think your Letter founded upon some misconceptions I cannot refrain from sending you a few lines of explanation. It seems to me that your objection to form Part of the Government which I am endeavouring to construct does not rest upon any Difference of Political Principle, nor upon any Diversity of opinion upon any practical Question now pressing for Decision, but is founded upon the apprehension, that at some time or other, some Question or other may arise upon which for want of the aid to be derived from the Counsel of Lord Aberdeen & Lord John Russell you may be at a loss for a sufficiently guiding Clue to a right Decision ; or else that the Cabinet may from the same Cause be led away to some Decision which you would disapprove. Now surely the first apprehension is an Injustice to yourself, or it implies an assumption which nobody can admit, as to a deficiency in your own Powers of Investigation and judgement ; and the second apprehension seems to be the Shadow of a future Shade.

If the Time should come when you should differ from a majority of the Cabinet then would be the Time for you and those who agreed with you to act upon the difference of opinion which would then have arisen ; but can you really reconcile it to the high sense of public Duty which has invariably guided your Conduct to refuse to afford the Crown & the Country the justly valued advantage of your public services merely because you imagine that on some future occasion and in some possible conjunction of events, which have not yet arisen, you might find yourself differing in opinion from some Portion of your Colleagues in the Government. I can scarcely think that upon full & mature Consideration you can think the ground on which you would thus take your stand, broad and substantial enough for the important Conclusion which you would thus build upon it. Hitherto the Cabinet have been entirely agreed as to the Terms of Peace to be proposed to Russia in the present state of affairs ; and the Cabinet have equally agreed to record and declare an opinion that the Events of the War must determine whether in the Course of the negotiations, let those negotiations take place now or hereafter any other or different Stipulations should be proposed to Russia. At the present moment therefore there is no practical Difference of opinion upon which you can place a Determination to abandon the Government. With regard to the future to speak plainly and forcibly you distrust my views & Intentions, and you think that I should be disposed to continue the War without necessity for the attainment of objects unreasonable in themselves, or unattainable by the Means at our Command, or not worth the Efforts necessary for their attainment : in this you misjudge me. If by a Stroke of the wand I could effect in the Map of the world the Changes which I could wish I am quite sure that I could make arrangements far more conducive than some of the present ones to the Peace of Nations, to the Progress of Civilization to the Happiness & Welfare of Mankind but I am not so destitute of Common Sense, as not to be able to compare Ends with Means, and to see that the former must be given up when the latter are wanting ! And when the Means to be brought to bear for the attainment of any Ends consist in the Blood & Treasure of a Great Nation, those who are answerable to that Nation for the Expenditure of that Blood & Treasure must well weigh the value of the objects which they pursue, and must remember that if they should forget the just Proportion between Ends & Means the good sense of the People whose affairs they manage will soon step in to correct their Errors, and to call them to a severe account for the Evils of which they would have been the Cause

31   *Gladstone to Palmerston*

Downing Street
Feb^r. 6. 1855.

I thank you very much for your letter of this morning : and I have availed myself of Lord Aberdeen's offer to converse with you. I have seen him since his visit to you.

In my letter of yesterday I said that I regarded Lord Aberdeen's presence in his Cabinet as having been all along a vital element with respect of the question of war and peace. I now am, as I was then, willing to recognise his confidence in the Cabinet as equivalent to his presence. I write frankly, without fear of offending you although you speak of mistrust a word which does not truly describe my feelings. It is I hope enough for me to say that I have acted with Lord Aberdeen all my life, that I am deeply attached to him, that I feel with him more nearly than with any other man on the one great question of the Hour, and that I should do nothing but wrong to you, to myself and to the State, by doing anything which would bely this feeling.

But as to yourself I hope you will infer my sentiments from what is imperfectly and hastily expressed in a sharp and difficult passage of public affairs, so much as from what has passed between us on some former occasions of less overpowering pressure. I have the happiness however of finding, that Lord Aberdeen will be in a condition to make such declarations on the subject that fills all our thoughts, as to remove any bar to my entrance into your Cabinet with the feelings and intentions I could desire, if you continue to wish it.

In so doing I shall have no conditions to ask. I know that if you seek me, you seek me with a view to the continuance of our financial policy in the same spirit, in which it has hitherto been conceived. But I ought to add that my constituency is in some respects peculiar : and I think they might not unjustly expect of me, as matter of honour, that if the policy of any Government to which I might belong, were not marked by a friendly and kindly spirit towards the Church of England (by which I do not mean any favour to encroachments either on civil or on religious rights) I should resign my seat into their hands.

32   *Gladstone to Palmerston*

Most Private.

As you are good enough to name to me that it had occurred to you to consider whether Layard[1] might be made U. Sect^y. for the Dept. of War, I ventured to suggest that the matter sh^d. be mentioned in the Cabinet. I feel that this requires some apology for it is not acc. to general rule : but the case is peculiar for the part played by him has been very marked, with reference to the late Gov^t. or the present Gov^t. in its late form, and with reference I think to Ld. Ab^n. in particular. I venture therefore at all events to hope that this important matter will be very carefully and maturely tho' it may have to be also promptly cons^d.

D. St. F. 6. '55.
    aft. midn.

---
[1] Sir A. H. Layard, M.P.

33   *Palmerston to Gladstone*

18 Feby. 1855

Your suggestions about the Purchase and Sale of Commissions in the army deserve to be well considered ; and I have sent your Letter with that view into Circulation.

34   *Gladstone to Palmerston*

Draft—
Ld. P. came in as I
was about to send
this off.
    F. 19.   Downing Street
Feb. 19/55.

Mr. Hayter [1] whom I have just seen is under an impression that you propose to acquaint the House of Commons to-day that the Cabinet have agreed to grant Mr. Roebuck's Committee [2] in some form.

I think he must have mistaken you, but the matter is of such extreme importance that I trouble you with this note to say that I understood on Saturday that the whole subject was to stand over for our meeting to-morrow. I think also that (at least) several of your colleagues are under the same impression.

Doubtless if we had come to that conclusion there might have been convenience in making it known at once : but under the circumstances I have stated I rely on your kindness to make no statement which will commit the Government.

35   *Palmerston to Gladstone*

21 Feby 1855

After the Cabinet had separated I found that Roebuck would not put off the naming of his Committee and

---

[1] Chief Whip.   [2] Committee of Enquiry into the conduct of the war.

persisted in moving it Tomorrow but he was afterwards persuaded by Vernon Smith[1] to put it for Friday for which day it now stands.

36   *Palmerston to Gladstone*

94 P[iccadill]y. 21 June 1859

This Paper has been given me by Borthwick of the Morning Post who represents the Interests of this Telegraphic Company. He says that they are bound by their agreement with Denmark to lay down their Cable in the Course of this week, and that the Admiralty are bound by their orders from the Treasury to make instant war upon the line if laid down by cutting it or otherwise destroying it. I wish you would look into the merits of the matter, and in the meanwhile it might be well to impose a Suspension of Hostilities on the Admiralty until we have come to a Decision on the Matter.

37   *Palmerston to Gladstone*

94 P[iccadill]y. 30 June 1859

Independently of the value of direct Telegraphic Communication between Gibraltar & England for Defensive Purposes in the Event of war, we ought to consider its usefulness in Peace for Commercial objects. We have an immense Quantity of Commerce by Sea to and fro between the United Kingdom on one Hand & the Mediterranean the Adriatic & the Black Sea & the Mouths of the Danube on the other. All this Shipping passes close to Gibraltar, and would it not be of great Importance to Merchants now concerned in the voyages of such Ships that Gibraltar

---

[1] Robert Vernon Smith, M.P. (afterwards Lord Lyveden), President of the Board of Control.

should be a Port of Call, from whence they might receive instant advices with respect both to outward bound & Homeward bound Ships & Cargoes? it seems to me that the Commercial utility of Such a Line would be very great.

38   *Palmerston to Gladstone*

P[iccadill]y. 14 July 59

What answer shall we authorize FitzRoy[1] to give to Thwaites? I asked him in answer to his first note, whether we have not the Right and the Power to stop up the Connection between the offending Sewer and the Serpentine, because if we have then the Limit of our Contribution to Thwaites ought to be the Expence of such Stoppage. It seems however from FitzRoy's second note that we have not such a Right.

39   *Palmerston to Gladstone*

94 P[iccadill]y. 2 Aug 1859

I have received this from John Russell I agree with him & with Hammond[2] that if we are to go to the Expence of a new Building we ought to make it large enough for the Purpose to which it is destined.

I had desired Mr. Scott[3] to communicate with Hammond and to correct some Faults in his internal arrangements. If we could contrive to lodge the Foreign Indian and Colonial offices in one Building it would no Doubt be a Convenience but I doubt the Possibility of doing so upon Scott's Plan.

[1] H. Fitzroy, M.P., First Commissioner of Works.

[2] Edmund (afterwards Lord) Hammond, Permanent Under-Secretary of State for Foreign Affairs.

[3] George (afterwards Sir) Gilbert Scott.

40   *Gladstone to Palmerston*

Hawarden
Chester
Sept. 12. 59

. . . I read with extreme grief the sad news from China.[1] That or something else will I suppose now draw us together. I cannot but continue to hope more than I fear for the Italians of the four associated districts.

Mr Cobden is here, very anxious for a reduction of wine duties with a view to improved relations with France. He is going to Paris.

41   *Palmerston to Gladstone*

Broadlands
15 Sept. 1859

. . . This China affair is very unpleasant. I doubt our Commander having shewn as much discretion as valour. One should have thought that the ground and the batteries and the Force opposed to us might have been better ascertained, but those who acted on the spot must probably have been the best judges

We cannot I think avoid avenging so unprovoked and faithless an outrage. There seem to be three Things which might be done.

Firstly an attack and occupation of Pekin. This would require a strong Military Force : perhaps we and the French who will probably be desirous of co-operating with us, might without much Inconvenience furnish ; and such an operation if successful would settle all matters finally. But this could not be done before the Spring

Secondly we might take Possession of Chusan and hold it till the Chinese did what we wanted, or we might make it a Place of Rendezvous for any Force intended to enter

[1] The repulse of Admiral Hope at the Taku Forts.

the North of China but this alone would be a feeble proceeding

Thirdly we might blockade China by Cutting off Communication by the Grand Canal, either by establishing ourselves on the Yang tse Kiang at the Point where the Canal cuts it, or by taking Possession of Tien sing the Place where the Canal enters the Peiho : the first operation on the Yangtse Kiang would be chiefly a Naval one The other would require a strong Military Force. Perhaps the Yang tse Kiang operation might at once be determined upon, leaving other Matters for further Consideration

42   *Palmerston to Gladstone*

Broadlands
28 Oct 1859

As The Queen passes so much Time every Year at Balmoral I think it would be very desirable that we should have the means of Telegraphic Communication with her ; and if you concur I will have the Thing done.

43   *Palmerston to Gladstone*

94 P[iccadill]y. 15 oct 1859

There is certainly some Force in what Liddell says as to the Possibility of cutting off deep sea Telegraph Lines, but nevertheless the Mediterranean abounds with such Lines and a Line with Gibraltar & Malta would be very useful to us on many occasions in Time of Peace to say nothing of its great Importance to our commercial interests by giving Information as to arrival to & fro of Merchantmen between England & Mediterranean Countries. Moreover Liddell represents a rival Interest

KEEP THE DOOR-CHAIN UP!

BRITANNIA (going out of Town). "Now, Pam, there are a great many bad characters about just now, mind you look out well—and always keep the *door-chain* up!"

44   *Palmerston to Gladstone*

Downing Street
25 Nov[r]. 1859

I have received the inclosed from the Duke of Somerset,[1] and I think we ought to authorize him to take the steps which he proposes to take. The French are making great Progress in the Construction of Iron plated ships and if we do not in some Degree keep Pace with them we Shortly find ourselves standing to a great Disadvantage. I think the Duke right in proposing to build Iron plated Ships of a smaller size and therefore less expensive than the Two Which were begun by the late Government. There are some Doubts whether this Iron-plating would resist the heaviest shot delivered at a short distance but it will certainly stand any shot beyond 4 or 500 Yards, and ships so armed would therefore beyond those distances have an immense advantage over ships not protected in the same manner.

45   *Gladstone to Palmerston*

Downing Street.
25 Nov. 1859.

I entirely and cordially concur in the Duke of Somerset's suggestion. It seems to me of the utmost consequence that our means of defence should be the most formidable and efficient which it is in our power to employ.

I would ask you, however, to consider in return with him whether it is really wise to continue the present outlay on so great a scale for the building of those maritime castles which we call line of battle ships and which seem to be constructed on the principle precisely opposite to that of all land fortifications, and to aim at presenting as large a surface as possible to the destroying fire of an enemy.

[1] First Lord of the Admiralty.

HP

I do not *now* speak with any view to the reduction of our outlay on building as a whole though I may think something might be desirable in that sense : but rather to the transfer from an apparently inferior to a probably superior mode of applying our resources.

46   *Palmerston to Gladstone*

94 Piccadilly

29 Novr. 1859

With Reference to what you say in your Letter of the 25 there are good opinions both ways as to Line of Battle ships but I own I think the Balance of argument strongly in Favor of having as many of them as needed to over match those which could be brought against us. I take it the Command of the Ocean will still be with the Power that can fit out the strongest Fleet of Line of Battle ships. Smaller vessels may be useful as auxiliaries in the narrow seas or to defend Coasts & Colonies, but the heavy Battery of a First or Second Rate will always be too much for smaller vessels.

Whether Iron plated ships will stand such shot as improved Science will bring to bear against them remains to be seen but even then it will be some Time before they can be completed in sufficient Numbers by any Power to constitute the Main arm of Naval Warfare.

47   *Palmerston to Gladstone*

94 Piccadilly

4 Decr. 1859

I Send you a Letter and its Inclosure which I received some little Time ago from the Prince about some proposed Magnetical observations.

The Subject is one in regard to which more of the

mysteries of Nature are to be dived into by such observations than in any other Department of Science and the Expence does not seem to be considerable as it would be only 32000 to be spent in six years. What shall I say to the Prince about it ?

48   *Palmerston to Gladstone*

THE ELECTRIC AND INTERNATIONAL
TELEGRAPH COMPANY

The following Message forwarded from Foreign Office Station and received at Chester Station, Dec. 15, 1859

FROM   TO
Lord Palmerston   Mr. Gladstone
                             Hawarden Castle
                                   Chester
Dec. fifteenth.

You are requested to attend a meeting of the Cabinet at three oclock on Friday the sixteenth instant Lord Palmerston especially wishes you to come.

49   *Palmerston to Gladstone*
[Printed, *Ash.* II. 168–72]
94 Piccadilly 15 Decr. 1859

Sidney Herbert[1] has asked me to summon a Cabinet for Tomorrow that we may come to a Decision on the Fortification Question, and I am most anxious that the arrangements which he has proposed should be adopted.

The Main Question is whether our Naval arsenals and some other important Points should be defended by Fortifications, or not ; and I can hardly imagine Two

[1] Secretary of State for War.

Opinions on that Question—It is quite clear that if by sudden attack by an Enemy landed in strength our Dock-yards were to be destroyed our Maritime Power would for more than half a century be paralysed, and our Colonies, our Commerce, and the Subsistence of a large Part of our Population would be at the Mercy of our Enemy, who would be sure to shew us no Mercy—we should be reduced to the Rank of a Third Rate Power if no worse happened to us. That such a Landing is in the present State of Things possible must be manifest. No Naval Force of ours can effectually prevent it. Blockades of a hostile Port are no longer possible as of yore. The blockading squadron must be under sail because there would be no means of supplying it with Coal enough to be always steaming, while the out-rushing Fleet would come steaming on with great advantage and might choose its moment when an on shore wind had compelled the Blockaders to haul off. One night is enough for the Passage to our Coast, and Twenty Thousand men might be landed at any Point before our Fleet knew that the Enemy was out of Harbour. There could be no security against the simultaneous Landing of 20,000 for Portsmouth 20,000 for Plymouth and 20,000 for Ireland our Troops would necessarily be scattered about the United Kingdom, and with Portsmouth and Plymouth as they now are those Two dock yards and all they contain would be entered and burnt before Twenty Thousand Men could be brought together to defend either of them.

Then again suppose the manœuvre of the first Napoleon repeated, and a large French Fleet with Troops on Board to start for the West Indies ; what should we do ? Would the Nation be satisfied to see our Fleet remain at anchor in Torbay or Portland leaving our Colonies to their Fate, and if we pursued the French, they might be found to have doubled back, to have returned to the Channel, and for Ten Days or a Fortnight to have the Command of the Narrow Seas. Now the use of Fortifications is to establish for a certain number of Days 21 to 30 an Equation between a smaller inside and a larger Force outside, and thus to give time for a relieving Force to arrive. This in our Case would just make the difference between safety and Destruction

But if these defensive works are necessary, it is manifest that they ought to be made with the least possible delay; to spread their Completion over 20 or 30 years would be Folly unless we could come to an agreement with a chivalrous Antagonist, not to molest us till we could inform him we were quite ready to repel his attack—we are told that these works might, if money were forthcoming be finished possibly in three at latest in four years. Long enough this to be kept in a State of imperfect Defence

But how is the Money, estimated in round numbers at Ten or Eleven Millions to be got? There are Two Ways, annual Taxation to raise for this Purpose over and above all other Expences, a Third or a Fourth of this Sum, or the raising of a Loan for the whole amount payable in Three or Four annual Instalments, and repayable in annual Instalments with Interest in Twenty or Thirty Years. The First Method would evidently be the best in Principle and the cheapest, but the Burthen would be heavy and the Danger would be that after the First year the Desire for financial Relief might prevail over a provident sense of Danger, and the annual Grants would dwindle down to their present insufficiency, and the works would thus remain indefinitely unfinished—The Second Course has the advantage of being financially as light or nearly so, as the present system because the annual repayment of Principal and Interest would be but little heavier than the present annual votes, while we should gain the same advantage of early Completion of Works which would be secured by the greater financial Burthens of the first Plan.

Arrangements of this kind have been deemed by the deliberate judgement and action of Parliament wise and proper for private Persons, why should they not be so for a

Nation in regard to outlays of the same Nature as those for which private Persons have by Law been enabled to charge their Estates. The objection to borrowing for Expenditure is Stronger for Individuals than for a Nation. The Individual if he went on borrowing for annual Expences would end by having no Income left to live upon or to assign to a fresh Lender. A Nation would perhaps in the end come to the same Standstill, but its Power of increasing its Income is greater than that of an Individual but still Parliament has encouraged and enabled private Persons to borrow money for permanent Improvements of their Estates the Money so borrowed to be repaid in a limited number of years.

If we do not ourselves propose such a Measure to Parliament it will infallibly be proposed by somebody else, & will be carried ; not indeed against us, because I for one should vote with the Proposer whoever he might be, but with great Discredit to the Government for allowing a Measure of this Kind involving one may say the Fate of the Empire to be taken out of their Hands. People would say, and justly too, that we and the Proposer ought to change Places, and that he and his Friends had shewn themselves fitter than we were to assume the Responsibility of taking Care ' *Ne quid detrimenti Respublica Capiat* '.

50   *Palmerston to Gladstone*

Broadlands
19 Decr. 1859

I do not think that a Desire to retain Patronage ought to stand in the Way of an administrative Reform which would save any sum worth saving and at the same time provide for the efficient Discharge of the Duties now performed by the officers whom it is intended progressively to suppress.

I should like therefore to see Laing's [1] Scheme.

[1] Samuel Laing, M.P., Financial Secretary to the Treasury.

51   *Palmerston to Gladstone*

Broadlands
19 Decr. 1859

Many thanks for this from Cobden, which seems encouraging.

52   *Palmerston to Gladstone*

1859
Broadlands 22 Dec^r.

This proposed visit of the Prince of Wales to Canada, and of course from thence to Washington seems to be a politic and useful Measure, but it will be attended with some Extra Expence, and I conclude that the Queen would expect us to provide the means of defraying it. What shall I say to the Duke of Newcastle[1]? I apprehend that the Revenues of the Duchy of Cornwall cannot as yet be applicable to such a Purpose ; Parliament would probably not object to vote a Moderate Sum but who would frame an Estimate ?

53   *Gladstone to Palmerston*

Private.
Hawarden Dec. 23/59.

I have just had another and still more encouraging letter from Mr. Cobden : I have sent it to Lord John Russell begging him to send it on to you, and I inclose herewith copy of a letter which I have written to Lord John. In it I have endeavoured to sketch slightly the course of proceeding.

Let me thank you, as one of the public, for your excellent speeches at Romsey.

Will you kindly return Mr. Cobden's letter to me.

[1] Colonial Secretary.

54   *Palmerston to Gladstone*

Broadlands 2 Jany 1860

I ought sooner to have returned you the inclosed I trust we may be able to make some satisfactory arrangement with the French Government.

55   *Gladstone to Palmerston*

Most Private.

D[owning] Str[eet] Jan 6/60.

I was at Pembroke Lodge last night when your note came saying you were about to circulate a Memorandum on our position with regard to the Italian question at this moment.

Forgive my troubling you with one word as it seems to me important.

I had on Wednesday two very long conversations with the Prince at Windsor. I have told the whole to Lord John as well as I could, but I now mention only a single point of a practical character.

The Prince spoke of the possible engagement with France as equivalent to doing what England refused to do in the Spring, before the war of Solferino. I replied that the overture made was not, as I understood it, now, as it was then, an overture to take up arms, but to engage to prevent some one else from taking up arms—in fact an overture to keep peace, not to break it.

Upon this he explained what he understood the overture to be—to the following effect—'What must happen will be this—you will make the engagement : Sardinia will then march into Central Italy : Austria must go there to oppose her : and the contingency will then have arrived in which you are to oppose Austria by force.

I replied that as I understood the matter without any doubt (and I was confirmed at Windsor by Herbert, and since by Lord John,) *this* was not the overture made now, though it was a question put and not pressed about a month ago.—That what was now proposed was an engagement to resist the use of foreign force in Central Italy—That according to the natural meaning of the proposal, which of course must be elucidated and placed beyond doubt if communications should proceed, it implied that the Pope might if he could recover the allegiance of his revolted sub-jects.—That they, and doubtless the people of Tuscany and the Duchies who are in the same boat, might baffle him if they could—but that no one else should interfere—and I admitted that Sardinia could make no title on any ground of European law, or any recognised principle of policy to interfere in the strife, which would not also entail and justify the interference of Austria.—Therefore that both were alike excluded—' To all this I understand Lord John to agree.—

But it was quite plain that the whole subject had been understood at Windsor in the other sense, nor did it appear to be doubted that the construction which I stated gave to the whole matter a new and different aspect.

I afterwards quoted words which you had used in the Cabinet of Tuesday and which as I conceived excluded by necessary inference the idea that Sardinia was to enjoy an exceptional permission to interfere.

Remembering what was read as well as what was said, in Cabinet on Tuesday, I thought it material to apprise you of the misapprehension I have described, as I think it was not without important consequences in incumbering our path.

A good article in the " Daily News " traverses the very bad ones in the " Times ".

56   *Palmerston to Gladstone*

94 Piccadilly
1 Feby 1860

Could you without Inconvenience come to me at Twelve Tomorrow? I should like to have a little Talk with you about our Financial arrangements on Parts of which I wish to have a clearer Idea.

57   *Palmerston to Gladstone*

94 Piccadilly
6 Feby. 1860

I have fixed your Statement for Friday, so that we are under no obligation to Gentlemen Opposite. I will summon a Cabinet for Thursday at one at your House. Some of our Colleagues wish to have more discussion & Explanation about the arrangements, and also to endeavour to come to an Understanding about the Fortification Question upon which like me, they have a very strong Feeling

Of course the Bill to authorize the periodical Issue of terminable annuities to cover the Expence could not be brought in till after the financial Arrangements are adopted by the House but will those Arrangements leave Room for the Charge of Interests on the terminable annuities?

58   *Palmerston to Gladstone*

94 Piccadilly
6 Feby 60

I think it is better to give you Law till Friday, and I shall so settle it today. This will avoid the necessity of interfering with Notices on Thursday, and the Delay of one Day will not make any material Difference

59   *Gladstone to Palmerston*

11, Downing Street,
Whitehall.
Feby. 7th, 1860.

Secret.

I have just received your kind note and return you many thanks for the arrangements you have made.

I have no doubt of being ready on Friday, but I shall have no strength either of head or lungs to spare.

There are I fear the most serious differences amongst us with respect to a loan for Fortifications, and this being the case I had thought it clearly for the interest of all that we should reserve that question until we had got through the French treaty, the Budget, and the chief Estimates.

As I understand the present arrangement, it will include a sum in gross for Fortifications out of which sum if the Cabinet shall hereafter decide upon a loan, either upon annuities or otherwise, provision can be made with perfect ease for the first years interest.

I thought this matter had been concluded for the present, but if the time has come when you wish to carry it farther, I must avow, that for many reasons it would be vain for me to enter upon the discussion on Thursday. In truth we have had a good deal of discussion already, and I have also reflected constantly and anxiously upon the subject.

My mind is made up and to propose any loan for Fortifications would be on my part with the views I entertain, a betrayal of my public duty. I may add that only under the full belief that the subject of fortifications was postponed did I become a party to the Military and Naval Estimates as they now stand.

The course which I should be prepared to follow was discussed in my conversation with you last Thursday, but I need not now enter upon particulars.

60   *Palmerston to Gladstone*

94 Piccadilly
7 Feby. 1860

I have received your Letter of this Morning—we will let the Question about the Fortifications rest for the present, as there will be Room left for them in your Budget— I conclude that when you come to work out the Details of your Budget you will take the Lease of the House upon the increased Income Tax, and make Sure of that being passed into Law, before you propose the Repeal of the Paper Duties ; for we should be awkwardly circumstanced if we had given up the Paper Duties without having got the increased Income Tax.

61   *Palmerston to Gladstone*

H[ous]^e [of] C[ommo]^{ns} 6 oclock

I have just received your note and am glad to learn that Ferguson is so liberal ; but I have been asked by Hy. Lennox across the House whether you would be well enough to make your Statement Tomorrow, and I said that it was, as I was then informed doubtful but that I expected to know this Evening, but I said that I trusted that if you should not be quite well enough the House would give you till Monday, as though Delay might be inconvenient it would be much more inconvenient that you should find yourself in the middle of your Statement to come to a Stand, from Failure of voice—The House fully acquiesced & they are quite prepared to learn that the Statement will be put off till Monday.

I said however that the Treaty would at all Events be laid Tomorrow.

I wish you therefore to consider and let me know whether you feel quite sure of being strong enough in voice for Tomorrow or whether you will take advantage of the Disposition of the House to give you till Monday.

62   *Gladstone to Palmerston*

Private.   Downing Street
                                         Feb. 8. 60.

I think the uniform and indeed necessary practice is in a case like that of the Financial Scheme is, to state it as a whole and not allow any distinction to be drawn as between its leading proposals. The Cabinet you will remember decided on the Estimates the Remissions and the Income Tax all separately but all as alike parts of a whole.

So much for my statement. As to the order of proceeding it is clear I think that we must take first the remissions of Customs Duty, giving precedence among them to those which fall under the Treaty.

A question might then arise whether to take next the Excise Resolutions or the Income Tax.

My opinion is that the House will probably decline to vote the Income Tax until it has voted the Principal Estimates.

In any case you would gain nothing but rather lose by postponing the Excise Resolutions : for while under this head we shall resign a million on the Paper Duty we shall gain more than a million and a half on Malt and Hop Credits and minor changes.

But on the other hand you will lose nothing in point of power by taking the Excise Resolutions after the Customs Duties Resolutions—for *they* will not take effect immediately, and if any event should happen to alter essentially its position the Cabinet might consider whether it should drop or proceed with any of them.

The only way in which the House can be effectually committed to the 10d Income Tax will perhaps be by their voting first the principal Estimates.

The whole subject is complex : but in rough outline this I think will be the safest order of proceeding.

    1. Customs remissions (These take effect *immediately*).

2. Excise and Inland Revenue Resolutions. These resign 1 Million and get for us 1,750,000. They will not take effect till Acts are passed.

3. Tea and Sugar Duties to be continued : and other Customs Charges say £420,000 to be imposed. To take effect April 1.

4. Principal Estimates.

5. Income Tax.

I have thought over the question of the order very much and this seems to me the best. You might put No. 4 the Estimates before No. 3 but I think it would rather weaken than strengthen the position, and it would postpone the time when we should get new taxes into play. To put the Income Tax early would I think be very dangerous to it.

63   *Palmerston to Gladstone*

94 Piccadilly
13 Feby 1860

I hope you are none the worse for that Triumph on Friday for which the Government is much the better. On looking through your Resolutions it seems to me that the one about Game Licences would require that a Licence should be taken out for every Beater employed in beating a Cover for a Shooting Party : this I imagine can hardly be intended.

64   *Gladstone to Palmerston*

Feb. 13. 60.

Many cordial thanks for your kind note. I am glad you think the Government is the better for the speech & plan. It would have been deeply painful to me, and it would still be so, after all the kindness I have received, were matters to take a different turn.

You need be under no apprehension for the beaters.

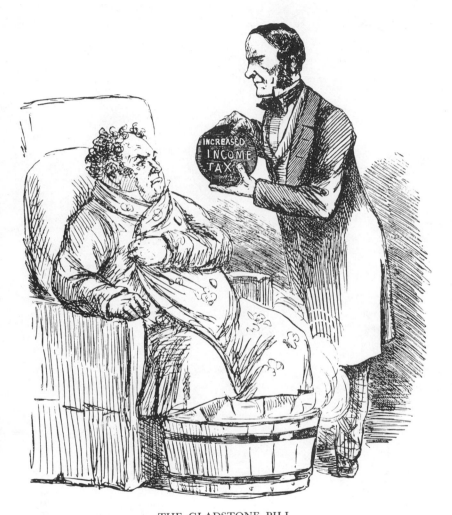

THE GLADSTONE PILL

DR. GL-DST-NE. " There, Mr. Bull—swallow it at once, and it will relieve your chest
directly."

Square-headed Mr. Simon [?], of the Inland Revenue, has one of the best noses for his game I ever knew ; and when he is on the moor for birds, nothing will induce him to break away after a hare. His words I am assured are those of the present law.

65   *Palmerston to Gladstone*

94 P[iccadill]ʸ. 14 Feby. 1860.

I was asked yesterday in the House of Commons a Question which I was unable to answer, namely in what way the assent of Parliament is to be asked for and obtained to the Eleventh article of the Treaty, which article will not apparently require any Resolution similar to the Resolutions necessary for the other articles. I own I was somewhat taken aback at finding that article in the printed Treaty, as I do not remember its having been discussed and assented to by the Cabinet ; and it certainly appears liable to the grave objections which were urged against it last night ; moreover under the Garb of reciprocity of Engagement it is obviously a concession made by England alone, as much as it would be a Concession to England if China & England agreed not to prohibit or lay a Duty on the Exportation of Teas or as it would be an Engagement binding only on the United States if we were to make with them a similar Stipulation about Cotton.

66   *Gladstone to Palmerston*

11 Downing Street
Feb. 14. 60.

I mentioned the export of Coal in the Cabinet with the observation that the reciprocal covenant seemed almost absurd, and that I had told Cobden it seemed to me if there was to be a stipulation at all it would be almost better to make it one-sided.

This was before authoritative and official communications had *begun* and before we were pledged to anything.

Mr. Gibson [1] who happened to be with me when your note came recollects my having spoken as above.

No difficulty was raised nor even if I remember was any observation made in the Cabinet on that when named among the other heads of the Clauses of the Treaty.

The question as to the assent of Parliament is much wider and embraces many more articles. For example, the duration of the Treaty.

I am not aware of any way in which the stipulations of the Treaty could be brought to an Aye or No in Parliament unless as to duties.

Even as to duties it is only a constructive pledge that Parliament gives for it can give no pledge to bind even itself much less succeeding Parliaments and it would be able to reduce the duties to-day and raise them to-morrow. I suppose Mr. Pitt meant by his Address [2] to pledge Parliament up to the highest point and even that was not high enough.

67   *Palmerston to Gladstone*

94 Piccadilly
19 Feby. 1860.

Would you be ready to answer Disraeli Tomorrow? leaving John Russell and me to come in afterwards? that would perhaps be the best arrangement

Charles Wood [3] has written to me pointing out the Difference between Pitt's Course & that which we propose to follow—and he tells me he has written also to you. The difference seems to consist in this, that he did Twice over that which we propose to do only once & in so far our Course seems better than his. The only doubt seems to be whether we might propose Resolutions in a Committee on

---

[1] T. Milner Gibson, M.P., President of the Board of Trade.
[2] On the Anglo-French Commercial Treaty of 1786.   [3] Secretary for India.

the Treaty which do not involve changes of Customs Duties.

If that was thought desirable it might be done after we have disposed of the Customs Resolutions applicable to the Treaty.

68 *Gladstone to Palmerston*

Feb. 20. 1860.

I will be ready to follow Disraeli.—Like you I do not see the difficulties which suggest themselves to Wood.— Mr. Pitt seems to have submitted nothing to the House of Commons but (1) Resolutions respecting duties and (2) respecting the privileges of the most favoured nation.

69 *Palmerston to Gladstone*

It will be well to look at the printed announcement of the Rewards offered
1st. for the Discovery of the N.W. Passage
2d for the Discovery of the Remains of Franklin's Expedition, & for ascertaining his Fate.
If any of the latter Sum remains unappropriated the officers & Crew of the Fox seem intitled to it.

As to the latter Point the He. of Cns would probably with cheerfulness vote Two or Three Thousand Pounds for the Erection of a suitable Monument to Sir J. Franklin, recording upon it (what Ly. Franklin wishes), the Efforts made by Ly. F. to ascertain his Fate. She sent Four Expeditions for that Purpose

P. 23/2–60

70 *Palmerston to Gladstone*

94 P[iccadill]y. 7 March 60.

John Russell and I incline to think that it will not be necessary to consult the Law Officers about the Eleventh

Ip

Article of the Treaty. The Engagement not to lay an Export Duty on Coals is within the Competence of the Crown
because no new Tax can be laid on, without the previous
Consent of the Crown ; and the Engagement not to forbid the Export of Coal is an Engagement relating to an
Exercise of the Prerogative of the Crown.

Still if you think there is any Point on which a legal
opinion is desirable we could ask the Law Officers to meet
us in the Chancellor's Room at the House of Lords at half
past one Tomorrow at which Time I hope you mean to
be there to vote Labouchere[1] into the Trusteeship held
by Macaulay.

71   *Palmerston to Gladstone*

D[ownin]ᵍ S[tree]ᵗ. 21 March 60

Brougham wanted his Brother William to be made a
Peer in order that his (Brougham's) Peerage might be
perpetuated in his Family. I could not do that but I settled
with him that he should have a new Patent with Remain-
der to his Brother William. He now writes as by the inclosed
begging that the Stamp Duty on the New Patent may be
remitted to him. What answer shall I give him ?

The Truth is that he and his Brother ought to divide the
Expence between them.

72   *Palmerston to Gladstone*

94 P[iccadill]ʸ. 22 March 1860

Borthwick and Mr. Ridout the latter a great Paper
Maker wish much to see you for a few minutes to state to
you the Grounds on Which Mr. Ridout urges a Small
Impost Duty on French Paper to countervail the Export
Duty on French Rags.

[1] Lord Taunton.

AN UNCOMMONLY CIVIL WAR

Mr. Bull. "Allow me, my dear Emperor, to introduce to your notice these beautiful diamonds !"
Emperor. "And let me, *cher* M. Bull, offer you a glass of this excellent light wine !"
(N.B. We know who has the best of it.)

73   *Palmerston to Gladstone*

94 P[iccadill]ʸ. 29 March 1860

I see that one of the Bills about the Paper Duties stands
for tonight. I think it would be desirable for many Reasons
to put off the Whole Paper Question both as to Excise Duty
and Import Duty till after Easter.

74   *Palmerston to Gladstone*

Brocket 12 April 1860

I hope the elastic Progress of the Revenue will enable
us to find the £150,000 that Sidney Herbert wants.

We must not part with him for so small a Sum. He is by
far the best administrator of Army Matters I have ever
known, and I am sure I should not know where to look
for another Half as good.

I do not like the aspect of European Affairs ; it looks as
if we should have a disagreeable Summer

Armaments going on in all Quarters, Insurrections
breaking out or announced to come off in the Course of
the Spring, French and Russian Intrigues active in many
Quarters, and serious Designs attributed not without some
show of Foundation to those Two Powers afford altogether
a tolerable Stock of Elements of Uncertainty.

75   *Gladstone to Palmerston*

Downing Street
13 April 1860.

By the time I come back from Edinburgh I hope to know
what are the Estimates of Revenue, and Expenditure for
the year, and what (either in augmentation or diminution)
has become of the Surplus as it appeared to stand in
February.

I did not understand you on Wednesday to recede in any
manner from the opinion you had formed that, contrary to

the opinion of the Cabinet last week, this £150,000 should be placed upon the Estimate but only to agree with me that under the circumstances of the case it was desirable that the production of the altered Estimate should be postponed.

A very short delay would enable us both to know how we stand as to Revenue and likewise to consider the bearing of this proposal on the larger and more important question which stands for early consideration.

I send a copy of this to Herbert.

76   *Palmerston to Gladstone*

94 Piccadilly

20 April 1860

Brand[1] tells me that you intend to take the Customs Bill this evening in Preference to the Paper Duties Bill which stands earlier in the List. This is I think a good arrangement, as it would be better not to go on with the Committee on the Paper Duty till after the Cabinet To-morrow.

It would be easy to provide the £150,000 we want, by postponing for a couple of months the Date at which the Repeal of the Excise Duty on Paper is to take effect; and the Truth is that for many Reasons there would be great advantage in putting that Repeal off altogether till next year when we shall have a rather formidable Deficit to encounter.

77   *Gladstone to Palmerston*

Downing Street.

April 20. 1860.

I think you have been misinformed. It was on consultation with Mr. Brand that I concluded it would be much better to go on with the Paper Duties Bill at once : how

[1] Sir Henry Brand (afterwards Viscount Hampden), Parliamentary Secretary to the Treasury.

could we recede when we have got the equivalent in the shape of the full Income Tax ? would not this seem to stand in the light of a fraud upon Parliament ?

P.S. Being detained here I have asked Gibson to go up and explain to you how in his view the question lies as to proceeding with the Bill. If it is a question of getting £150,000 there are certainly better ways of doing it.

78   *Palmerston to Gladstone*
94 Piccadilly
24 Ap 1860

The Statement which you made at the last Cabinet of the Reports you have lately received as to Corrections to be made in our Estimates of Revenue for the present year seems to indicate that our Surplus is likely to be changed into a Deficit before the Year is over.

In this State of Things would it not be prudent to hold our Hand as to reduction of Taxes, and to allow the Repeal of the Paper Duties to stand over to form Part of the general arrangements which we shall have to consider for the Budget of next year.

I see no Hope of any diminution of Expenditure this year ; on the Contrary the China Operations may for the Moment add to our Expence, and the European Horizon is by no means reassuring.

79   *Palmerston to Gladstone*
94 Piccadilly
3 May 1860

It would be desirable that in your Speech tonight you should not represent the Six Pound Franchise as an indispensable Condition of our Reform Bill because it has become sufficiently apparent that the Bill will not pass into Law with that Franchise in it—From all I hear I am led to think that if we were at Liberty to announce the Substitution of Eight for Six, and some Increase of the County Franchise our Difficulties would disappear, but we cannot ourselves do that although we might submit to it, if done for us by either House of Parliament.

I shall ask the Cabinet to meet at one on Saturday on account of the early Hour at which the Academy dine and I wish on that Day to ask the Cabinet to consider our financial Position with Reference to the very unpleasant Condition of European affairs and to the Prospect of what may happen this next Summer & autumn

I shall be glad if you will put off the Third Reading of the Repeal of the Paper Duties to next week.

80   *Gladstone to Palmerston*

Downing Street
May 3. 60

I take due notice of what you say about the £6 Franchise and I think a higher authority than mine I mean that of Lord John Russell has already made it clear to the House that we are not tied to the particular form of any enactment in the Bill.

Of course after the intimation you have given me it is right that the Paper Duties Bill should stand over until after Saturday.

81   *Palmerston to Gladstone*

94 Piccadilly
18 May 1860

I fixed your Wine Licences Bill as the first Order of the Day for Monday according to your strong wish but I hope that if it should lead to discussion you will adjourn the Debate to the next day, Tuesday, as I had distinctly promised the Attorney General,[1] that he should have Monday clear for the Bankruptcy Bill, and Changes of arrangement on Matters of this Kind, if not absolutely necessary are much to be avoided.

The Bankruptcy Bill is a Measure of very great Importance to all the trading & Commercial Interests, it is the only one of the Three great Measures of Law Reform which were announced in the Queen's Speech, that we have any chance of passing, and it would be very discreditable to the Government if nothing were to follow the announcement made at the opening of Parliament. The Attorney General has made in the laborious Preparation of the Bill great Sacrifices of Time and of professional Income, and if he cannot have a full evening for launching his Measure before Whitsuntide it will be Stuck fast in the Quicksands of Reform after the Holydays, and we shall all incur the Discredit of inexcusable Failure.

82   *Palmerston to Gladstone*

94 Piccadilly
1 June 1860

I see that some Question is to be asked of you today as to Remission of Taxes in Lieu of the Paper Duties ; but in the present state of affairs and with the accounts we have received of the Determination of the Chinese Govt who seem to say *je veux qu'on me batte,* any Repeal of any Tax or any Reduction of any Tax Seem for the Moment to be wholly impossible

83   *Gladstone to Palmerston*

Cliveden,
Maidenhead.
June 3, 60.

Private.

The confusion of business in which we unfortunately find ourselves adds greatly to the difficulty wch. measures may

[1] Sir Richard Bethell, Q.C., M.P.

present in themselves. As I understood the Cabinet yesterday we are again to discuss the *order* of proceeding after we
shall have had two or three days experience of the temper
of the House about the Reform Bill. I wish however to
mention what I think an urgent demand upon the attention of the Government in addition to all the others already
before you.

In consequence of the news from China, and of the
number of troops dispatched thither which is far beyond
that decided last autumn by the Cabinet we shall probably
require to vote two millions and a half for the services in
that quarter over above the £850,000 voted in March,
and the £1,700,000 (in round numbers) for this financial
year which were included in the arrangements of the
Budget.

I should not like to hand over to a successor the task of
providing this £2,500,000 of which a part at least ought
it seems to me to be provided by new taxes. If the money
were simply to be borrowed, that I might very well leave
to other hands. But especially considering that the whole
Chinese charge for the year proposed up to this time is to
be met from extraordinary resources and not from taxes,
I think all will be of opinion that something should be
done by taxation, even independently of the decision to
which the Cabinet came yesterday about fortifications.

By Wednesday or Thursday when I suppose the Cabinet
will meet I will be ready with the particulars of a proposition but I may now say it would be to raise a million and
a half, or more, by new taxes before the 1st of next April.
I should also propose this to be done at an early date.
This I am aware raises the question anew how much time
we can afford to spend on the Reform Bill, but the necessity
seems to me a real one and should not be kept out of view.

I think it was clearly understood that the declaration is to
be made at the moment of laying the Fortification Report

on the table, about the extent to which the Government adopt it, but that that is to be reserved for the day which you may fit for declaring your plan. If I am not right in this pray inform me as much for me depends on it.

I have a letter from Mons. Duv. de Hauranne who desires to be particularly remembered to you.

84   *Palmerston to Gladstone*

94 Piccadilly
3 June 1860

I wish very much to have half an Hours Conversation with you upon the Subject discussed in Cabinet yesterday; Could you call here at any Time between Three & Four today?

85   *Palmerston to Herbert*

94 Piccadilly
20 June 1860

MY DEAR SIDNEY HERBERT

I return you Gladstone's Letter. You may assure him that I Shall at all Times be ready to consider in Connection with other Candidates at the Time, any Oxford Man whom he may think deserving of Promotion in the Church— With Regard to Waldegrave [1] my choice of him was chiefly influenced by the opinion given to me by the Bishop of London who on being consulted by me as to several Persons whom I had heard mentioned said that from his Knowledge of Waldegrave and of the Diocese of Carlisle where he had been Dean, he thought Waldegrave would suit the Northern Diocese better than any of the other Persons who had been named—as to Waldegrave's politics I am not particularly acquainted with them but I understood that he is generally liberal in his views.

[1] Bishop of Carlisle.

86   *Minute by Mr. Gladstone*

July 1. 1860

1. It appears to me absolutely necessary to seek a remedy for the late act of the Lords.
2. I see no advantage in Mr. Collier's[1] or any other Resolution, except as introductory to action : and if action can be had a Resolution may perhaps be needless.
3. Lord Palmerston's objections to placing a large or considerable part of our taxes on the footing of annual grants appear to me conclusive.
4. I cannot agree with Sir Geo. Lewis[2] that the Income Tax with the Tea and Sugar Duties give us by expiring a security for next year. Those are subjects so weighted with interests or difficulties of their own, that the odds (I think) are greatly against its being practicable to handle them freely as tools for operating on other questions.
5. The principle of combining in one the financial measures of the year is good : but I fear it would often be found so inconvenient as to be unavailable.
6. Difficulty I admit surrounds us on all hands : nothing can now succeed without union, effort, & determination : but even with them I see no way of ultimate hope or safety, except some plan of action founded on the principle, that the Lords are not to tax the people without their consent.

87   *Gladstone to Palmerston*

11, Carlton H[ouse] Terrace

July 3. 60.

Thanks for the copy of the Resolutions, I have been examining them, and apart from the personal matter, I have two points to notice.

[1] Robert Collier, Q.C., M.P. (afterwards Lord Monkswell), Counsel to the Admiralty.
[2] Home Secretary.

THE PAPER CAP

1. It would I think greatly improve the *second*, if it were to say ' Bills of several descriptions relating to taxation ', instead of ' Bills relating to taxation '. For in truth it is only certain descriptions of those Bills, in regard to which the power has been exercised.

2. The first resolution, following an ancient precedent of 1692, uses the word ' Supplies ' which *included* Ways and Means. But the second Resolution distinguishes between Supplies and Ways and Means. The effect is to make the first Resolution ambiguous : the language of the one proceeding on the old model, that of the other on the new. Now it is the first Resolution only that asserts the exclusive right of the Commons. It might be cured by inserting Ways and Means in the First Resolution, or the word exclusive in the second. I say consider this for it is really material with respect to the clearness and consistency of the Resolutions.

The third Resolution also distinguishes between Taxation and Supply. I think it shows the real meaning but only by a circuitous argument.

88   *Gladstone to Palmerston*

11 C[arlton] H[ouse] Terrace.

Jul. 4. 60.

Before the Cabinet meets I wish to explain to you the view I take of the Taxing Bills question in its present position, in order that you may decide how far it is admissible.

The Cabinet has decided by a great majority *not* to announce to the H. of Commons any intention of proceeding at this time to vindicate its right by action. On Monday indeed I understood the intention to be that the direct contrary should be stated. It was to that statement that I could not be a party.

I have little hope that the H. of Commons, unless led by the Gov^t., will *so* vindicate its rights : and therefore I do not desire in the debate on your Resolutions to bind myself to that course. But I could not without a breach of what I think the highest political duty resign, either tacitly or expressly, my personal liberty to concur in any proposal with that view when your Resolutions are disposed of, if it sh^d. seem likely to produce any beneficial result.

I think the Resolutions themselves deserve support.

89   *Gladstone to Palmerston*

Private.   11 D[owning] S[treet] July 5. 60

There is a point connected with the decision of the Cabinet yesterday on which I should wish to know your wishes.

It was, I think rightly, determined that the proposal of a new duty should follow *immediately* upon the China Vote. It will therefore be proposed *before* the Cabinet can submit any proposal which it may hereafter adopt with respect to Fortifications and to whatever charge they may entail. In acting on the Resolution of yesterday I should infallibly be met with the remark " this is all very well, but we have not yet got the whole *charge* for the year before us, in as much as we have been told that something is to be proposed about Fortifications, and that something may involve charge for which no provision has been made : but before you ask us to vote any new impost, you ought to tell us the whole charge for the year ".

The answer I should suggest (which might be given by anticipation) would be that it was not the intention of the Cabinet to propose the imposition of *any* further burden on the finances or rather the taxes of the year. That the mode of proceeding would be explained when the Fortification Vote is moved or on some other early opportunity, but that at present I could only say this would be the last demand we meant to make upon the Taxpayer.

They would be told at the same time of the necessity of taking a borrowing power in some form for China etc., and they would be left to speculate upon the question whether this should extend to Fortifications, or not—until the day for your explanation had arrived.

No other way occurs to me of dealing, at least from my lips, with this subject.

90   *Palmerston to Gladstone*

94 P[iccadill]ʸ 9 July 1860

You will see by the inclosed that no further sum than that taken in the Army Estimates this year will be required for this year for the Fortifications.

91   *Palmerston to Gladstone*

94 Piccadilly

13 July 1860

I see by the Votes that you are going to propose that the Import Duty on Paper shall intirely cease. I never understood that this was to be ; I understood that all that was to be done was to reduce the Import Duty to that amount which would be consistent with the Stipulations of the French Treaty ; that is to say to the amount of the Excise Duty, with such an addition as may be equivalent to the Money value of the Inconvenience arising to Paper Manufacturers from the Excise Regulations—To abolish the whole of the Import Duty of Paper would be unfair by the Manufacturers at Home, and would look like an Endeavour to Drive them to Petition for a Repeal of the Excise Duty, the Continuance of which they do not at present complain of.

92   *Gladstone to Palmerston*

D[owning] S[treet] 13 July 60.

I explained a few days ago in the House of Commons that
my notice on the Paper Duties stood on the list in its
original shape, that it would not be proposed in that shape,
and that I would as soon as possible amend it. This however can only be done when the Government have agreed
on the precise amendment to be proposed and adhered to.
It would be well that this should be done as soon as possible. The natural thing would have been to withdraw my
notice for the time but this I could hardly do as a family of
amendments had grown up about it which were not of my
parentage or property.

Your observations are most just and unquestionable.

93   *Palmerston to Gladstone*

To fortify London by works is impossible—London must
be defended by an army in the Field, and by one or more
Battles,—one I trust would be sufficient ; but for this Purpose we must be able to concentrate in the Field the
largest possible Military Force. In order to do so we must
have the means of defending our Naval arsenals with the
smallest possible Military Force, and this can be accomplished only by Fortifications which enable a small Force
to resist a larger one. Thence it is demonstrable that to
fortify our Dockyards is to assist the Defence of London.

As to Time we have no Time to lose. I deeply regret that
various circumstances have so long delayed proposing the
Measure to Parliament, but it would be a Breach of our
public Duty to put it off to another year. There may be
some Persons in the House of Commons with peculiar
notions on Things in General and with very imperfect
notions as to our National Interest who will object to the
proposed Measures, but I cannot bring myself to believe

that the Majority of the present House of Commons, or the House of Commons that would be elected on an appeal on this Question to the People of the Country would refuse to sanction Measures so indispensably necessary.

The Sum required is small for its object. Compare it with the Cost of any of the least Important warlike operations— The Caffre War, the China Wars the Canadian Rebellion while on the other Hand the object to be attained is Protection for the very vitals of the Country—I have written this very hastily. I fear it is hardly readable.

16 July 1860   PALMERSTON

94   *Gladstone to Palmerston*

11 C[arlton] H[ouse] Terrace
July 19. 60.

The same motives which made me anxious to propose the additional Spirit Duty, operating in a minor degree lead me to submit to you whether *I* should make the proposal as to Customs Duty on Paper.

If you wish the matter to remain in my hands perhaps you will arrange for our taking that subject on as early a day as possible.

The Resolutions I have no doubt will be ready this evening : I should be quite ready to proceed to-morrow if it suited the general convenience, but unless this were acceptable on both sides a longer notice would be requisite.

95   *Palmerston to Gladstone*

94 Piccadilly
19 July 1860

It would certainly be desirable that you should dispose of the Paper Duty of Customs but to make use of Guizots favorite expression " *Je n'accepte pas* " the implied Reason which you hint at for proposing to do so.

96   *Palmerston to Gladstone*

94 Piccadilly
19 July 1860

I have by Inadvertence kept much longer than I ought to have done your Letter about the Oxford Professorship.

I send you a Letter which I have received on the Subject from George Grey,[1] for your Consideration.

I do not know that generally speaking the advisers of the Crown know better Means than University Authorities have for making a good Choice. But I know from Cambridge Experience that local Jobs are often perpetrated in the filling up of University offices by University Election.

The Responsibility attaching to the advisers of the Crown is sometimes a Security if not for the best Choice, at least against a very bad one.

97   *Palmerston to Gladstone*

94 Piccadilly
20 July 1860

It seems to me, who have not seen and do not know Sir Culling Eardleys Picture that the Sum which Sir Charles Eastlake[2] mentions would be quite enough to give for it.

As to the second Point we should probably not be disposed to allot more than the £6000 for Pictures this Year.

98   *Gladstone to Palmerston*

11 Carlton H[ouse] Terrace.
July 20. 60.

The necessity of altering the Customs Duty upon Paper appears to me undesirable. General policy, justice to particular interests, and the positive obligation of Treaty form

[1] Chancellor of the Duchy of Lancaster.   [2] Director of the National Gallery.

in this case the threefold cord which it is proverbially so difficult to break.

I hope your Cabinet to-morrow if there is one may be early rather than otherwise.

99   *Palmerston to Gladstone*

94 P[iccadill]y. 20 July 1860

Brand thinks we shall have a good deal of Difficulty about the Paper Customs Duties, & advises that the changes should be put off till next Session. Could this be done? He thinks the Proposal of the French to reduce their High Export Duty on Rags will have a bad Effect.

100   *Palmerston to Gladstone*

94 Piccadilly

23 July 1860

It is quite clear from what passed this Evening in the House of Commons that the Conservatives are bent upon beating us about the Paper Duties, and will muster all their strength to do so, while on the other Hand I am told by Brand Dunbar and Laing that Many of our Friends will vote against us on that Question—would it not be prudent that we should try to persuade the French government to consent to allow the whole of the Paper Duties to remain as they have been? Cowley[1] in a private Letter to John Russell which I read this Evening says the French Govt. do not care about those Duties and we might fairly put it to them that no good could arise to the Relations of the Two Countries from an adverse Vote of the House of Commons.

But if any thing is to be done it must be done at once. I was asked three or four Times this Evening to name the Day on which the Paper Duties would be brought on.

[1] Ambassador in Paris.

KP

101   *Gladstone to Palmerston*

July 24. 1860
11 Carlton H[ouse] Terrace

I thought that the question had been finally decided by the Cabinet about bringing on the Paper Duty and I confess that I could not defend a recession from an intention we have so long and so repeatedly announced, and which we have founded on a Treaty engagement.

I quite agree that delay only aggravates the matter and I should suppose it best to proceed on Thursday or Friday.

In saying this I must add that I have not yet learnt whether Gibson has got the opinion of the Queen's advocate which was thought by the Cabinet a fit or necessary supplement to that of the Attorney and Solicitor General. This may be an objection to your fixing anything to-day.

I must not write on this subject without confessing to you that I do not know how to reconcile the terms of your Resolution on Fortifications, moved last night, with the arrangement to which I understand you and the Cabinet had kindly come on Saturday, and the essence of which I understood to be limited to the execution of certain selected works within the year, and that no legislative sanction was to be asked for the plan as a whole. From this I thought it followed that the Government would not as a body be committed to their course next year, and I believe all these conclusions were warranted by the communications made to me ; but as I have said I know not how to reconcile them with the terms of the Resolution, especially as construed by your speech. All this I shall endeavour most carefully to consider, but I thought it only fair to state the first aspect which in my eyes the proceedings bear.

102 *Palmerston to Gladstone*

94 Piccadilly
24 July 1860

It is quite true that the Cabinet, against my advice, came to the Decision to go on with your Paper Duty of Customs Bill, but I conceive that this does not preclude me or any other Member of the Cabinet from representing Difficulties and Dangers which the Reports of our House of Commons Staff officers may lead him foresee as threatening that Course. These authorities all tell me, and they have again told me this Morning in the House that they consider Defeat as nearly certain ; that all the Opposition will come to the Post, that many of our Friends will vote with them, and that many more of our Friends who may not like to desert us, will in their Hearts condemn us for making them vote against their Convictions and opinions— as far as the Government is concerned the Defeat on this Question would involve no other Consequences than the bad effect of closing a Session with a Defeat on a Question to which Importance enough would appear to have been attached, to make us persevere in spite of all warnings from Friends and unmistakeable Indications from antagonists ; but it seems to me that if there is an easy and creditable Escape from such a Result it would be better to take advantage of it—That Escape appears pointed out by Cowleys Letter to John Russell which I saw last Night, & which reports that the French Government do not care at all about these Paper Duties. If that is so why should we not ask them to allow those Duties to remain in all Respects as they have hitherto been, and on all Kinds of Paper ? but ask our out of Cabinet Men in the House of Commons what they know & think.

If the Question is to be brought on I agree with you it is better and fairer to bring it on this week, but in that Case Notice should be given at once.

As to the Fortifications we have taken the Course which was agreed upon that is to say we have proposed a vote of Two Millions only for the year ending July 1861, out of the Nine Millions ultimately to be asked, and our Bill to be brought in after the Resolution is reported will not go beyond those Two Millions. But I never intimated that I should not open the whole Scheme to Parliament, and endeavour as far as my speech and the Debate in the House could go, to pledge Parliament to the Adoption of the Whole.

In Fact to have proposed the Two Million only, and those works only which the Two Millions would begin & execute would have been to fall intirely short of the Recommendations of the Commissioners, and to have virtually thrown the Two Millions away—

Most Things begun and left imperfectly finished are in some Respects worse than if they had never been begun, but works of Defence are peculiarly so, because they are liable to be taken by an Enemy and to be turned against those whom they are meant to defend ; but nothing that we have done binds Parliament beyond the present ending Twelve Month.

We had thought on Sunday that we might take a vote in Supply instead of in the Committee of which I had on Friday given notice, but on Communicating with the Speaker and May we found that such a Course would not be right and we fell back on that which had before intended to take.

103   *Palmerston to Gladstone*

94 Piccadilly
5 August 1860

It will I think be advisable at the Meeting Tomorrow, and in the Debate in the Evening to avoid reviving the Question between the two Houses.

104   *Palmerston to Gladstone*

94 Piccadilly

8 Aug 1860

I have received this from the Prince ; I have asked Lowe[1] about it, and he says that some of the valuable Collections of works of art at Kensington are in great Danger of Damage unless the Recommendation of the Committee is adopted. What shall I say to the Prince? it seems to me that it would be unwise not to take at once those Steps which are necessary for the safe Custody of the National Property in Question.

105   *Palmerston to Gladstone*

D[ownin]g S[tree]t 11 Aug 1860

The Queen asked me some little Time ago in anticipation of the vacancy at Westminster, to appoint to it when it should happen the Revd. Mr Nepean, for whom she felt much interested, among other Reasons on account of his having been for many Years attached to her Aunt the Duchess of Gloucester—I do not much like the Practice which prevailed greatly in the time of former Sovereigns of turning church appointments into the Channel of Royal Favor, but as there was no personal objection which could be urged against Mr. Nepean I could not do otherwise than comply, and I have accordingly directed that Mr. Nepean should be appointed to the vacant Canonry at Westminster—

I state this for your own Information, but it will be enough that you should say to the Dean of Peterborough that I am sorry that an arrangement already made prevents me from giving effect to his wishes.

[1] R. Lowe, M.P., Vice-President of the Board of Education.

106   *Palmerston to Gladstone*

Confidential.
                              94 P[iccadill]ʸ 16 aug. 1860

I have settled the matter with Derby ; Granville will move Tomorrow to suspend the Sessional order for the Purpose of reading the Savings Banks Bill a second Time, and Derby's friends will not attend in sufficient numbers to make any effectual opposition to the motion.

He was very well disposed to avoid creating needless difficulties—It will be best to keep this to ourselves lest there should be Mutiny in Derby's Camp if it was proclaimed that he had come to a private understanding with us.

I shall tell Brand to ask Mellor to put off his Motion upon the Ground that Granville is going to Moot the Matter again Tomorrow in the Hᵉ. of Lords.

107   *Palmerston to Gladstone*

                              94 Piccadilly
                              21 aug 1860

I find that Argyll[1] has recommended to the Treasury that the Letter Carriers of the Post Office should henceforth be appointed, not by Selection by the Postmaster General but upon their own application if approved by the Civil Service Commissioners ; it seems to me that such an arrangement ought not to be adopted without very full and mature Consideration— It would establish a new Principle which would on similar Grounds apply to other Branches of the Public Service and its Expediency seems to me to be very questionable.

[1] Lord Privy Seal.

108   *Palmerston to Gladstone*

St Giles s 5 Oct 1860

I have received the inclosed from Azeglio.[1]

These Irish volunteers for the Pope have violated our
Law, and have gone to help the Pope in violating by cruelty
and oppression towards his Subjects the Laws of the Roman
States ; but they thought they had evaded and not broken
our Law, and they were led by their Priest to believe that
the States of the Pope were a Terrestrial Paradise about
to be disturbed by an Inroad of unclean spirits from Revolutionary Quarters without. They did wrong but from
good and generous Feelings. At all Events they are our
Countrymen placed by the Course of Events in a most distressing Condition—we can hardly expect that the Sardinian Government should pay the Expence of sending
them Home to Ireland, the Pope ought to do so but the
Fate of War has taken them out of his holy keeping. It
seems to me that it would be right and creditable for the
English Government to take charge of these men and to
pay for their Passage Home, which might easily be done
out of civil Contingencies and it would not only be a kind
and generous act but it would be politic and useful as
regards the Catholics of Ireland.

If you agree I will desire the Foreign Office to instruct
Hudson[2] to make arrangements and to draw on the
Treasury for the amount of Expences incurred.

109   *Palmerston to Gladstone*

Broadlands

6 October 1860

. . . I spoke to the Queen about Pressly when I was at
Osborne just before She started for Germany—She suggested that it would be more in accordance with the Rules

---

[1] Sardinian Ambassador in London.   [2] British Ambassador to Sardinia.

of the Bath that he should begin by being a Companion, as Larcom did ; and I have moreover found upon Inquiry, as appears by the inclosed Paper that the number of Knights Commanders is limited to Fifty, and that there are already Fifty appointed—under these Circumstances I fear that Pressly must be satisfied with one step at a time.

110   *Gladstone to Palmerston*

Hawarden.

Oct. 7. 60.

I will inquire at the Treasury and let you know whether there is any precedent on record, which would afford a ground, as far as usage is concerned, for the proposal you make to pay out of Civil Contingencies the expences homewards of the Pope's 600 or 700 Irish Volunteers. I must however confess that at first sight it seems to me open to great objections. In the first place it goes *beyond* the demand of the Sardinian Government for in asking for a ship I presume Marquis d'Azeglio means that the Sardinian Government would bear the other charges of the passage. In the second place we should be aiding those at the charge of the State who have broken its law and all whose friends exult in what they have done. In the next place I know very well that if they come home at the public cost, they will come at a much greater actual outlay than if their passages are found in any other manner. But what chiefly alarms me is the breadth of the precedent (if a novel one) to be established, and its effect upon similar enterprise in future—of which we may have further examples.

I do not doubt that this is a case of distress brought on probably in a great degree by an honest fanaticism. It seems to me one of those cases which ought to be met not out of the pocket of the English people but by private subscription ; and for one I should be very happy to subscribe.

This mode of proceeding would I think not fail to be appreciated by the Roman Catholics generally : I am not so sure that they would think highly of the other. And it has above all this recommendation that it would lay down no evil precedent for private individuals would always remain masters of their own money and would use it at their own discretion.

As I have said much seems to me to depend on usage but I give my first impressions on the supposition that the question is about a novelty.

111   *Gladstone to Palmerston*

Hawarden
Oct. 16. 60

I should in no case have thought of pressing the opinion which I stated to you in my letter of the 7th, on the matter of the Irish *Papalini*, in contrariety to yours. But it is reported to me from London that the spirit and course of precedents, although I imagine it is chiefly of cases where one or a very few have been in question, is favourable to your plan. By this post I desire that a brief note of them may be sent to you forthwith and I cheerfully leave the matter in your hands. . . .

112   *Gladstone to Palmerston*

Downing Street, S.W.
Private.   Nov. 16. 1860.

I have heretofore shrunk from recommending to your notice any particular person among my constituents as qualified to be advanced to a Bishopric : but bearing in mind the terms of a very kind note which you addressed to Herbert in the month of June, I feel that on the occasion offered by the decease of the Bishop of Worcester I ought not to omit to make known to you the signal merits of Mr. Claughton[1] the Vicar of Kidderminster alike well known and generally beloved in the Diocese of which the See is now vacant.

I do not know of a single point in which I could not speak with the utmost confidence of Mr. Claughton as a person who if known to you personally would command your warm approval.—He is an experienced and a most effective parish priest, a highly accomplished scholar, an excellent preacher, eminently judicious in his dealings with men, calm in his judgement and moderate in his opinions, and qualified in a very remarkable degree not only to give satisfaction by his preferment to the Diocese and the public generally, but also to exercise as a Bishop that *weight* which depends upon well balanced character, and which is often so difficult even in men who are otherwise of signal merit.

As to his politics I am not particularly informed beyond the fact that his brother-in-law, Lord Dudley I think answers for them, and that he is as you know, one of your warm admirers and very decided adherents.

113   *Palmerston to Gladstone*

94 Piccadilly
22 Nov[r]. 1860

I am much obliged to you for your Letters and for the Testimony they bear to the Merits of Mr. Claughton of whose deserved Popularity I have heard Much. I feel however bound on the present occasion to look for a Cambridge Man, of the seven Bishops whom it has been my Lot to recommend to the Queen five have been Oxford Men ; and though I by no Means am disposed to revert to the old Practise of taking alternately a Cambridge and an Oxford Man for the Bench, yet I should be unwilling to expose myself to the imputation of sending Cambridge to Coventry

[1] Bishop of Rochester, 1867.

in Resentment for my having been dispossessed of my Seat for that University.

In good Truth I have no such Feeling, I had represented the University long enough, and it has been an advantage to me to have changed to other Constituencies. But I am grateful to my University for many Benefits and should be sorry to be thought unmindful of obligations.

114   *Palmerston to Gladstone*

Broadlands
22 Decr 1860

Lewis has sent me the inclosed Letter from the Regius Professor of Greek at Oxford observing that the arguments contained in it deserve a careful Consideration before the Measure to which it refers is introduced into Parliament.

I am not sufficiently acquainted with Oxford affairs to be able to Judge as to the Bearing of What Mr. Jowett says ; but my Cambridge Experience convinces me that it is inexpedient to leave appointments like those of Professorships to be made by the Majority of resident Voters. I have seen at Cambridge very unfit men elected by personal or College Partiality

Majorities incur no Responsibility, the advisers of the Crown are held in check by their Responsibility

I think however that your scheme of three Ministers and two University Men would sufficiently check local abuse.

I should be glad however to have your Remarks upon the Professor's Letter.

115   *Gladstone to Palmerston*

Hawarden
Dec. 27. 60

Professor Jowett sent me his letter to you in the first instance and I saw him on the subject. Having acted as the medium between the Executive and Initiative power of the University on the one hand, and you on the other, and Professor Jowett's letter having come in after you had accepted in general terms the proposal tendered, and as I also had acted in the matter more as a Burgess of the University than as a Minister, I was a little embarrassed as to the point of form, and I recommended the Professor to go to Sir Geo. Lewis. At the same time I told him all I had to say on his letter, and I will now repeat it to you. I told him frankly that I thought his comments were somewhat invidious, because including nothing (as is the fact) with reference to the liberality which the University has shewn. *You* are asked to make a concession in return for what the University does : but to Mr. Jowett their act is one of pure gift without any equivalent : & it would have been, I think, the more becoming to acknowledge this, because as you may know he has been the subject of controversy in the University and his opinions are highly distasteful to the great majority. . . .

116   *Palmerston to Gladstone*

94 Piccadilly
19 Feby 1861

Some of our Colleagues with whom I have talked about the Course to be pursued on Hubbard's Motion agree with me that it would be best for the Government and for yourself that we should resist the Motion, even if it should be carried against us. There is, as you are no doubt aware, a very unjust Impression among many that the Government acting under your Impulses are disposed to make important Changes in the Bearing of Taxation, throwing a larger Portion of it on accumulated Capital and there would be a Danger that if we agreed to Hubbard's Motion, that Impression might be encouraged—on the other Hand if we resist it on the ground that previous Inquiries have shewn the Impossibility of drawing the Line of Distinction which the Hubbardites wish to Establish our being beat would not be of much Consequence.

Our Chief Difficulty in that Case would be to find some-body who on the Part of the Government would be competent to watch and direct the Proceedings of the Committee, and who would have Time at his disposal to do so.

117   *Gladstone to Palmerston*

11 C[arlton] H[ouse] Terrace
Feb. 25, 1861.

I have just had your box marked " Pressing " which has come to me first on its circuit. As this is so, and as I am obliged to put in a strong paper of objection, amounting at one point nearly to complaint, I think it best to ask your Messenger to take the box back to you that you may see my memorandum at once.

I Keep the pamphlet to run over hastily.

p. 24 of the pamphlet.

" There is much to be done before our maritime frontier shall be in a state to meet the two duties of defence and of aggression."

p. 26. Recent changes ' have carried over to the side of the attacking force an undesirable superiority '.

31. Contemplates fleet of 94000 men wh. it w^d. take from 25 to 20 years to realize.

(Enclosure)

ON LORD PALMERSTON'S MEMORANDUM
of Feb: 25, 1861.

This sudden demand for a fresh Naval Outlay of Three Millions is made within a fortnight or three weeks of the time when the Cabinet had arrived at its decision on the scale of Expenditure for the year, and had announced it to Parliament.

I am not opposed to our applying a larger *share* of our Ship-building force and expenditure to iron-cased or shot-proof vessels : for, within a few months after the Administration was formed, I wrote to the Head of the Government, and I think also to the First Lord of the Admiralty, recommending such a course. But that was with a view to the substitution of work on Shot-proof Ships for a part of our vast expenditure on Wooden Line of Battle Ships, of which I doubted the utility.

I am obliged to object to our coming at the present time to the conclusions proposed in Lord Palmerston's Memorandum, for the following reasons, which I must state hurriedly.

The plan would create great alarm, and would in itself be more a danger than a guarantee for peace.

It would give rise to many and just complaints of our having deceived Parliament and the country by the recently published Estimates.

No sufficient evidence has come before me to show that the French Government intend the immediate outlay of four millions on iron or Shot-proof vessels : or to show within what time, even if it did intend to strain every nerve for the purpose, that object could be accomplished.

It would be uncandid to conceal my opinion that, in the office I hold, I ought to be supplied with further means of considering such evidence, than have been afforded me by the circulation of one or two manuscript papers, for the most hurried perusal as they have passed from hand to hand. Nor could I undertake to dispose of this question between Monday and Wednesday afternoons.

I believe however that in the papers I refer to there was matter to cast much doubt upon the execution if not the existence of the French plans as they are now represented.

Great inconvenience, if not some danger, I think, occurred last Summer from the relation established—perhaps of necessity—by declarations in Parliament, between the plan of Fortifications and supposed designs of French aggression. I am disinclined to be a party to its repetition : especially as repetition, in such cases, is apt to become practical aggravation.

Though most anxious for the effectual prosecution of Shot-proof Ship-building, I hold, and it is to *some* extent admitted by the Duke of Somerset's letter, that our knowledge and experience, with respect to several most important questions of construction and use, are not such as to justify immediate decision on the immense orders now proposed.

It does not surprise me, that a Ship-building Loan is suggested : for it was always my belief that the measure of last year, instead of remaining an exception, had the strongest tendency to become a precedent. But I am wholly unable to concur in the suggestion.

It is true that the French Government are dangerously adding to their public Debt ; which is now nearly one half of ours. In a later stage of national experience, we have thus far been in great part preserved from a similar course. By an alteration in this respect, we should compromise the financial strength, which is the first among all the material conditions of permanent national defence.

In conclusion, my objections, as I have stated, do not apply to any measures which may be taken for assigning, after sufficient consideration and experience, a large proportion of our contemplated strength and expenditure, as settled by the Estimates, to Shot-proof Ship-building. Those Estimates provide for the permanent maintenance, with a view to Wooden Ship-building, of establishments which were devised when we had, and meant to have, only a wooden Navy : and they would admit, I apprehend, of considerable transfers to iron-casing, the method

(I believe) thus far pursued by the French, which transfers might take place, without noise or alarm, during the immediately impending financial year.

W. E. G. Feb. 25. 61.

118   *Palmerston to Gladstone*

94 P[iccadill]ʸ. 25 Feby 61

I have only time to make one or two hurried Remarks on your Paper.

The Reason why the Admiralty Recommendation was not made before the Estimates were framed is that the great Increase of the French Navy was ordered only a Short Time ago.

As to Transferring to Iron Ships the Sums taken in the Estimates for Wooden ones, I apprehend that would go a very little Way and would deprive us of some Things which are still essential.

No doubt a full Exchequer is a good Foundation for National Defence but if the superstructure is wanting, the Foundation would be of small avail and if the French had the Command of the Sea they would soon find means to make a full Exchequer empty—

Our Measures of defensive Preparation may doubtless make the French angry, but only because they render us Secure against the effects of French anger

The anger of a Power no stronger than ourselves may be borne, with Regret if you will but without alarm. The anger of a Power greatly and decidedly stronger must cause apprehension, and is likely to lead to disaster or Humiliation ; and no People are more prone than the French to make an arrogant abuse of predominant Power.

"BEGGAR MY NEIGHBOUR"

Pam. "Is not Your Majesty tired of this foolish game?"

119 *Gladstone to Palmerston*

Most Private. 11 Carlton H[ouse] Terrace.
Feb. 26. 1861.

[1] This letter withheld
on finding that the
project started in the M[emorandum]
was not likely to go
forward.

W. E. G. Mch. 1. 61.

Your Memorandum of yesterday, and the accompanying circumstances, I think require from me in answer more than remarks upon the particular proposal.

You have a right to expect the services of a Chancellor of the Exchequer with whom you can take counsel upon all measures of finance, whether military or other, in their beginnings.

Not merely reasons affecting myself, but a sense of what is due to you, make me feel the unseemliness of my renewing during the present Session a series of struggles such as were those of last year upon the Fortifications, the Paper Duty, and the Question of Taxing Bills.

By what is due to you I mean what is due not only to your station, and to the credit of your Government, but to the kindness and consideration with which you have treated me on many occasions.

The most natural sequel to what I have said would be at once to place my resignation in your hands.

But one strong public motive, over and above many which are personal, disinclines me to any such step at the present juncture. I earnestly desire, and I feel it to be a duty unless it is crossed by some other duty yet more imperative, to render my account of the measures of last year ; which, whether they were good or bad, were in their bulk sufficient to stamp a character on the Session. This

---

[1] Endorsed in pencil.

account can only be rendered in full by means of the Budget ; which, in proposing measures for the future, will also wind up the past and will offer to objectors the legitimate occasion for asking the judgment of Parliament.

Any such question must be disposed of shortly after Easter ; and I desire to be in at the death, even though it should be my own. But in at the death I cannot be, if our plan of Naval Expenditure for the year is to be abandoned within a fortnight after its announcement : and in that case it would be better that you should at once commit my duties to other hands, than that a struggle such as those to which I have referred should begin in the Cabinet of to-morrow.

My Memorandum in the Cabinet box will explain to our colleagues what I have to say in relation to the immediate questions : this letter of course is for you as Head of the Government.

120   *Palmerston to Gladstone*

94 P[iccadill]y. 19 March 1861

If you are to bring on your Budget Statement soon after Easter, and I think you have announced it for the 13th April, the Cabinet would very much wish that the outline of it should be explained to them on Saturday next, in order that they be able to consider the Scheme before it is stated to Parliament.

Let me also remind you that we shall want in the Course of the Session to ask for a further Issue of terminable annuities.

Herbert will I imagine want something more than Two Millions to defray the Expence of the works to be completed by the Summer of 1862 ; and Somerset will require for casing with Plates some of our wooden Liners, and for building new Iron Sea-going Ships to put us on a Par with the French a Sum of about the same amount. I should fear that you may not be able to Screw this last sum out of the

Revenue of the year and in that Case, the best way of meeting the want would probably be to make the advance out of terminable annuities to be repaid from annual vote next year or the year after.

121   *Gladstone to Palmerston*

Private.   11 C[arlton] H[ouse] T[errace]
                    Mch. 20. 61.

I fear from the tenour of your note that we may have some difficulty in settling the items of a financial [scheme : for although I consider myself bound in honour to act this year upon my reluctant but deliberate assent to the measure for fortifications which you proposed last year][1] plan : for I do not understand it. You have now decided that there shall be the further provision which you name as remaining to be made for the Navy over and above the sum required for fortifications under the Act of last year ; and I have hitherto looked upon that sum as expressing the amount which in addition to the Estimates already presented and the Militia Estimates was to dispose of the question of Military and Naval Expenditure for the year.

Apart however from any anticipation of difficulty on this subject I do not think we can make any real progress in Cabinet on the matter of finance before the recess. It will not be possible for me to frame any plan until after the close of the financial year on the 31st of March. The revenue of the country has been in so singular a state for the last few months that I do not venture to ask the Department for an estimate of what it may be next year until the present one shall have closed. Even within the last few weeks, the Board of Inland Revenue have added £250,000 to their estimate of Excise deficiency for 1860-1 ; and I have never known a time when it would be so essential to proceed with great caution and in full possession of the best *data*. One

[1] The words printed within brackets were deleted by Gladstone.

or two important items affecting the side of expenditure are also as yet unfixed. Of course I am busy in collecting all the materials so as to be in a condition to put them together and to be ready with my proposals for the Cabinet as promptly as possible after most materials are in my hands. But I do not think that I can submit them sooner than either Monday the 8th or at the very earliest Saturday the 6th of April.

You will probably therefore consider in Cabinet what day we should definitely name for the Budget. Though I have spoken of Thursday the 11th, it is understood by the House that nothing has been fixed, but that it *will* be fixed before we adjourn. On account of the Income Tax it is most desirable to have it at the earliest moment. In no case, I think can it involve a very large number of items or be of complex structure like that of last year.

122   *Palmerston to Gladstone*

Broadlands 6 ap 1861

I understood it to have been settled that we were to have a Cabinet about Budget and Finance on Wednesday next, and summonses have been sent out accordingly—If however the unexpected Requisitions which you mention, or any other Circumstances should make it desirable that such Cabinet Should be put off to a later Day, it must be fixed for Friday and not for Thursday, because our Committee on public business meets on Thursday to consider Report, and the Cabinet Ministers who are Members of that Committee must be there on that Day. But if these inevitable Delays occur, it may be worth while for you to consider whether it would not be better that your Budget which was for an early Day, I believe Monday, in the Week after next should not be put off to a later Day.

I send you a Letter which I have received from Edward Ellice about financial arrangements he has probably written to you to the same Effect.

No Doubt we should be placed in a better Position if Taxes which form a considerable Part of our Revenue were not for so short a Time as one Year.

123   *Gladstone to Palmerston*

Carlton H[ouse] Terrace
8 April 1861.

I return Mr. Ellice's letter. Let me assure you that his memory entirely deceives him as to his communication with me last year ; I never said, or thought, anything like what he puts into my mouth.

Having myself asked Parliament in 1853 for an Income Tax for seven years I am the last person to be insensible to the benefit of obtaining that Tax for more than one year at a time.

But Mr. Ellice proposes something different from this. He proposes to take 7d for three years : and to leave it to be settled in each year, by a separate demand and separate Act, what should be the number of additional pennies. In this I confess I see no benefit. But I see some danger ; namely this, that if we were to say to Parliament give us the tax at 10d for this year, and at 7d for two more years, we should perhaps incur the charge of bad faith—however unjustly—on asking next Session an addition to the 7d.

On the other hand Parliament would not like to vote 10d for three years : and on the whole I do not see any way, while I am quite open to conviction and think the subject one very proper for discussion.

124   *Gladstone to Palmerston*

11 Carlton H[ouse] Terrace.
8 April 61.

I think I can be ready by Wednesday—especially if not called early in the day.

But your notice is at present out *for to-morrow at 12.*

It is only China that has held me back. I am desirous
either to see or hear from Elgin.

The account will not stand so well as I could wish ; but
neither will it be by a great deal so bad as some people
seem to expect.

I enclose a note on Mr. Ellice's.

125   *Palmerston to Gladstone*

94 Piccadilly 14 April 1861

I have acquiesced reluctantly in your Proposal of Yesterday that the Tenth Penny of Income Tax, and the Excise
Duty on Paper should both be repealed ; reducing our
Surplus for this Year to something less than Four Hundred
Thousand Pounds, and affording the Prospect of a Deficiency of more than that amount for the Year beginning in
April 1862. But I think it proper to record in writing the
opinion which I have more than once expressed verbally
in Cabinet in our Discussions on these Matters, namely that
the financial arrangements of the Country ought to have
been framed upon a Principle different from that on which
your Proposal has been founded.

My deliberate opinion is that a larger Surplus than that
which your arrangement will give ought to have been left
to meet the many Contingencies which the unsettled State
of affairs in Europe may give Rise to ; and that if a large
Part of the Estimated Surplus could be spared, it ought to
have been applied to pay off a Part of those Exchequer
Bonds, to the Payment of which out of Income, the Faith of
the Government and of the Country is pledged.

That is the Course, which, in my opinion sound Policy
on the one Hand, and good Faith on the other pointed out.
The Cabinet at your Recommendation have agreed to a
Course founded on different Principles, and I have acquiesced in that Course being proposed to Parliament. But

MASTER BULL AND HIS DENTIST

DENTIST. " Don't cry, my little man ! I'm not going to draw any more this time, and
there's a penny for you ! "

I think it right to say beforehand that, as far I am concerned, I do not intend to make the Fate of my administration depend upon the Decision which Parliament may come to upon your Proposal.

126   *Gladstone to Palmerston*

11 C[arlton] H[ouse] Terrace.

Ap. 14. 61.

In reply to your letter which I have just received, I have to say that there is not a word of it, of which I have either any wish, or any title to complain, though there is one expression, namely that of " good faith " as applicable to the payment of Exchequer Bonds, which, if this were the place for argument, I would venture to contest.

I thankfully admit the conciliatory spirit in which you have become a party to the proposals that are to be made to-morrow. On my own part I only ask you to believe that I did not submit them to the Cabinet without a full *belief* that they would be beneficial to your Administration.

As regards your intimation that you do not mean to make the fate of your Government depend upon that of the proposals, I assure you that, reserving my own freedom, I never should have presumed to advance any such claim against you or the Cabinet. That in a matter of such moment the decision of the Cabinet will receive a loyal and united support in Parliament I am perfectly aware : and I entirely disclaim all idea of asking more.

I do not speak of circulating your letter, because that, if you think it proper you will doubtless do yourself.

127   *Palmerston to Gladstone*

94 Piccadilly

1 May 1861

I quite agree with you that it will be best that you should make a Statement Tomorrow in moving the

Resolution you will thus answer by anticipation Horsfall's amendment, while his amendment moved after your Speech will give you an opportunity of replying later in the Evening.

Brand tells me that Taylor says that Disraeli wishes the Debate to end Tomorrow night ; and I believe Brand is right in thinking that we have no Interest in putting off the Division till Monday. He is of opinion that we shall have a fair Majority.

If a Cabinet is wanted on Saturday it should be at one, on account of the Academy Dinner.

I have just received from Brand Hubbard's amendment to the Motion for the Speaker leaving the Chair Tomorrow. This will probably interpose a Night's Debate before we get into Committee.

128   *Palmerston to Gladstone*

94 P[iccadill]y. 5 May 1861

On looking back to what took Place on the 18th and 22d May 1857 about the Marriage of the Princess Royal, I See that I presented the Message on 18th and fixed its Consideration for the 22d ; but that on the 22d it was the Chancellor of the Exchequer who moved the Resolution for the annuity to the Princess on her Marriage. I conclude that the same Course should be followed with Regard to the Princess Alice.[1] The Consideration of the Queen's Message stands fixed for Tomorrow and it would I am sure be a great disappointment to The Queen, if that Matter were to be put off to a later Day—you have probably thought of this but in Case it should have slipped your Memory I send you this Note to remind you— . . .

[1] Betrothed to Prince Louis of Hesse-Darmstadt.

129   *Palmerston to Gladstone*

94 P[iccadill]y. 6 May 1861

I think you are right, and I will move the Resolution accordingly.

130   *Palmerston to Gladstone*

94 P[iccadill]y. 16 May 1861

I think you are making a Mistake in insisting upon going on with your Budget on Thursday of next week. The House of Commons allows itself to be led, but does not like to be driven, and is apt to turn upon those who attempt to drive it. Everybody on each side of the House is disappointed at our not adjourning to the Monday. An adjournment to that Day would have enabled men to go to distant Homes or to run over to Paris. The shorter adjournment is neither one Thing nor the other. But a great many Men have determined to take what we do not give, and to be away till the Monday. If you persist in forcing them back for Thursday the Result will be that the Opposition will come back with increased bitterness and anger, and our own Friends will come sullen and sulky and discontented. But the Spirit of attack being more energetic than that of Defence the Opposition will come up in greater proportional Numbers, than our Friends, and as our Majority was only 18 on the last Division, you may find yourself either defeated on a Division on Thursday, or what is perhaps more likely, compelled by the spinning out of the Debate to be on the Monday much in the same Position as to Progress, in which you would have been if you had with a good grace yielded to what we all know to be the wish of the House in general.

You must be aware that your Budget is not much liked in the House except by the comparatively small Band of Radicals below the gangway, who are thought to be your

Inspirers in financial Matters, and I happen to know that many of our own Friends voted with us on the last occasion against their wishes and opinion, and simply and solely on account of their unwillingness to appear to desert the Government. These Men will not be conciliated by your forcing them back as they will think prematurely. After all there can be no great public Injury in the Delay of four Days ; and it is a Delay which the Opposition can compel you to submit to, if they chuse to do so.

131   *Gladstone to Palmerston*

D[owning] S[treet] May 16. 61.

I assure you I have not the least wish to press my own opinion as to the day when we are to go into Committee on the Finance Bill. I have stated the argument of public convenience pretty high, according to what I believe to be the truth : and it would be difficult for *me* to be the person to postpone the Committee until Monday : but after the opinion you have expressed, which I find Brand fully concurs in, I cheerfully leave the matter in your hands.

I may say a few words in speaking, on the general subject of delay, but if so it will be with the object of making the postponement easy, and of placing the responsibility for our slowness generally in the right quarter.

132   *Palmerston to Gladstone*

94 P[iccadill]y. 24 June 1861

This Death of Lord Campbell[1] is a sad Thing personally and politically and so totally unexpected.

We must bethink ourselves of finding a Successor. John Russell agrees with me that Bethell[2] is pointed out by his professional Eminence and great ability. If Bethell were to

[1] Lord Chancellor.
[2] Richard Bethell (afterwards Lord Westbury), Attorney-General.

be appointed, Atherton [1] would of Course become Attorney General, unless possibly Roundell Palmer [2] could be brought into Parliament for the Seat that Bethell would vacate—I am not versed enough in Legal Etiquette to know whether Roundell Palmer would consent to come in as Solicitor General in the event of his being able to get into Parliament or whether Atherton could be expected to consent to let Palmer come in as Attorney General. I am told however that the Etiquette of the Profession would require that the Solicitor should become Attorney—Steps have been taken to ascertain whether Palmer could be brought in for Wolverhampton and therefore nothing should be said today as to who will be Campbell's Successor.

begun last night
finished today

133   *Gladstone to Palmerston*

June 6. 61

At my suggestion, and with the knowledge of Lord Stanley, [3] Sir Rowland Hill [4] will call upon you to explain to you his present position in the Post Office. I hope you will make yourself, by careful inquiry, thoroughly master of it. I am afraid we are in danger of losing him, and I desire not to be responsible in any degree for bringing so great a misfortune on the public service.

The difficulties which he states to me are partly connected with certain controversies that arose last year respecting the pay and position of the Metropolitan Establishment, and partly go beyond them.

As respects the former branch of the subject, I am sorry

---

[1] Sir W. Atherton, Q.C., M.P.
[2] Roundell Palmer, Q.C. (afterwards Lord Selborne).
[3] Postmaster General.   [4] Secretary to the Post Office.

to say there are serious differences of opinion between the Postmaster General and myself, which I fear must come before you and the Cabinet. He has made a proposal some part of which I think it *absolutely* incompatible with my duty to adopt : while I understand him to decline to recede from any part of it. The bulk of the papers and correspondence is great ; and I am afraid we can hardly ask you, especially at this period of the year, to go through them. Suffice it for the present to point out a specialty in the case. Lord Stanley naturally enough views & argues it as the head of a Department. But the constitution of that Department places it in subordination to the Treasury in a manner more akin to that of a pure Revenue Department than is that of a Secretary of State. . . .

134   *Palmerston to Gladstone*

94 P[iccadill]ʸ. 18 July 1861

I ought to have returned you these Papers sooner. We spend public Money liberally but usefully for the Encouragement of art ; we buy Pictures, and medieval Curiosities ; we pay for Frescoes, Statues and Galleries ; but we do comparatively little for Science. And yet Science is fully as deserving of public Encouragement, and the Knowledge which it imparts and the Truth which it establishes redound quite as much to the Honor and Fame of a Nation as the Triumphs of art, and are often attended with Results of more practical usefulness.

I am quite for giving the Money asked for.

135   *Palmerston to Gladstone*

94 P[iccadill]ʸ. 19 July 1861

I Send you a Memorandum of the Proceedings taken in the Hᵉ. of Cⁿˢ last year for bringing in the Bill which authorized the Issue of Terminable annuities to provide two Millions out of the aggregate Sum required for certain works & Fortifications for our Dockyards and other Places.

I find on Inquiry that between this Time and the End of August of next Year the probable Progress of these works may require one Million more, making three Millions out of the five Million at which those works were estimated. I therefore propose to take now, only one Million more on account of those works. But the Naval Question is extremely pressing and important. The French will have by next Spring six formidable Iron Cased Ships ready and fit for Sea, all of them being now launched and afloat—They are also building Ten more which however will not be ready for a year and a half unless great and extraordinary Exertions are made to complete them

We have now in Hand seven Iron platcd Ships which will not be fit for sea till some Time next Summer. It is absolutely necessary that we should take immediate and active Measures to keep Pace with the French ; and having much urged the Duke of Somerset on this subject I send you a Letter and Estimate which I have received from him.

What I propose to do on this Matter is to take another Million of terminable annuities to enable him to set to work immediately in preparing the Iron Cased and Iron built Ships mentioned in his estimate. This will enable him to go on at once and the Expencc to be incurred by him after the End of this financial year will he says, probably be met in great Part by Reductions on other Heads which he may be able to effect.

But no Time is to be lost These wooden ships which are to be cased with Iron Plates cannot well be finished under eighteen Months, and if we were to put off beginning them till next year, we should be disastrously behind the French who would have sixteen powerful Iron plated Ships to our Seven. This would be a Disproportion for which I never would consent to be answerable if it was possible by any means to prevent it ; and those means are ready at Hand by the Course above-mentioned. The House of Commons has shown by the Discussions which have taken Place on this Subject that they feel the full Importance of the Matter.

I Send you also a Memorandum of a Report which the Prince Consort sent me two Days ago.—I am disposed to think the Statement premature, because I doubt the French Emperor Shewing his Hand before he is ready to play his cards. I wish it may be true, because then the People of England will have their Eyes opened and will see by practical Illustration what is the real purpose for which Cherbourg has been created, and that it never was intended for a Building yard like Brest L'Orient and Toulon, but is destined as a Place D'Armes, for the assembling of a Naval & Military Force for our Benefit, if at any Time it should suit the Policy of the French Government of the Day to favor us by the Honor of a visit.

What I should propose to do is to give notice tonight of moving the preliminary Resolution on Monday.

136   *Palmerston to Gladstone*

94 Piccadilly 19 July 1861
6 p.m.

My attention was attracted last night at the latter End of the Sitting to some Remarks made upon a Paper which had yesterday Morning as it was said, been delivered to Members bearing upon the Bill brought in on the Part of the Government for the Consolidation of the Law Courts. I have been so much occupied all Day with matters which could not be postponed that it is only late this afternoon that I have been able to pick out of my daily Supply of House of Commons Papers, the Document to which Reference was made last night or rather this Morning about Two oclock I conclude to be a Treasury Minute dated the

16th of this Month, and which seems to have been laid before the House of Commons and to have been ordered to be printed on the following Day namely the 17th instant. It is needless for me to say that I had no previous Knowledge of this Minute and was no Party to its being made and laid before Parliament although as First Lord of the Treasury, and therefore first Member of the Board by which this Minute was framed I am virtually and responsibly a Party both to the Minute and to its Presentation to Parliament.

The Minute appears to me to be a formal Protest by the Board of Treasury against a Measure submitted to Parliament by a Member of the Government on Behalf of the Government—It is an appeal by the Board of Treasury, and therefore by the First Lord of the Treasury to the opponents of the Government in the House of Commons against a Measure proposed to the House of Commons sanctioned by the First Lord of the Treasury, and in Fact greatly approved by him, and which had been adopted by the Government after long Deliberation and much Discussion. I am therefore in my official Capacity made to enter into factious opposition to my own Self and the Government of which I am the Head—The Statements in the Minute are many of them purely conjectural, and many of the arguments & Conclusions drawn from them have little or no weight. Those Statements and that Reasoning might be or, if my Memory does not deceive me, they were, fit Matters for the Consideration of the Government, before a Decision was come to on the Subject to which they relate ; but I own it seems to me strange that when a Government has come to a Decision and has proposed a Measure to Parliament that Government should go to the Trouble of furnishing its opponents with a detailed Brief to guide them in their Endeavours to throw that Measure out—So much for the general and Corporate objections to what has been done : but my personal objections are these. I conceive that as First Lord of the Treasury I am intitled if I chose to put forward my Rights to be the effective as well as nominal Chief of the Financial arrangements of the Country. Sir Robert Peel when he was First Lord was so, and both concocted and brought forward the great and leading financial measures of his Government to what extent he directed the more detailed arrangements of the Board of Treasury I do not know—I have no wish or desire to follow his Example ; in asking you to take Charge of the Exchequer I clearly understood that the Management of the Finances of the Country subject always to the Concurrence of the Cabinet should be left to you— I have in regard to those Matters treated you with perfect Confidence. I have never required as I was intitled to do that you should consult with me beforehand the financial Measures which you were about to propose to the Cabinet. I have often in the Discussion of your proposed Measures in the Cabinet given up opinions which I happened to entertain and yielded them to yours ; I have not made it my Practise to interfere with the detailed Business of the Board of Treasury of which I am the Head ; but I wish it to be clearly understood between us that I do not intend to be set aside as I have been on this occasion, and to be made without my Knowledge and Consent a virtual Party to Proceedings of which I intirely disapprove

137   *Gladstone to Palmerston*

                      11 Carlton H[ouse] Terrace
Private.   July 19. 61.
                                      Night.

I have read with much regret your letter of to-day. I think my best course is, avoiding all retrospective discussion, to tender you a frank explanation, which I am sure you will construe in good part.

I understand you to reprove me

1. For having framed a minute of Treasury hostile to the Law Courts Money Bill.
2. For having presented it to Parliament without your knowledge and assent.

As respects the first point, the Minute is in my view a paper correcting in detail the defective financial calculations of the Commissioners, and giving the view of the responsible department in regard to them.

It also suggests on prudential grounds a large margin in the estimate of charge : and brings out as the *possible* or *maximum* cost of the plan to the public a sum of something over a million.

It appears to me that it was my absolute duty to take care that in passing the Bill the House of Commons was made aware of our view of this maximum charge. Most unfortunately, as I think, this great and important measure was carried into Committee without previous discussion in the House of its principles and provisions. On finding this to be the case, I asked Cowper [1] to lay before the Committee a paper which would have given the necessary intimation to the House of what it was about. Before this had been fully discussed between us, the Committee reported, and a Treasury Minute laid before the House then appeared to be the most convenient vehicle for the discharge of a duty, the omission of which would I think have drawn on us, now or hereafter, severe and merited reproach.

But I do not stand upon the fact that this was *my* view of our duty. And here I must say I think you must have written in momentary forgetfulness of most important facts, which in truth determine the whole case, for I at once admit that it would have been most improper to you, though I do not think the minute hostile to the plan, in me gratuitously to take into my own hands the settlement of the question whether the maximum charge was to be made known.

---

[1] Hon. William Cowper, M.P., First Commissioner of Works.

MP

That question was in effect settled months ago *by you and by the Cabinet* at my suggestion. I drew a paper submitted it, obtained your approval, that of our Colleagues, and that of the then Attorney General, and supplied him with a copy of it and all this was for the purpose that the substance and facts of it might be embodied in the statement, with which the Attorney General was to introduce the Bill or explain it to the House of Commons. It set forth as the outside charge this very figure of a million.

I say then that the Cabinet unanimously decided on making known to Parliament our views of the possible maximum charge. That I might exactly adhere to your and their decision, I wished to do this by the very same paper you had expressly approved. Cowper however thought that this contained matter unfit (as I understood him) for the purpose, hence the substitution of a minute omitting such matter, and containing explanations in detail, but in sum having precisely the same effect, namely to present the maximum charge, and the mode in which it was to arise.

I think I have given, in outline, a complete answer both to the reproof for hostility, and to that for having acted without your assent.

I admit however that we were obliged, as to the form, to proceed with inconvenient haste. The sole motive as far as I was concerned, was to enable Cowper to proceed without loss of time, as he seemed anxious on the subject ; though individually I am very doubtful how far the success of the plan was or is likely to be promoted by any endeavour to pass the Bill without, or with only partial, discussion.

You say truly you took an interest in the plan : and I reply that, seeing this to be the case, I thought it my duty to waive many scruples and difficulties of my own, and to do all I could for putting the matter in train for favourable discussion and for settlement.

I must add that, hurried as I was, I did not omit to communicate with Cowper at every point, and did not

(I believe) adopt a single step without his knowledge ; and I may further add, that, from your close communications with him on matters relating to his department and his knowledge of your wishes, I have commonly assumed that in communicating with him I was in effect doing it with you. [1]

After this explanation I proceed to give you the assurance, which I hope is needless, that I have had no intention either of hostility to this great and interesting though necessarily complicated scheme, or of proceeding otherwise than under the full cover of your authority.

At the same time, meaning to speak without reserve, and not being *certain* that your letter has been written in momentary forgetfulness, and under the pressure of affairs, of the facts I have related, I cannot omit to say that its language appears to me to be of equivocal construction, and suggests the idea that you may have meant by its tone to signify that you thought the time was come when the official connection between us ought to cease. If such is your intention I beg by this letter to leave the matter entirely at your choice, and I shall feel that at the close of the session, in the present state of our finance and our affairs, it can be done without any public inconvenience— If you had no intention of this kind, please to consider the last sentence as never have been written. I shall expect to hear from you before any Cabinet is held.

P.S. I have referred to the Minute I laid before the Cabinet : it was approved finally on May 29. It mentions as the probable charge £1,055,000. It was to be communicated to the Chancery Monies Commissioners : and this continues with my clear recollection and above all with the nature of the facts to confirm me in stating that it was proposed and adopted as embodying information that was to be made known to Parliament along with the plan.

[1] W. Cowper was Lord Palmerston's step-son.

138   *Gladstone to Palmerston*

Private.   11 C[arlton] H[ouse] T[errace]
                                                    July 20. 61.

I have received to-day at half past four your intimation
that you propose to take another million of terminable
Annuities by an Act to be now introduced for the purpose
of the Fortifications Act of last year, and likewise to apply
the principles of loan by Terminable Annuities to the
building of iron ships : as also that you propose to give
notice to-night that you will move a resolution accordingly
on Monday.

In the midst of a day of close and incessant pressure I
should thus, while still holding the office of Chancellor of
the Exchequer, be deprived of all power of examining and
considering proposals which I deem to be in some points
open not only to grave, but as at present advised I must
add to insurmountable objection.

I may further add I observe that the Duke of Somerset's
letter is dated on the 15th. And that the principle of borrowing for the construction of iron ships has not to my
knowledge been adopted or considered by the Cabinet.

I hope I may without being unreasonable ask for a postponement of your intention to give notice until Monday
and for copies of what you may consider the material
information in the case.

139   *Palmerston to Gladstone*

                                             94 Piccadilly
                                             20 July 1861

I have only Time for two Lines in answer to your Letter
just received.

I do not admit that the Cabinet determined that the
Paper which you read to us in May should be converted
into a Treasury Minute and be laid before Parliament, nor

do I think that any Communications which may have passed between yourself and Cowper could be considered as implying my assent to that Proceeding. But I can with great Truth assure you that although I regret what I think a precipitate step with Regard to the Treasury Minute, I should consider the Termination of our official Connection, as a real misfortune to myself, to the Government and to the public Service.

140   *Gladstone to Palmerston*

11 C[arlton] H[ouse] T[errace]
Jul. 20. 61.

What I conceived you and the Government to have decided was the communicating of the vital fact to Parliament. The form of the Treasury Minute was adopted by me on Cowper's observation that the Cabinet minute was inconvenient. It was done in haste occasioned solely by a desire to forward your wishes by not delaying the Bill.— I am sorry if it was done ill.

After the kind expressions which close your note, I shall come to the Cabinet. I forward to you a Memorandum which I have just done in haste on the two Loan questions.

Time forbids, but I think I can, without raising any controversial matter, explain to you the preparation of the Budget—*Now* however there is not a moment.

141   *Palmerston to Gladstone*

Brocket 21 July 1861

With Reference to the Conversation which passed at the Cabinet yesterday,—I cannot refrain from saying that I am uneasy about the relative Positions of England and France with Regard to Naval Strength.

Two Things must I think be admitted by all. First that it would be dangerous to England that France should for any Period of Time have a superiority at Sea either in the amount or in the Quality of her Naval Force, Secondly that Ships cased with Iron must in an Engagement have an advantage over ships not so protected against shot and Shell. I have no doubt that Guns are making and will be made that will throw elongated shot so heavy and striking their object with such momentum that no Thickness of Iron Casing which a Sea-going Ship can carry will resist the Blow, but such Blows would be much more damaging to a wooden ship unprotected with Iron Casing ; and such Cannon must be so heavy that they could not be used as Broadside Guns between Decks, and could only be put one or Two at the utmost, as Pivot Guns on the upper deck where they would be exposed to an Enemy's Fire : such Guns would indeed or rather will be of great value in land Batteries where additional weight has no other Inconvenience than that of requiring some few additional Hands to work the Gun. The great advantage of Iron cased Ships over Ships not so cased is that wooden Sides are easily penetrated by Shells which explode within the Ship, whereas the Iron Plates resist such Shells.

Well then starting from my two Premises what are the Facts from which a Conclusion is to be drawn ? The French have now launched and afloat in water six Iron plated Ships one of them the Gloire has made several voyages and is therefore in Sea-going Condition. One of the others is I believe equally complete. The remaining four will probably be in Sea-Going Condition by next Spring, and two of them the Magenta and Solferino are Two-Deckers carrying a very heavy Battery—In addition to this Force the French have in Sea-going Condition, eleven Floating Batteries, as they are called, but which are Sea-going Ships of smaller size than Frigates and with less strength of Steam Power, but cased with Iron, and perfectly fit for operations in the Channel. They will thus have next Summer 1862 17 Iron Cased ships of War of various Sizes, of which two will be Two-Deckers ; this will be their Condition in Summer 1862. We may hope by that Time, though I much doubt it, to have in Sea-going Condition Six out of the seven Iron Cased Ships now building ; the seventh, the Achilles will scarcely be finished so soon, and we have besides nine Iron Cased Gun vessels built for the Crimean War, not very good or serviceable and certainly not as good as the best of the eleven of the same Kind which the French have. Thus in the Summer of 1862 we shall have $6+9=15$, or possibly $7+9=16$ against the 17 of the French. But there lies concealed under this apparent approximation to Equality, what I consider a Serious Inequality on our Part.

The French Ships with one Exception, the Couronne, are built of wood like ordinary Ships of War and are coated, most of them the whole of their length, some not quite to the end of their Bows or quite to their Stern with Iron. The Couronne is built like ours with an Inside Shell of ¾ of an Inch of Iron like a Packet or a Merchant Ship, and outside of that first a wooden skin of about 2 Feet, and then an Iron Covering of 4½ Inches. The Consequence is that the Part which is Iron Cased will resist ordinary Shot, and the Part which is not Cased will be pierced by ordinary Shot just as an ordinary Ship of war would be ; a Hole being made in the wood which is easily stopped up by a wooden Plug driven into it, and if a Shell pierces the wooden End and bursts within, there are strong Partitions closing in the Iron Cased Parts, within which the Crew will have retired to work the guns within the protected Part and not much Damage will have been done.

But our Iron Cased Ships built on the Model laid down by Pakington's [1] Admiralty are in my opinion sadly wrong in Principle. They consist like the Couronne of an internal Skin of ¾ of an Inch of Iron ; but this Skin is not protected

[1] Sir J. Pakington, M.P., First Lord of the Admiralty in Lord Derby's Government.

all the way from Stem to Stern—The Middle Part has like the Couronne, or I believe I ought rather to say that the Couronne has like them, over the Iron Skin a coating of Teak wood 18 Inches or 2 Feet Thick, and outside of that an Iron Casing 4½ Inches thick. But this Protection does not extend the whole way from Stem to Stern as it does in the Gloire, and I believe in most of the other French Ships ; and on a considerable Part of the Side of our Iron Ships towards the Bow and towards the Stern consists of Nothing but the thin Iron Skin of ¾ of an Inch of Iron. My Belief is that if the Gloire or one like her were to lie alongside of one of ours of Equal Force, the Gloire would before many Broadsides had been exchanged, have smashed to Pieces those Parts of our Ship Warrior Black Prince or other, which consists only of this ¾ of an Inch of Iron. It is true that the protected Part is shut in at each End by a strong Partition supposed to be shot proof, and it is alleged that as the Crew would in action be all withdrawn within the Protected Part no essential Damage would be done by the smashing of the Fore and after Part of the Ship. And it is said that all that Part of the Fore and after Portions thus unprotected, which are under the water Line, and which might be struck by Shot, are divided into Compartments by Water-Proof Partitions so that only one Compartment at a Time could be filled by water. But this seems to me a very unsatisfactory arrangement ; if the Fore and after Part unprotected by Casing were Shattered away the Ship would become a Mere Box floating on the Water, and if several of the water tight Compartments were pierced by Shot, and filled with water, the Ship would by the additional weight of the water sink deeper and become what is called Waterlogged and would be comparatively unmanageable. The Reason why this manner of Construction was adopted was, that our Admiralty People thought that if the armour extended the whole Length of the ship, the Bow would plough too deeply into the water, and the

Ship would be too heavy and would not carry her Guns high enough out of the water, to admit of her Port Holes being left open when the Sea was rough. I have repeatedly and strongly remonstrated with the Duke of Somerset against this Paste Board Construction of our so called Iron Ships of War ; and the Iron Cased Ships henceforward to be built will be so shaped in their Hulls as to have Buoyancy enough to bear being Iron Plated along their whole Length from Stem to Stern—

I have entered into this long detail to shew that our nominal approximation to Equality with the French towards the End of the Summer of 1862 will have concealed under it a real inferiority of Quality in our Iron cased Ships —and this seems to me to render it the more Important that we should lose no Time in adding to our Numbers and improving the Quality of the Ships so to be added.

Now the first operation which the Duke of Somerset proposes to set to work upon, is to complete Five or Six wooden ships of which the Frames and Timbers are partly ready in our Dockyards, and to finish them in such a Form as to give them Buoyancy enough to carry their Iron Coating from Stem to Stern, and to keep their Port Holes high enough out of the water to admit of their Guns being fired in rough weather as well as in smooth. These six ships will therefore be an important addition to the Quality as well as to the amount of our Iron Plated Force—When I inquired some Time ago how long it would take to complete these ships and to put them into Sea-going Condition, I was told it would require eighteen Months from the Time when they might be begun ; perhaps by great Exertion that Time might be shortened, perhaps by Departmental Delays not unusual in all Services, it might be lengthened —assuming eighteen Months to be required from the present Time these six Ships would not be fit for Sea till the Beginning of 1863.—Supposing these six wooden Ships cased with Iron to be fit for Sea in the Spring 1863, we should then have an apparent Superiority over the French, because we should have $7 + 9 + 6 = 22$ against $6 + 11 = 17$—But we must bear in Mind that the French have two or three months ago (I think the orders were given in December & January last and operations were begun in May) laid down and begun building ten more Iron Cased Ships, all of them intended to be of great Force. Ships of this Kind require about two years for Completion, but no Doubt by great Exertions they might be finished in 18 months and the French might turn the whole Strength of their Dockyard work upon these ships and there are many Parts of the work upon which any tolerable workman might be employed, so that the French Government would have no Difficulty in adding from the general Labour Market any Number of Hands that might be wanted for quickly finishing these ten Ships. But supposing two years to be required these ten new Dramatis Personae would make their appearance on the Stage in May 1863, and thus our just mentioned Proportions of $7 + 9 + 6 = 22$ English against $6 + 11 = 17$ French would be altered, and the French would come into the Field in 1863 with $6 + 11 + 10 = 27$, to our 22 : while moreover our 22 would consist of Iron Frigates and Floating Batteries or Gun vessels, of which some would be inferior in Quality to those of the French. This inferiority in Number and Quality would certainly exist from Midsummer 1863. Now this it is, which seems to render it important and urgent to lose no Time in beginning to construct six additional Iron ships which the Duke of Somerset and his Naval associates recommend us to sanction.

Experiments have got to be made as to the Sea-going Qualities of the Warrior, and as to the relative Powers of Sides intirely Iron but of considerable Thickness, or of Sides partly wood and partly Iron, to resist heavy Shot. These Experiments will scarcely lead to any satisfactory conclusion before next autumn. But the Questions to be determined by these Experiments relate only to the manner in which the Coating of the Ships Sides should be made. There is no Doubt as to the Manner in which the Keel, the Stern Posts, the Stem, and the Ribs of the Ship should be made, and these Things being large and Time being required as well as Care & Skill to forge them it would be desirable that no Time should needlessly be lost in ordering them. If these six Iron Ships could be begun in this autumn of 1860, they might be finished by the autumn of 1863, and there would then be but a short Interval between the Time when France would have a Superiority of Five Iron Cased Ships over us, and the Time when we should in numbers, at least, be above the French by one Ship—If they were to be much longer delayed, no probable Exertions on our Part would enable us to complete them in 1863.

Now it cannot be denied that Peace and Good understanding between England and France are a great Security for the Peace of Europe as well as for the welfare of England & France and that Peace and Good understanding between England & France are most likely to be permanent when France has no Naval Superiority over England—This needs no answer, it is only a written Conversation and a Statement of my views upon what seems to me a very important Matter

142   *Gladstone to Palmerston*

11 Carlton H[ouse] Terrace
Aug. 10. 61.

At the time of the last vacancy on the Episcopal Bench, I ventured, in compliance with a very kind suggestion of your own, to mention to you the very remarkable qualifications of Mr. Claughton, the Vicar of Kidderminster, for a seat on that Bench. You gave me an answer of which I felt the force : that, under the circumstances, it must be a

Cambridge turn. I therefore would now recall the subject to your memory. Nor does it require much detail to state these qualifications. He is a scholar as well as a divine, a person of refined mind as well as of devoted piety, an excellent preacher and a most effective and experienced parish priest, lastly a man of so much discretion and moderation that he is admirably qualified to acquire that rather rare advantage, *weight* in a diocese with all classes and parties, and to prosecute at once the work of active religion and the work of peace.

You would I have no doubt obtain a confirmation of this report from the Bp. of Worcester, from Lord Hatherton, or from any one who knows the diocese and the man. I do not mention Ld. Dudley as being his brother in law.

For myself I can truly assure you that I should not have obtruded upon you any case of *ordinary* merit and qualification.

143   *Gladstone to Palmerston*

Hawarden

Aug. 15. 61

Although I apprehend it is our intention to prosecute with all due dispatch the preparatory measures requisite for the erection of a National Gallery (whether by extension or *de novo*) yet I am disposed to give way to the recommendation of the Lords Committee that the Turner Pictures should at once be placed in Trafalgar Square ; for I think that if we do not act thus, we shall have a new source of broil and shall be less able to carry on with the requisite care our inquiries respecting the plans and cost which though they should not be remiss should not on the other hand be precipitate. What do you say ?

144 *Palmerston to Gladstone*

Walmer Castle
27 August 1861

The Bishopric of Gloucester and Bristol will become vacant by the Removal of Dr. Baring to Durham, and I mean to propose the See of Gloucester to Doctor Thompson, Head of Queen's College Oxford who is I think one of the Persons whom on a former occasion you mentioned to me as an Oxonian worthy of Promotion—

It might perhaps be agreeable to you to make to Doctor Thompson the Communication of the authority which I have received from the Queen to offer him the See of Gloucester, and if so, I would ask you to write to him to that Effect.

145 *Gladstone to Palmerston*

Penmaenmawr
Aug. 29. 1861.

I am very glad to receive under your hand a confirmation of the accounts in the newspapers about the new Bishop. For although I am not intimate with Dr. Thompson I know quite enough of him to have formed the opinion that the appointment is one which will do you credit, and just credit in every quarter. I believe him to be an able, temperate, well instructed, and earnest man : he is certainly a striking preacher.

It is extremely kind of you to make me the channel of communicating with him. Had I been at your side I should perhaps, none the less thankfully, have tried to induce you to write to him yourself : but you are two days off, and time is of value in these matters, so I shall at once convey to him in your name the offer which you have in so considerate a manner authorised to be made.

I hope you are enjoying the sea breezes at Walmer : perhaps amusing yourself with the inquiry how the old Britons should have prevented Caesar from landing there or hard by as I believe he did.

146   *Palmerston to Gladstone*

Walmer Castle
2 Sept 1861

I return you the inclosed Letter. There is much to be said in Favor of dividing many of our existing Dioceses, but the Question is a large one and cannot be dealt with Piece Meal ; and I am not prepared to take it up.

There would be no Difficulty in finding any additional Number of Bishops, but I do not know where we should find additional Salaries suitable to the Rank Position and Duties of a Bishop.

147   *Palmerston to Gladstone*

Broadlands
7 Oct 1861

I ought long ago to have returned to you the accompanying Papers, but they have accidentally gone astray till now.

The Queen's desire to do a kind Thing by Mrs. Byng was very natural, and the arrangement which Her Majesty proposes is such that it appears hypercritical to make any objection to it.

But small as the Matter is in itself it belongs to a larger Category, and to Questions which it is very desirable not to give the House of Commons additional opportunities of meddling with.

The Estimates and Votes for Parks and Palaces are invariably the opportunity for a Field Day for Men of small Capacity of limited Knowledge and of vulgar Minds ;

but such men there are in the World and unluckily but unavoidably they find their way into the House of Commons, and what they say often makes more Effect out of the House than it deserves.

One annual Topic of Declamation is the lodging of private Persons in Palaces and Buildings maintained at the public Expence, and ill natured Remarks are often made upon that subject. Members say that nobody can object to any proper Expence necessary for the Comfort and Dignity of the Royal Family, but that they do not see why the Public are to pay for keeping up Buildings which are occupied not by any Members of the Royal Family, but by private Persons who are put into them by Grace and Favor and who make these Buildings in some sort Alms Houses.

We are always able to make fair Head against those attacks when confined to Hampton Court, but it is very desirable and in the true Interest of the Royal Family that the Range of such Criticisms should not be extended, and as it is important to keep House of Commons Cavil as much as possible out of Windsor Park, I should strongly recommend that the proposed arrangement by which a Lodge in that Park should be applied in the same Manner in which the apartments at Hampton Court are applied should not be carried into effect. A Discussion about a Matter so apparently small but still new in Principle as applied to Windsor Park would let in the narrow End of the Wedge, and might probably lead to other Discussions about that Park unreasonable and groundless no doubt but which would be disagreeable to the Queen & the Prince Consort.

148   *Palmerston to Gladstone*

Bᵈˢ. 7 Oct 1861

I have written my other Note upon the Principle of objecting intirely to extending the Alms House System to Windsor Park but if you think that Fredᶜ. Peel's Plan would do, I would defend it. I believe however the best Course would be to object to the Principle.

149   *Palmerston to Gladstone*

Broadlands
13 Oct 1861

I return you the inclosed Letter which you may send to Phipps.[1] There will be no Harm in its being shewn that the Chancellor of the Exchequer is not the *most* hard hearted of Men.

150   *Palmerston to Gladstone*

Broadlands 18 Oct 1861

With Reference to our Conversation of yesterday about the Treasury, I should like to have a Copy of the Treasury Establishment as it now stands stating the Classes, the number in each Class, and the Scale of Salary for each Class, and including also the Clerks on temporary Service ; and then a Statement of the Alterations proposed, with the Reasons for which those alterations are recommended. Any Change for the worse would of course create Dissatisfaction and give Rise to Remonstrance, and it is better to consider such Things well before hand, than to have to defend afterwards arrangements hastily made.

151   *Palmerston to Gladstone*

94 Piccadilly
16 Novr. 1861

The People who are employed to fix assessments of Income Tax upon Land have been amusing themselves by

---

[1] Sir Charles Phipps, Private Secretary to the Prince Consort.

making exorbitant Demands, trusting to the neglect or Ignorance of Land-owners who might fail to appeal in Time. I happen to know Cases of this Kind in Hampshire, in Derbyshire and Nottinghamshire, in which unjust Charges founded upon nothing but Capricious assertion have been abandoned the moment they were complained of, the Persons who made them having no Ground on which the Charges could be maintained. I am afraid we shall hear of this System when Parliament meets, if it has been general. The Income Tax falls more heavily and unerringly on Land, than upon Mercantile Manufacturing and Trading Income, and it therefore ought not to be exacted beyond the legal amount.

152   *Gladstone to Palmerston*

Chatsworth
Nov. 17. 61.

What you say of the gripe of the Income Tax on the land is most true, & it is a peculiarly hard case if the assessments upon it are vexatious : but you know we have *no* authority over the officers who make the assessments, nor any authority to demand more tax than the Local Commissioners impose. And there is this difficulty that, while we have no authorised power over them, any vague or general complaint proceeding from the Executive might do much mischief in begetting laxity. But if you can find that in any case a Government Officer is complained of (their function is to object before the Commissioners if the Assessors are neglectful) then we can interfere with effect & without danger to remove the grievance.

The accession of Fould to office seems under the circumstances to be a great event and beneficial to us and to all Europe as well as to France.

Np

153   *Palmerston to Gladstone*

94 P[iccadill]y. 29 Novr. 1861

I have requested the Law officers to be in attendance in Downing Street today at half past Two, in Case we should want any further Explanations from them. Perhaps it would be well if you would ask Phillimore [1] to come.

154   *Gladstone to Palmerston*

(*Fragment, endorsed 1861*)

. . . I found also that when the Estimates had been completed, I believe entirely on *their* basis, there was a probable deficiency of four or five millions, for a year of which nearly one-third had passed. And the expenditure was I think nearly seventy millions, or some fourteen millions more than in 1853. This was not the act only of the Government. The Opposition hallooed them on ; and the country seized with a peculiar panic was in a humour even more lavish than the Opposition.

My view was, and I stated it, that we ought to provide for this expenditure in a due proportion between direct and indirect taxes. I showed that this proportion had not been observed : that we had continued to lay large amounts of war tax on tea and sugar, and had returned to the scale of 1853 for Income. I proposed to provide the necessary sums chiefly by an increase of Income Tax. But neither then (in July 1859) nor for nearly two and a half years before, had I ever (to my knowledge) presumed to speak of any one as bound to abolish the Income Tax or to remit the additional duties on Tea and Sugar.

I fully expect from *you* the admission that as to these measures I could not in the altered circumstances be bound absolutely to the remissions. But you say I was bound to give them a preference over all other remissions.

[1] Robert Phillimore, Q.C., afterwards Queen's Advocate.

No where I believe can one word to this effect be extracted from any speech of mine. I found in 1860 that all the reforming legislation, which had achieved such vast results, had been suspended for seven years. We were then raising by duties doomed in 1853 from twelve to thirteen millions. It would in my opinion have been no less than monstrous on my part to recognise the preferences you claim for these particular duties. All of them indeed would have been reliefs, even the Income Tax which is I think proved to be the last relief of any. But, though reliefs, they were hardly reforms : and experience had shown us that reforms were in fact double and treble reliefs.

I may be wrong, but it is my opinion, and I found it on experience that, the prospects of the removal of the three collectively (Income, Tea extra, and Sugar extra,) being in any case very remote, it is less remote with than without the reforming measures of the last and (I hope I may add) of the present year.

Had the expenditure of 1853 been resumed, there would notwithstanding the Russian War have been in my opinion room for all these three things 1. abolition of Income Tax by or near 1860, 2. remission of increases on Tea and Sugar within the same time, 3. the prosecution of the commercial reforms.

It may be said that having set my face against an excess of Expenditure, I ought to have considered that a holy war, and not to have receded. Although however I place public economy somewhat higher, as a matter of duty, than many might do, I do not think it would have been right, I do think it would have been foolish and presumptuous in me to have gone beyond these two things, first making an effort to the utmost of my power, at the critical moment (as I took it to be) and secondly on being defeated to watch for opportunities therafter. Since it should be remembered I do not recommend or desire sweeping and sudden reductions.

As you have gone so far and so kindly into the question, I hope you will tell me what you think of this narrative as an argument, presuming it to be true as fact.

The chief errors that I see myself to have committed are these.

In 1853 when I took the unusual course of estimating our Income roughly for seven years, and assuming that our expenditure would either continue as it was, or only move onwards gradually and gently, I ought no doubt to have pointed out explicitly that a great disturbance and increase of our expenditure would baffle my reckonings.

Again in 1857 the temper of the public mind had undergone a change which I failed to discern : and I attacked the Government and the Chancellor of the Exchequer of that day for doing what the country desired though I did not.

I name these as specific errors, over and above the general one of excess of heat.

The Budget of last year I cannot admit to have been an error. People say it should have been smaller. My belief is that if it had been a smaller boat it would not have lived in such a sea. I speak of the period of the Session before the China War became certain. When it did so, we were in a great strait about the Paper Duty. We felt the obligation incurred by the vote on the second reading, and we construed it according to the established usage. We took the more arduous but I think the more honourable course for a Government to pursue. Had we abandoned the Bill, I know not how we could have looked in the face those who had acted and invested on the faith of our unbroken practice.

I admit that political motives greatly concurred to recommend the Budget of last year. It was a Budget of peace, and peace wanted it. The Budget of this year followed from the Budget of last, given the other circumstances. At the same time I can understand how the claim of Tea could be set up with a motive : but not well, after the occurrences of last year, how it could be supported, though I know it was supported, without what I call by that name.

This is a long egotistical story. But when you consider that it contains my whole story (except *pièces justificatives*) in answer to so many speeches in both Houses and elsewhere, for never to this hour have I opened my lips in personal defence, you will understand why I might be garrulous.

There is one most kind, and overkind, sentence in your letter, beside the immediate subject, and about which I had rather speak to you.

P.S. Notwithstanding the mild doctrine I have held about expenditure I admit it may be said I ought not to have joined a Government which had such extended views in that direction, even though they were the views of the nation. Much may be said on this. I may however remark that when the Government was formed, I did not fully conceive the extent to which in this matter we should proceed.

155   *Palmerston to Gladstone*

94 P[iccadill]y. 9 Jany. 1862.

I think that these mourning Expences[1] ought to be defrayed by the Civil List and not to be charged against any vote of Parliament. It is very important that we should be able to Shew that the Queen has not without real necessity come to Parliament for special aid and certainly not for small objects

You will have seen that the Trent affair is satisfactorily settled and that the Prisoners[2] are given up. But *uno avulso non deficit alter*. Not indeed *aureus* ; but I hope it will not be *ferreus*.

[1] For the death of the Prince Consort.
[2] Messrs. Slidell and Mason, Confederate envoys, arrested by U.S.S. *San Jacinto* in the British mail-steamer *Trent* and subsequently released.

Upon every Principle on which the Federals give up the Men taken from the Trent, they ought also to give up the Men taken from the Eugenia Smith, and I hope and trust they will do so.

As to your Speech you need no Suggestions from any Body as to what to say or what to avoid.

156   *Palmerston to Gladstone*

Broadlands 21 Jany 1862

. . . I want to draw your attention to the Circumstances connected with the appointment of Knights of the Garter

The Fees payable by a Knight upon his appointment vary from upwards of six to eight or nine Hundred Pounds, or indeed I believe to a Thousand, according to the Rank of the Person appointed. Now it seems to me to be a Relic of an age gone by, and to be in itself a great Injustice and abuse, than an Honor conferred by the Crown, often as a Reward for public Service should be the Cause of inflicting a heavy Money Fine upon the Person so rewarded, and to whom the Payment of so large a Sum, is in many Cases very inconvenient. The Question arises now immediately with Reference to appointments which I am submitting for the approval of the Queen.

There are five vacancies and I propose to fill up Four of them by Men whose Services in various ways must be acknowledged by all, but to all of whom the Payment of a heavy Fine would be a Burthen extremely inconvenient.
Lord Canning is certainly not a rich man, and I under-
stand has been able to save but little in India.
The Duke of Somerset is far from wealthy—
Lord Russell we know has very Limited Means.
Lord Shaftesbury has a very Slender Income.
Lord Fitzwilliam the Fifth is of Course well able to pay
any Price which he may think the Garter worth.

Don't mention any of these names at present for some of the Persons do not know that I am asking the Queen's leave to offer them the Garter.

If I mistake not an arrangement was made a few years ago, by which this abuse, as I think it, was removed from the Order of the Bath, and a fixed Salary was given to the officers of the Order instead of the Fees on appointment.

Now what I wish you to consider is, whether a similar arrangement might not be made about the Order of the Garter. It is to be borne in Mind that there is I believe no Power on the Part of the officers of the Order to compel the Payment of these Fees, except by declining to put up the Banner of the non-paying Knight over his Stall in St. George's Chapel at Windsor.

The non-paying Knight cannot be prevented from wearing the Insignia of the Order, and is equally summoned to Chapters for electing to Vacancies ; but of Course no Man likes to refuse making a Payment which by Prescription is due to those who claim it. I should be very glad if any arrangement could be made on this matter.

157   *Gladstone to Palmerston*

11 Carlton H. Terrace.
Feb. 1. 1862.

I have been hard at work with Pressly and Anderson on the Revenue and Expenditure of 1862-3, and I think it may interest you to know the result without loss of time. I mean the result as we think it would be, on the assumption of Naval and Military Charge as proposed by the respective Departments.

I give you merely the totals to save time.

Estimate of Expenditure	£70,293,000
Revenue	£69,390,000
Deficit	903 m.

You will see that the choice lies between a reduction of a million on these Estimates (in round numbers from 28 million to 27) and additional taxation. I stated yesterday though very briefly why the latter alternative is in my view inadmissible.

I should add that we all consider the Estimate I have given as a sanguine one : though of course it cannot pretend to certainty or precision.

158   *Palmerston to Gladstone*

94 P[iccadill]ʸ. 17 March 1862

I hope you will be ready tonight with your Sledge Hammer in Case of Need.

159   *Gladstone to Palmerston*

Early.   11 Downing Street
                                        March 24. 62.

This Memorandum is intended to express the views which appeared to be taken by the Cabinet on Saturday with respect to future provision for the Royal Family.

If it meets your approval you will perhaps circulate it.

It appears to me to deserve consideration whether, if and when approved by the Cabinet, it should be sent to the Queen as in draft, before being finally transmitted for Her custody.

I find that Marlborough House is at the charge of the Prince of Wales.

160   *Minutes on Telegraphs with America*

1 April 1862.

Though it is very desirable to obtain telegraphic communication with N. America, I consider that Government

cannot prudently embark at the present time in this undertaking. Every month gives us additional knowledge, and
adds to the probability of ultimate success.

S.[1]

I should likewise be in favour of waiting
Ap. 1.   R.[2]

I concur with the Duke of Somerset & Ld. R. and I do
not think we should give any pledge as to the future, for
it is quite possible that, if the parties can cure themselves
for a while of the vicious habit they have contracted of
looking for Government money in order to overcome the
difficulties of novel enterprises, knowledge on the subject
may reach such a point as to bring capital forward freely for
the purpose without the great mischief of State intervention.

It will be borne in mind that the Telegraph to America
offers the prospect if successful of such immense returns,
that in almost every other case we might be pressed more
strongly for aid, on the ground that the inducement in the
event of success was less & therefore the need for help greater
Ap. 2. 62.   W. E. G.

161   *Gladstone to Palmerston*

11 April. 62.

. . . Not having heard anything of my draft about the
arrangements (prospective) for the Royal Family, I venture to remind you of it " now that you have some leisure "
as so many kind correspondents say when one is hoping
for a holiday.

162   *Palmerston to Gladstone*

Broadlands 17 Ap. 62.

I have received your Letter about the Cabinet on Saturday, but I am not the Culprit who summoned it, and I have

---

[1] Duke of Somerset, First Lord of the Admiralty.
[2] Earl Russell, Foreign Secretary.

written to Russell who I presume is the guilty Party to ask what it is about. I will suggest to him two or half past instead of three, but those who have to come to Town that Morning can hardly arrive sooner.

I send you two Letters from Phipps about Wolsey's Chapel. It seems from them that the Queen means the ornamenting of that chapel to be paid for out of the annual vote for Palaces, and that she expects a much larger Sum than fifteen Thousand, to be voted by Parliament for a Memorial to the Prince Consort. I wrote to her yesterday a letter which crossed the last Letter from Phipps which reached me this morning. I said to her that I doubted whether I rightly understood her views about the Wolsey Chapel. That if the ornamenting of that Chapel was to be the Parliamentary Tribute to the Memory of the Prince I could not doubt that Parliament would vote the Sum, from 15 to £20 000 required for the Purpose but that if She meant the work as simply a Part of the Decoration of Windsor Castle, it did not seem to me to be so sure that such a vote would be passed without objection. That moreover the estimate for this year for the Royal Palaces was voted some weeks ago, and there might be much objection to proposing now a supplementary vote for that Service, and that consequently I feared the matter must stand over till next year, if that was the Footing on which the Proposal was to stand

It appears now from Phipps's last Letter that this is the Queen's view.

(*Enclosures*)

Private.

Osborne,
April 14th, 1862.

MY DEAR LORD PALMERSTON,

The Queen has spoken once or twice, with some anxiety, on her not having received any further answer with regard to the plan for decorating Wolsey's Chapel at Windsor as a Memorial Chapel. This would she supposes come under the head of the Windsor Vote, for the Castle, and its appendages, as this Chapel is entirely distinct from St. George's, and is an integral part of the Palace in the charge of the Office of Works and Lord Chamberlain.

The Queen seems to be very anxious upon this subject, and I think would almost have been inclined to carry out the plan for the Chapel out of Her own means—but with her greatly increased expenses, and having taken upon Herself the cost of the Mausoleum, it would, I know, be impossible for her to do so.

The Queen has more than once mentioned this Subject, upon which I believe you spoke to her when you saw Her at Windsor, and since that She had, I think, written twice upon the Subject, but had received no answer, I thought that I might as well mention the Subject *confidentially* to you.

She always mentions this plan as entirely distinct from a public Memorial, and as a Work within the Castle, like the decoration of the Waterloo Gallery—only called for by this particular sad occasion.

Believe me,
faithfully Yours,
C. B. PHIPPS.

Osborne,
April 16, 1862.

Private.

MY DEAR LORD PALMERSTON,

Since I wrote to you upon the 14th, the Queen has, this day, received a letter from Lord Sydney,[1] from which it would appear that he supposes that the sum necessary for the restoration and decoration of Wolsey's Chapel, was to be obtained from Parliament as a Vote for the National Memorial to the Prince Consort.

The Queen thinks that he must be mistaken in this supposition, as, in the first place, the sum which it is estimated

---

[1] Lord Chamberlain.

would be required for this work, fifteen thousand pounds, would be, as a national memorial, as unworthy of this great Country, as of the object to which it was destined, and in the second place, a National Memorial could hardly consist of the execution of certain works within the Queen's Palace.

A further objection which the Queen would entertain very strongly to such a proposal, would be that in the execution of a Work, destined to be the National Memorial, for which the funds were voted by Parliament, the House of Commons would very probably, and not without reason, desire to exercise some superintendence and direction, and this the Queen could not assent to.

Her Majesty would, on no account, wish that the plans, with regard to this Chapel, should in any way be blended, or interfered, with the provision of a National Memorial, but would prefer that the works necessary to complete the design should be carried on gradually and slowly, extending over three or four years, and a small Vote, on account, being taken annually in the usual Estimate for works in Windsor Castle.

> Believe me,
> My dear Lord Palmerston,
> faithfully yours,
> C. B. PHIPPS.

163   *Gladstone to Palmerston*

> 11 D[owning] S[treet]
> Ap. 17, 62.

Sir C. Phipps has sent me copy of his letter to you—by the Queen's desire. I shall of course say nothing at present on the merits, in acknowledging its arrival.

It seems to me that the Queen has fallen into an excess, natural enough under the circumstances, but still of such a nature that the whole question will require your best care for its successful treatment.

You will judge far better than I can of the best mode of dealing with the Queen on this very tender subject. It appears to me however that there is one side of the question which suggests considerations that she would feel to be at once weighty and inoffensive. We are a people having deeply rooted traditions in the matter of monuments as well as in other matters : and it seems to have been our fixed practice to limit very greatly the intervention of the State in such affairs, and to leave them, in the main, & beyond narrow limits, for spontaneous movements. The latter are a true index of feeling, which it is the object of the memorial to express and record. The former would run great risk of becoming first mechanical and then false. If this be so, it would seem that in proposing to do twice as much as has been done before (The charge would be not £15000 but nearer £19000) we have made a sufficient step in advance, and to do more might seem to be doubtful alike in principle and in policy.

The true *national* monument to the Prince Consort will be the Subscription Monument : though that will be the *State* monument, which is erected by votes of Parliament.

The very fact of the virtual exclusion of the Peers from any share in the decision of such votes is a welcome if secondary argument against permitting them to become too prominent.

I leave town on Saturday and go to Manchester on Monday for public occasions. You will not I presume most probably have a Cabinet before Monday the 28th.

164   *Palmerston to Gladstone*

[Partly printed in *Ash*. II. 222–5 ; *Glad*. II. 48–9]

Private   94 Piccadilly 29 April 1862

I read with much Interest as I came up yesterday by the Railway your able and eloquent speeches at Manchester ;

but I wish to submit to you some observations upon the financial Part of the second speech. You seem in that speech to make it a Reproach to the Nation at large that it has forced, as you say it has, on the Parliament and the Government the high amount of Expenditure which we have at present to provide for. Now I do not quite agree with you as to the Fact, but admitting it to be as you state, it seems to me to be rather a Proof of the Superior Sagacity of the Nation, than a subject for Reproach.

The main Causes which have swelled our annual Expenditure have been, increased Demands for Military and Naval Purposes. The Civil Service estimates have been to a limited extent increased by the Transfer to them of Charges for the Collection of the Revenue formerly paid out of the Revenue in its way to the Exchequer, and there have been some Transfers from local Taxation to General Taxation, but these nominal additions add nothing to the real Burthen of the Nation. The main sources of increased Expenditure have been Army Navy and Education—as to Education the Increase has arisen from the working of a self-acting system. We may not have had the full value of our Money, but we have derived great advantage from the outlay.

Now as to the augmentation of our Military and Naval means of Defence I cannot give to the Nation as contradistinguished from Parliament and Government the exclusive merits of having demanded them. It appears to me that the merit, as I call it, or the Reproach as you seem to consider it, is equally to be shared by Nation Parliament and Government. Successive Governments have taken the Lead by proposing to Parliament such Estimates as acting upon their Responsibility they thought needful for the public service ; successive Parliaments have sanctioned those Estimates, and the Nation has ratified these acts by their approval. It is therefore a mistake to say that this Scale of Expenditure has been forced upon Parliament or upon the

Government, and it is a still greater Mistake to accuse the Nation as Cobden does of having rushed headlong into Extravagance under the Impulse of Panic. Panic there has been none, on the Part of any Body. There was for a long Time an apathetic Blindness on the Part of the Governed and the Governors as to the defensive Means of the Country compared with the offensive Means acquired and acquiring by other Powers. The Country at last awoke from its Lethargy, not indeed to rush into extravagant and uncalled for Exertions, but to make up gradually for former omissions ; and so far, no Doubt, to throw upon a shorter Period of Time Expences which earlier Foresight might have spread over a greater Length of Time. The Government the Parliament and the Nation acted in harmonious Concert ; and if any Proof were wanting that the nation has been inspired by a deliberate and sagacious appreciation of its Position with Respect to other Powers, that Proof has been afforded by the long continued and well sustained Sacrifices of Time and Money, which have been made by the 160,000 volunteers, and by those who have contributed to supply them with requisite Funds. If the Nation has, as you say, urged upon Parliament and the Government increased means of Defence for the Country the Nation has at least given the most conclusive Proof of the sincerity and Deepness of its Conviction that such increased Means of Defence were necessary, by the spontaneous Devotion of so large a Number of its youth to defensive organization— But have the Government, or rather have both Liberal and Conservative Governments have the Parliament and the Nation been wrong, and have Bright and Cobden and yourself been right ? I venture to think that the Government the Parliament and the Nation have taken the juster view of what the state of Things required.

We have on the other side of the Channel a People, who, say what they may, hate us as a nation from the Bottom of their Hearts, and would make any sacrifice to inflict a deep

Humiliation upon England. It is natural that this should be. They are eminently vain, and their Passion is Glory in Wars. They cannot forget or forgive Aboukir, Trafalgar, the Peninsula, Waterloo and St. Helena. Increased Commercial Intercourse may add to the Links of mutual Interest between us and them ; but commercial Interest is a Link that snaps under the Pressure of National Passions ; witness the bitter enmity of England lately freely vented, and now with difficulty suppressed by those Northern States of America with whom we have had a most extensive Commercial Intercourse.

Well, then, at the Head of this neighbouring nation who would like nothing so well as a retaliatory Blow upon England, we see an able, active, wary, counsel keeping, but ever planning sovereign ; and we see this Sovereign organizing an Army, which including his Reserve, is more than six Times greater in amount than the whole of our regular Force in our Two Islands, and at the same Time labouring hard to create a Navy equal to, if not superior to ours— Give him a Cause of Quarrel which any foreign Power may at any Time invent or create, if so minded ; give him the Command of the Channel which permanent or accidental Naval superiority might afford him, and then calculate if you can for it would pass my reckoning Power to do so, the disastrous Consequences to the British Nation which a Landing of an army of from 1 to 200,000 men would bring with it. Surely even a large yearly expenditure for army and navy is an Economical Insurance against such a Catastrophy.

This being my view of the Matter I cannot but regret that you should by speeches in and out of Parliament invite an agitation to force the Government of which you are a Member to retrace steps taken upon full Deliberation and in Fulfilment of Duties, for the faithful Performance of which it is responsible to the Crown and to the Nation. When fourteen or fifteen men are brought together to deliberate upon a Course of action it is scarcely possible that all should take exactly the same view of the matter discussed, but some Decision or other must be come to, and those who have yielded their own opinions even if they have not been convinced do not when the Decision of the Body is acted upon, proclaim to the world their Dissent from the Course pursued.

Pray forgive these Remarks and take them in the friendly spirit in which they are given.

165 *Gladstone to Palmerston*

11 Carlton H[ouse] Terrace
Ap. 30. 62.

I have just received and have only had a moment to glance at yr. letter. I do not for a moment doubt the kind spirit in wh. it is written ; and my present purpose is a simple one. It is plain to me that the subject is one on which I ought to have a free and full conversation with you *before* I again reply to Northcote and Disraeli in the H. of C.

This cannot be, I fear, *before* to-morrow evening.

And it had previously occurred to me that a ferocious financial battle in the evening after the work of peace in the morning, might be thought mistimed.

Do you think it well that the House should have a holiday to-morrow ? It seems to me it would be reasonable, and generally approved of : and it might not be free from awkwardness to postpone the finance now, if the House sits. This is the suggestion I had to make. But if the House meets, I think it is almost necessary to postpone the finance with a view to the conversation, notwithstanding any awkwardness or [*illegible*] to which it may give rise.

Pray give directions as you may think best.
Op

166   *Gladstone to Palmerston*

11 Carlton H[ouse] Terrace

May 2. 1862.

Before we meet, I think I cannot do better than tell you in the first place what, before I received your letter, I intended to say in reply to Northcote.

It was as follows in point of substance.

That the first duty of the Chancellor of the Exchequer is, among his colleagues, and in his department, to object to what he may conceive to be needless or mischievous expenditure.

That when he has concurred or acquiesced in any proposal of public expenditure to Parliament by the Administration, he is responsible for the proposal alike whether he may have been an approving or an objecting party ; and indeed that he is more responsible for it, than any of his Colleagues, except first the Prime Minister, and secondly the Minister of the particular Department to which it relates. That he has no right to use any words which, rightly and fairly interpreted, disclose the objection he may have urged before his Colleagues, or assume on his part a separate position from theirs, with respect to the amount of the Estimates which he may have presented.

But that in common with them, he is entitled and bound, in considering what the Estimates and public charges are to be, to take into his view among other matters the state of public feeling and opinion, and that as in legislation, so in expenditure, the condition of public feeling and opinion justify and require his being a party to proposals far from being in precise accordance with his own individual views. He justifies the Estimates but he justifies them with respect to all the circumstances of the case ; and among those circumstances a main one, in this country so largely endowed with the power of self-government, must ever be the view of the nation itself.

That if he conceives that public opinion requires in matters bearing upon his department, to be either stimulated or restrained, it is his right and duty, subject to the conditions above laid down to improve as far as he can by any arguments couched in moderate and becoming language, and sufficiently guarded against misapprehension, the state of opinion and feeling which may at the time prevail among the public.

Further, that his duty thus to raise the warning voice is much enhanced, if in the department of Finance, for which after all he is especially responsible, he sees in the actual state and course of things, a real public danger or a serious mischief.

These being the general principles applicable in my view to the case I admit that I may most unintentionally have erred in their application. To whatever extent I may have done so, I confess my fault and deplore it. But I have really been without the means of judging whether I am guilty or not guilty : for those who have repeatedly charged me in this matter, have never cited any *words* of mine on which to found the charge.

But I cannot pretend that apart from such casual error as has been just described, I acted without case, nor can I promise to change my course. What I have intended to do has been to fulfil what I think one of my most distinct and solemn duties. As the Minister of War (for example), perceiving dangerous deficiencies in the establishments of the country, and finding Parliament and the public indisposed to exercise an adequate energy in supplying them, is bound to use all judicious means of bringing about a healthier state of mind, so it is with me in regard to the public expenditure. If I see that finance is in an unhealthy state : if I find that from the close pressure of expenditure upon resources the Parliament is from time to time betrayed or in near danger of being betrayed, into votes which tend to compromise its own dignity, and to raise in the public mind expectations that will have to be disappointed : if the special knowledge, which my department gives me, convinces me that there is considerable suffering among the people, or portions of the people, from the taxes, some part of which might be avoided ; if lastly I find reason to conclude that our system of defence, and our state of preparation for great efforts in war, is becoming silently impaired, in a greater or even a less degree, in what I hold to be one of its capital and primary particulars, namely the state of our finances : in each and all of these cases it is the duty of the Finance Minister in particular to lift up the warning voice, to exhibit the facts upon the knowledge of which a right judgement must depend, and temperately to endeavour to lead the public mind to a healthier tone.

Now each and all of these cases, I affirm to exist. Not perhaps in an immediately alarming, but in a sensible degree. I conceive I should betray my duty, were I to wait until the danger had become palpable and pressing in the view of all men. I do not believe there is any department of State policy, in which it is at once more obligatory and more practicable, than in finance, to resist evil in its beginnings. These are the opinions in which I have grown up, and I am too old to change them. I have now stated at great length what I believe to be in great part if not truisms, yet truths which nothing but an exceptional state of things and the presumed opportunities of party warfare would have brought into question.

In all good humour, I prefer not being classed with Mr. Bright or even Mr. Cobden, first because I do not know their opinions with any precision, and secondly because as far as I do know or can guess them, they seem to contemplate fundamental changes in taxation which I disapprove in principle, and believe also to be unattainable in practice : and reductions of establishment and expenditure for which I am not prepared to be responsible. My opinion is that by the firm hand of an united Government our expenditure might be and ought to be gradually reduced by some millions. It has undergone upon the Estimates some reduction this year. I do not ask the Government to controul circumstances in themselves uncontroulable, or to resort to the work of reduction in that hurry, which I think has done so much mischief in the extension of our expenditure. I think it a mean and guilty course to hold out vague and indefinite promises of vast retrenchment but I think it will be a healthful day both for the country and for the party over which you so ably preside, when the word retrenchment of course with a due regard to altered circumstances, shall again take its place among their battle cries. I believe the day is coming, when the two parties in Parliament will perhaps run a race for the possession of that word, and I am not without fear that the liberal party shall be the hindmost. But I wish to avoid the race altogether. I wish calmly and steadily to discountenance that *spirit* of extravagance, which is at present abroad with the school master, and which perhaps shows itself less, but operates more, in the mode of going about the formation and maintenance of our establishments, than in mere theories as to their scale. I cannot effectually discountenance that spirit without exhibiting and denouncing it.

To pretend conformity of opinion with you in some of the points touched in your letter, would on my part be dishonest. I think (though I have carefully avoided saying it in public) that the English people have by their conduct with regard to expenditure during the last three four or more years proved their spirit which had been proved by a thousand years of previous history, but that they have shown on the whole in the same matter, less than their usual high degree of political intelligence and self-possession. I think that there has been some panic, and much precipitancy. With no authority at all, I am in one sense sorry, and in another glad, to hold opinions widely apart from those, which you I admit with great authority, declare with respect to the spirit and intentions of France.

My aim in this letter, whether I succeed in it or no, is to lay out my mind before you without the least reserve that whatever you judge, may be a judgement not taken in the dark. I gladly acknowledge your kindness, and that of the Cabinet, in many discussions and many decisions with respect to expenditure. If there is any part of this letter satisfactory to you in substance, but which you may think I have not sufficiently expressed in my public declarations, I am ready to supply the omission by stating it in terms at least as strong as those which I have here employed. If there is any part unsatisfactory to you in substance, you —will I dare say ask me to explain it : but the intention with which it is written is one that has at all times been firmly rooted in my mind, and that seems to me to touch the very foundations of the duty of my office as it has at all times been understood.

The Tax Bill, and the assault, are put off till Thursday, because of the question of education on Monday. Saturday is a day of peace and pictures : Sunday I hope to be out of town. At any other time, I am at your command.

167   *Palmerston to Gladstone*

94 Piccadilly 7 May 1862

I ought sooner to have acknowledged your Letter of the 2ᵈ but I have been very busy—I have no doubt you will make a very good Defence against the intended Attacks of Northcote & Disraeli.

What I expect is, that they will say that in your speeches in Parliament and at Manchester you have expressed Condemnation of the amount of Expenditure which the Government of which you are a Member have deliberately and upon their aggregate Responsibility proposed as necessary for the public Service of the Country in the present Circumstances of this Country and of the world ; and that you have to a certain Degree indirectly at least invited a Pressure from without, to force the Government to Reductions which they may not be of their own accord prepared to make. The Fact is, that although some small Charges for half Pay Surgeons and Lieutenant Colonels and the Like, have been forced upon the Government by Discussions in the House of Commons, yet the Army and Navy Establishments which are the great Sources of Expenditure, have been fixed by the executive Government upon its own sense of what is needed, and have been *accepted* by Parliament and the Country, as in their opinion judicious arrangements : but it cannot be said that the Scale of those Establishments has been forced on a Reluctant Government by a Panic Stricken Nation—The Case which you put of a War Minister trying to bring public opinion round to his views is not exactly in Point—Such a War Minister would be trying to induce the Nation to agree to Measures of Defence which the Government thought necessary and wished to adopt ; but a Chancellor of Exchequer would not be acting in a similar Way by urging the Nation to force the Government to alter and diminish arrangements which that Government deemed to be requisite.

That which of course you will skilfully avoid will be the appearance of proclaiming or divulging to the Public Differences of opinion which may have existed in Cabinet Discussions, but which have been merged in an aggregate acquiescence.

It is quite true that ample financial Means are necessary for National Defence but if a War should suddenly come upon us, as it might have done with France about Tahiti, or with America about the Trent the want of Ships and Troops and Guns and Muskets and Dockyard Defences would be ill made up for by the Fact that some Hundreds of Merchants & Manufacturers had made large Fortunes, and had great Stores of Three per Cents, or large Landed Estates. This would only be offering to the Butcher a well fatted Calf instead of a well armed Bull's Head. You disclaim political community of opinion with Bright and Cobden, and justly, but you cannot but be aware that owing to various accidental Circumstances many People at Home and abroad connect you unjustly with them, and this false Impression is certainly not advantageous.

I hope your cold is better.

168   *Gladstone to Palmerston*

11 C[arlton] H[ouse] Terrace
May 8. 62.

I have received your kind letter and will endeavour to act in the same spirit as that in which you write. My difficulties are great : from the distance of prospective reduction neither honour nor (almost) decency would allow me to recede : but I hope I shall say nothing to disparage the expenditure of to-day for to-day, as far as it depends upon the Government.

169   *Palmerston to Gladstone*

94 P[iccadill]y. 8 May 1862

It seems to me subject to your own view of the Case, that your Position is pretty nearly as follows—

As Chancellor of the Exchequer it must be your wish and Inclination to diminish as far as possible the Burthen of Taxation. This cannot be done without reducing Expenditure. You see with Regret the obstacle to reduced Taxation which the present Scale of Expenditure opposes. But that Scale of Expenditure has been deemed necessary in the present State of Things by the Government the

Parliament and the Nation and you feel bound to acquiesce in their Decision. You nevertheless would see with Pleasure at some future Time such an alteration in the Circumstances upon which present opinions and Decisions are founded, as would in the Judgement of Government Parliament and the Nation justify and allow such a Diminution of annual Expenditure as would permit you to carry into effect your Wishes for a diminished amount of Taxation.

170   *Gladstone to Palmerston*

11 Carlton H[ouse] Terrace
May 9. *1862.*

This afternoon Mr. Baxter requested an interview with me on the part of Mr. Forster[1] and Mr. Stansfield[2] with himself : without naming the subject.

When I met them, they stated to me that from a conviction of the necessity of placing a check upon our expenditure, they had recently had it in view to call the attention of Parliament to the subject, and to move a Resolution having reference to the future : that their desire was to proceed in the manner most friendly to the Government, keeping the main purpose in view : but they had had no communication, directly or otherwise, as I understood them, before or since yesterday, with the gentlemen opposite : that they spoke for themselves alone, but that in their belief their sentiments were largely shared by others on the Ministerial Benches. Finally, they offered to show me some draft, more or less matured, of a Resolution in the sense described.

I thanked them for the spirit of their communication ; and stated that they had better [not] show me any draft they might have in preparation, that I could not offer them any advice or suggestion, inasmuch as I must consider and be

[1] W. E. Forster, M.P.
[2] James Stansfeld, M.P.

governed by other relations from which they were free ; and that my duty would begin and end with making known to you as the Head of the Government what they had said.

Previously to this conversation, I had no knowledge on the subject beyond what was conveyed by yesterday's debate. Of the significance of that debate you are far better able to judge, than I am : but judging as well as I can for myself, I imagine it to be probable that any movement in the sense of economy, which may once be commenced on the Government side, will, if only out of self-respect, be prosecuted with more persistence than the one of about eighteen months ago : while distress in the country may lend it greater favour out of doors, and there is on the part of important persons opposite an evident intention to turn anything of the kind as far as may be to account.

It is easy to foresee that a Resolution of this kind might place me in an embarrassing position, much as I dislike propositions of an abstract character : but I will not anticipate what may never happen.

Quite apart, however, from such a Resolution, and from the *immediate* fortunes of the Government, I must say a few words upon our financial prospects. We started both the last financial years with better promise in figures than the present one : but both ended by defeating my calculations. We met the extraordinary exigencies of the time, so far as was necessary, by extraordinary resources : those extra-ordinary resources are at an end. Should the aggravation of the existing distress or inclement seasons produce, as either might produce, a deficiency next year, we have no more of these resources to draw upon, and we should be obliged to ask Parliament for means to supply the void by an addition to debt. I do not now speak of what is to be done with next years Estimates though that question will be most serious when the time for it arrives : but I do feel it to be more desirable that the great spending Departments in particular should exercise every practical economy, in the absence of exceptional demands, with respect to the conduct of their ordinary business for the current year. In former times a considerable saving upon the military and naval expenditure as compared with the Estimates could be reckoned upon with tolerable confidence : but of late they have come much nearer the margin if they have not even exceeded it. I am desirous to place the state of the case, according to the best judgment I can form, before you, in order that you may consider whether it would not be well to suggest the careful avoidance of unnecessary expenditure in the Admiralty and the War Department : in both of which there is of necessity a good deal of room, except under real pressure of events, for the exercise of discretion, both as to establishments and as to materials. It is from you alone that the suggestion can come with effect. You will remember that when the Estimates were adopted about the beginning of February they were put upon a footing which left only a nominal surplus : such a position entails of course considerable risk of deficiency : such a risk would be reduced almost to *nil* by the application of a somewhat tighter hand than usual in the great departments : and my special reason for calling this to your mind at the present moment is because a deficiency this year might entail various inconveniences which we have hitherto escaped, and because there are signs, as far as I see, in the House, of an increased anxiety upon these subjects, which in the opinion of some extends to the country.

P.S. I ought perhaps to have explained the great practical difference of the effect of a deficiency on a Government *before* and *after* its temporary resources are exhausted. In the latter case it might be compelled to go to Parliament for a vote to supply the void, which would place it in a *most* assailable position. This might come to be our case.

171   *Palmerston to Gladstone*

94 P[iccadill]ʸ. 10 May 1862

You will see by the inclosed that the Queen has Notions
of the Liberality of Parliament which I fear would be far
from realized if we were to attempt what She wishes us to
propose. Might we not say that when we erect a new
National Gallery which may probably be on the Burlington
House ground that Building might be called the Albert
Gallery and might have a Statue of the Prince placed in
it in some suitable Part of the arrangement.

172   *Gladstone to Palmerston*

11 C[arlton] H[ouse] T[errace]

13 May. 62.

Here is the Memo : respecting the provision for the
Royal Family which I have this morning received from
the Chancellor.

I have substantially, written in his amendments of the
phraseology, leaving however one on the last leaf for you
to deal with : as Grey also wished to have some further
consideration of the language of the last paragraph.

When you are satisfied with it I think it should be written
out afresh before going to the Queen even in draft.

173   *Palmerston to Gladstone*

[Printed in *Glad.* II. 50]

94 P[iccadill]ʸ. 25 May 1862

You may not have seen how your Name is taken in vain
by People with whom I conceive you do not sympathise.

(Enclosure)

TAX PAYERS
READ
MR. COBDEN'S
NEW PAMPHLET, THE
"THREE PANICS",
AND JUDGE FOR YOURSELVES.

HOW LONG will you suffer Yourselves to be Humbugged by PALMERSTONIANISM, and Robbed by the "SERVICES", and others interested in a War Expenditure even in times of Peace?

A portion of our Press evidently finds its PROFIT in Artificial Excitements and WARLIKE SENSATIONS not scrupling to resort to MISREPRESENTATIONS and SUPPRESSION of the TRUTH in order to further its ends.

THE CHANCELLOR of the EXCHEQUER
APPEALS TO YOU
to help him.

You have the power in your own hands if you will only exert it.

REFORM
THE HOUSE OF COMMONS,
And do it thoroughly this time.

[Nisbet, Printer, 164 Trongate, Glasgow]

174   *Palmerston to Gladstone*

94 P[iccadill]ʸ. 27 May 1862

I have been reflecting upon your proposed Resolutions and the Course of Proceeding you have suggested for this Day week, and I am much inclined to think that our best Course would be that I should get up after Stanfield's Resolutions are put, and endeavour to get rid of all Resolutions by moving the previous Question and I am led to believe that such a Course would find the greatest Support in the House.

Stanfields Resolutions we could not agree to.

Lord Robert Montagu's Resolution is a Truism without any practical objects or application.

Horsman's Resolution is an assertion which no Member of the present Government could deny, and to which no Member of the late Government, nor any independent Member who has not opposed the supplies to which it relates could consistently refuse to agree. But at the same Time it is only a repeated affirmation of Decisions which the House of Commons has on former occasions come to.

I apprehend that the Course of Proceeding would be that after Stanfields Resolution was put, Ld Robert Montagu would move his amendment moving for that Purpose the omission of all the words after the word, " That ", and the Question put by the Speaker would be that the words proposed to be left out stand Part of the Question.

We should say " No " to that and the House would no Doubt carry the Negative. Ld Robert would then move to insert his words, which we might object to as being simply a Truism without practical application ; if that Resolution was set aside Horsman would move his Resolution or he would move it as an amendment to Ld Robert's.

It would require more Ingenuity than I possess to find a good Reason for refusing to assent to Horsman's affirmation. In Truth, to object to it would be to censure ourselves.

To your Resolution many objections might be urged. Some Persons would cavil at your preliminary Statements and we should have a financial wrangling from Disraeli and Northcote. For my part I think your last Resolution might be construed as holding out a Pledge of future Reduction of Expenditure which future Circumstances might prevent us from realizing at all Events to the Extent of the meaning that would by some be put upon it. No *great* Diminution of Expenditure can be made except on the

Army & Navy ; and I own that I do not foresee any change
of Circumstances likely to take Place between this Time
and next February which would justify any considerable
Reduction either of Army or Navy ; though we may
reasonably hope to make some Diminution of Expence
on those Heads—But those anticipatory Resolutions are
nothing but a Trap for a Government ; they tend either
to expose a Government to the Imputation of breaking
Faith with Parliament, or to compel them to provide in-
adequately for the proper Demands of the Public Service.

I am unwilling to place myself in Either of those Conditions.

It seems to me that I might get up immediately after
Stanfield's Seconder and move the previous Question
upon Grounds which I believe the Majority of the House
would be disposed to take stand upon but I must ascertain
from the Speaker whether this could be done.

175   *Gladstone to Palmerston*

Carlton H[ouse] Terrace.
May 27th, 1862.

I deeply regret to find that your reflections on the scheme
of Resolutions which I submitted to the Cabinet on Saturday have taken an unfavourable direction. I observe however that we seem agreed in thinking, though perhaps not
for the same reasons, that the Government ought not to
support either Stansfeld, L^d. R. Montagu or Horsman. I
also assent to your observations of Saturday that in whatever we do, we ought to have regard both to the desire for
defence, and also to the desire for economy. And finally I
admit that there is some inconvenience in what you term
anticipatory Resolutions.

But the time is peculiar and ' exceptional '. We have
presented a Budget without a surplus. This proceeding
would be wholly unjustifiable, if we could regard the

present expenditure as regular and normal. The justification of the finance of the year—on which the Cabinet was unanimous involves the admission, and justifies the assertion, that the present expenditure of the country is inconvenient. Even if the resort to Loan in the case of the fortifications left behind a necessity for any other proof of that proposition.

I regard the nature of the Budget of this year as a most important element in the case. In my opinion it justifies the H. of Commons in asking the Government formally, what it thinks of the Expenditure, and whether it considers that, apart from exigencies it may and ought to undergo some reduction.

To this *act* of the Government is to be added the declaration of the leader of opposition. And all this comes home with the utmost force to me, since I have held and must continue to hold the necessity of prospective reduction.

Judging in the first place for myself, and with reference to the course I have found it my absolute duty to take, which I admit may be separable from, though it is not in conflict with, that of the Government, I feel that for me to support the previous question would be an unworthy evasion of a difficulty.

And this the more when great distress prevails in a portion of the country.

There are other practical objections to the previous question. I apprehend there might be much difficulty in introducing the motion without a violation of the just rights of those who have given notice of amendments. And I may add that if I found it on reflection possible for me to vote for it, I should be under the necessity of reiterating in the most pointed manner in a speech, what I have heretofore said on the subject of retrenchment. A difference of tone in the declarations from the Treasury Bench on such an occasion would be very disparaging to the Government.

I confess I do not enter into the objections which you think might be urged against the Resolutions. The

allegations they contain are indisputable so far as they refer
to figures. The promise they hold out seems to be duly
guarded : and I was in hopes on Saturday that such was
the impression of the Cabinet, and your own. It may be
said they are bold. But I do not see in what way they involve any elements of rashness. I should think them likely
to do, what none of the other proposals would or could do,
namely to rally under your banner the *whole* of your party,
in a vote honourable to the Government, and satisfactory
to the country.

As the crowning merit of my Resolutions, I will add that
they would enable me wholly or substantially to withdraw
from the debate, and to leave the candid defence of our
position in other hands.

176　　　　　　*Palmerston to Gladstone*

94 Piccadilly 28 May 62

I find that by the Forms of the House we are precluded
from moving the previous Question on Stanfield's Resolution, and thus getting rid of the whole Lot. We must therefore deal with the Resolution and the Amendments one
after the other in the order in which they stand, and yours,
if it were moved could not be put until all the others had
been disposed of. The Course then would be to affirm in
the first Place that Stanfields Resolution should not stand
Part of the Question. The first Question to be put from the
Chair being upon Ld R. Montagus Amendment, That the
words proposed to be left out, namely Stanfield's Resolution, stand Part of the Question. I assume that the No's
would have it. Then would come L^d R Montagus Words
unless he were to withdraw them, which it is not impossible he might do. If he did not, we should have to
negative the Motion that his words be here inserted.

Then would come Horsman's Resolution the Question

Pp

then being that those words be here inserted—Now I hold that those words are a Statement of a Truth and not like Ld Robert's, of a Truism and I could not vote to negative them and there are many in the House who would vote for them, perhaps a Majority.

But the simple affirmation of that Resolution however true and however in Keeping with the Consistency of the House might be taken by some of our Friends below the Gangway as a Slap in the Faces, richly deserved indeed, but which it might not be useful in a Party Sense for us to administer. Russell has suggested & so has Brand a way out of the difficulty by proposing to add to Horsman's Resolution some words in the Sense of your proposed Resolution but shorter, and it seems to me that such a Course would be successful.

Your four Resolutions might be put as a separate String if we had cleared away all the others ; but as I have said there would be a Difficulty in effecting such a Clearance ; while, as I imagine, the Forms of the House would allow our proposing an addition to Horsman's Resolution.

The addition which I would suggest would be that on the inclosed Paper and I am led to believe that such an addition would satisfy Stanfield and those who act with him, who must by this Time have found out that they have made a mess of it.

I would be ready to move such an addition

177   *Palmerston to Gladstone*

94 P[iccadill]^y. 29 May 1862

You said yesterday that you meant to put into your comparative Statement of the Expenditure in the last three years something about the Loan raised for Fortifications, but that Loan has nothing whatever to do with the Expences which mean to compare and it can have no Place in your Comparison. The principal Sum raised was raised by Loan and not out of annual Taxation and the Interest payable upon the terminable annuities issued and to be issued forms Part of the aggregate amount payable for the Interest of our National Debt. If you were going to make a Comparison of the annual Charge on account of the Debt in different years the Interest payable on these terminable annuities would of course form a Part though a very small one of the general aggregate, but there would be no more Reason for including any Thing about these terminable annuities in your comparative Statement of annual Expenditure, than there would be for putting in the Loan raised for the Russian War or any other Part of our National Debt. Any such Insertion would be decidedly objectionable.

178   *Gladstone to Palmerston*

11 C[arlton] H[ouse] T[errace]
29 May. 62.

The following reasons strike me as conclusive against affirming Horsman's motion ; independently of what further reflection might suggest.

1. The past expenditure is not challenged by Stanfeld's motion ; and to make an affirmation respecting it which reaches over the last four years is wholly gratuitous.

2. Is there a precedent for this kind of sweeping and wholesale retrospective affirmation by the House of the Estimates for Defence of two or more than two Governments, and of two Parliaments ? I do not know one, and believe it would be a very bad one to establish.

3. In common consistency if any vindication of the expenditure were called for, it should touch the Civil as well as the Military, for Stansfeld makes no distinction : but this Horsman leaves to shift for itself.

4. I hold that in agreeing to public expenditure, a minister may and sometimes ought, within certain limits to take into view other elements besides the intrinsic merits of the proposition, especially the state of the national feeling. But Horsman's motion affirms the expenditure on its intrinsic merits alone, and requires of me, in this, I believe unprecedented, and sweeping proposition, what I have never yet given, and cannot give.

5. It appears to me with the light of experience to be plain, that great mistakes have been committed, for example the immense and costly conversion of wooden ships of the line. I objected to this at the time : but with my limited knowledge I gave way to your authority. To affirm now that this was right, and that all the money spent in the famous reconstruction must have been spent if we had directed more of our energies at an early date to iron ships, is in my view impossible. '

I return your " addition " which though more vague perhaps than I should *like* seems to me in principle sound.

179   *Palmerston to Gladstone*

Brocket Hall
10 June 1862

I have received the accompanying Letter from Sir Francis Baring, and I must say it seems to me full of good Sense. Much Damage must arise not only to the existing administration, but to the Government as an Institution by needlessly proclaiming to the Public Differences of opinion between different Departments of the Government, and more especially from setting up the opinion of a subordinate officer against the opinions of his superior. I am sorry to say that I have more than once heard that Clarence Paget is too free in telling People in private that he differs from his superiors and disapproves of things he has had to propose in Parliament. But Frederic Peel who is

a staid man ought to have more Sense, and a greater
Knowledge of Propriety and of public Duty than to press
the Committee to examine a Subordinate to contradict
his superior. Pray put a Stop to such a Proceeding.

180   *Palmerston to Gladstone*

94 P[iccadill]y. 18 June 1862

The Pasha of Egypt dines with us on Saturday. His
Desire is to meet and make acquaintance with leading
Members of the Government. I wish much that you and
Mrs. Gladstone would sternly cast aside any other En-
gagement you may have for Saturday, and that you would
come here to meet the Pasha—We cannot give him the
Cajoleries he received at Paris, but we ought to do for him
whatever we easily can.

181   *Gladstone to Palmerston*

Carlton H[ouse] Terrace
24 June 1862.

I send you herewith a copy of the Cabinet Minute on
the provision for the Princes and Princesses : which, upon
an intimation from Sir C. Phipps that the amendments
were satisfactory, I have sent to the Queen to-day.

182   *Palmerston to Gladstone*

94 P[iccadill]y. 15 July 1862

What is the State of the Matter to which the inclosed
Letter and Newspaper Extract relate ?

The Phoenix Park is undoubtedly as fine an open space
as is to be found anywhere ; so close to a large and important City ; and it has certainly received for many years

past less assistance from Art and Care than probably any other Metropolitan Park. The Irish may fairly claim to have their Park share in general Improvement.

183 *Memorandum on Border for North and South States of America*

I had a conversation last night with a Southern Gentleman, whose name I need not put on paper, with respect to the question always represented on the Federal side as physically and socially incapable of solution for political purposes, the question I mean of the *Border* between the Northern and Southern Republics, presuming there will be only two, of which he does not feel quite sure.

His view is as follows :

1. Maryland is Southern in sentiment and feeling but, isolated as it is by the Potomac, it must probably on a final settlement belong to the North.

2. Western Virginia, the tongue of land so called, should without hesitation be given to the North.

3. Tennessee is divided physically into Eastern, Middle, and Western : the three divisions having respectively Knoxville, Nashville, and Memphis, for their capitals or principal towns. Western Tennessee is as purely a Flax and Cotton district as Alabama. Middle Tennessee is a rich and Eastern a poorer and high district, both given to cereals, and *less* emphatically Southern in feeling than the West, but still so clearly Southern that it is plain the whole State must belong to the Southern Confederacy.

4. Kentucky has a kind of aristocracy in some of its Southern counties, and the families composing it are wholly Southern in feeling. But the bulk of Kentucky (which is at present in *both* Republics by formal vote) is necessary to the configuration of the North : and the South must be satisfied either with getting some of the

Southern Counties or with the emigration of the families southward which will take place if there is no such partial annexation to the South.

5. Missouri is capable, both geographically and socially, of an easy division into North and South, by a line running about East and West : and should be parted between the two Republics accordingly.

6. All this must take place, according to Southern sentiments, by the free action of the several States.

7. The question of the Territories involves no practical difficulty. Slavery, says my informant, is sedentary and not migratory. New Mexico is at present, by law of the United States, a Slave country : and New Mexico is all they want : with this exception the whole of the Territories will go to the North without dispute.

8. On my asking how far views of this kind are accepted in the South, he said he believed they were entertained among intelligent and responsible persons, and would at the proper time be acted upon : but they could not safely or advantageously be proclaimed in present circumstances, and what he had said to me on these heads was to be regarded as confidential information only.

W. E. G.　July 31. 62.

184　　　　*Gladstone to Palmerston*

Private.
Penmaenmawr N.W.
Sept. 7. 1862.

I have just read in the Globe that the Archbishop of Canterbury is dead.

As an individual I would presume to offer one word on such an occasion : but I represent a constituency which is in a position different from that of every other except one only, with respect to its deep, and immediate as well as deep, concern in the appointment of a successor to the Primacy.

I shall however I hope not appear to offend by any undue attempt to limit or suggest a choice, when I say that
I am quite certain the desire of nine among every ten in
that constituency is, that the Minister should freely and
conscientiously exercise his judgement, but that his choice
should fall on some one who from moderation as well as
piety and learning should carry real weight not with any
party in particular, but with the Church at large. It is for
the purpose of explaining my *meaning* rather than as any
departure from what I have above said if (as I think *age*
has for a long time been considered a needful qualification
in an appointment to the See of Canterbury) I point to the
single name of one whom you have twice preferred, the
present Archbishop of York,[1] and whose praise for wisdom
and goodness is in all parts and all borders of the Church.

185   *Palmerston to Gladstone*

[Partly printed in *Glad*. II. 76]

94 P[iccadill]ʸ 24 Septᵗ 62

It seems to Russell and me that the Time is fast approaching when some joint offer of Mediation by England France,
and Russia if She would be a Party to it, might be made
with some Prospect of Success to the Combatants in North
America, and Russell is going to instruct Cowley by a
private Letter to sound the French Government as to their
willingness to agree to such a Measure if formally proposed
to them. Of Course no actual step to such Effect could be
taken without the Sanction of the Cabinet But if I am not
mistaken, you would be inclined to approve such a Course.

The Proposal would naturally be made to both North
and South, if both accepted we should recommend an
Armistice and Cessation of Blockades with a View to
Negotiation on the Basis of Separation. If both declined
we must of Course leave them to go on ; If the South

[1] Archbishop Longley.

ONE HEAD BETTER THAN ONE

LOUIS NAPOLEON. " I say, hadn't we better tell our friend there to leave off making a fool of himself ? "

LORD PAM. " H'm, well, suppose you talk to him yourself. He's a great admirer of yours, you know."

accepted and the North declined we should then I conceive acknowledge the Independence of the South, but we ought, Russell and I imagine, to declare the maintenance of our Neutrality even in the Case of our acknowledging the Independence of the South. Ld Lyons would be going back towards the Middle of October, and his Return would be the fitting opportunity for such a Step if determined upon. It looks as if matters were rapidly coming to a Crisis and perhaps we may have to make the move earlier than the Middle of October. A great Battle appeared by the last accounts to be coming on. If Maclellan is badly defeated the Federal Cause will be manifestly hopeless, If Jackson should sustain a serious Reverse he will be in a dangerous Position so far north and cut off from his Supplies. But a few Days will bring us important accounts.

I saw the other Day that you are going to have some great Dinner given you in the early Part of next Month. I hope the Chancellor of the Exchequer will not be too sympathising with the Tax Payer, nor tell the Country that they are paying too much Taxation have too large Establishments, and ought to agitate to bring the House of Commons and the Government to more Economical ways & Habits. Those Topics suit best Cobden & Bright and their Followers. I am only up for the Day to see Russell on his Return and to inquire how the Sheep Disease goes on. I fear it will spread wide and be a great Evil. They say vaccination does not take in the Sheep. But what Graham used to call the Reason Why has not been explained

186 *Gladstone to Palmerston*

Private.

Hawarden Chester
Sept. 25. 1862.

I am glad to learn that in your opinion and Lord Russell's the time has arrived for coming to an understanding with some other principal Powers of Europe so as to be in a condition to take some part with a view to procuring a cessation of the deadly struggle in America. There are two reasons of a special nature, apart from others which might be named, that make me, for one desirous of such a proceeding. One is that the progress of the Confederate Arms has been such as, if it be continued for even a short time, may fairly authorise that Government with something like justice to ask of us prompt recognition, whereas it would appear to be desirable that we should not be brought to that step without having previously made a friendly effort to induce the North to recede. And indeed this rapid progress of the confederates threatens to raise at an early period other very serious difficulties. It would appear that up to a recent period they have been willing to give over to the North Maryland, Western Virginia, Kentucky, and great part at least of Missouri. But if their invasion of Maryland should lead to a powerful manifestation of Southern feeling in that State, they may no longer be inclined, and indeed it may become difficult for them in point of honour, to abandon that State in the final arrangement. Similar considerations may apply in parts of Kentucky and elsewhere. So that whereas up to this time the whole difficulty in obtaining peace has lain on the Northern side, a state of things may come about, if Europe does not speak at the right moment, in which she will find a new set of obstacles to accommodation set up on the side of the South, and these obstacles again reacting unfavourably on the disposition of the North.

The second reason is this. The population of Lancashire have borne their sufferings with a fortitude and patience exceeding all example, and almost all belief. But if in any *one* of the great towns, resignation should, even for a single day, give place to excitement, and an outbreak should occur, our position in the face of America, and our influence for good might be seriously affected : we might *then* seem to be interfering, with loss of dignity on the ground of our immediate interests, and rather in the attitude of parties than as representing the general interests of humanity and peace.

On the other hand, it will be a serious impediment, as it occurs to me, should Russia decline to join with France and England. British North American interests may always, where there is a bias, be held to detract something from our impartiality : and the recent Mexican policy of France tends to make her in some degree suspected by the United States : the accession of Russia would of all others be the one to stamp any effort you may make with the one great requisite namely moral authority.

With respect to the Dinner at Newcastle, and the speech it will require, I have no difficulty, known to myself, in giving you satisfaction. Indeed, your notice of the subject has only anticipated by two or three days a letter which I intended to write to you, had you not thus " prevented " me, in order to ask any counsel you might be disposed to give me on any of the topics which such an occasion will suggest.

Without drawing any distinction between military and civil, and without minutely determining the question whether excess of expenditure implies in any thing like the same degree excess of establishments, I have felt for a considerable time that not only the actual scale of our expenditure, but the prevailing temper of extravagance and the prospects which it opened to us, have constituted a public inconvenience, and have threatened to become a public danger. The House of Commons, guided by you, has declared its views on this subject in terms with which I for one am satisfied. I believe it to be exceedingly important for the interests of the Government and the country that we should be able next year to propose a reduction of taxes : and I am fully convinced that such a diminution of the Estimates as is necessary for the purpose may be safely and wisely made. But the H. of C. by its Resolutions has placed the matter in your hands : it remains to be dealt with in the Cabinet : but when it has thus been referred to you I do not think it either required by my duty to the country, or consistent with my duty to you and to my colleagues, to agitate as you term it, or in other words to act upon opinion out of doors. I am not therefore going to the North upon an economical crusade : I may unintentionally step aside, but I shall not intentionally say anything, if I refer to economy at all, except such as you might say yourself, which I hope you will take for a sufficient guarantee.

This dinner affair has risen in a great degree out of the French Treaty. It came to me through, and was recommended by, Headlam and Hutt : and Brand concurred in their view.

Forgive my troubling you with so long a letter and believe me

The crops in this country are good : with partial manifestations of the potato disease. I think the Revenue, which has thus far held up very well, begins to show signs of the distress which I apprehend has prevailed in Ireland as well as more severely in Lancashire.

187   *Gladstone to Palmerston*

Hawarden
Sept. 28. 1862.

I venture after some consideration to lay before you what appears to me to be the strong claims of the Bishop of Oxford to the See of York, become vacant through the translation of Archbishop Longley ; a measure which I believe will bring you a reward in the universal satisfaction of the Church and of the public.

The Bishop of Oxford [1] is probably the first preacher of

[1] Samuel Wilberforce.

the day in the Church of England—He is certainly by much the most famous ; and his fame is owing to his constant and exhausting labours. With respect to these labours he is entirely without a rival ; and the very places where he is most heartily welcomed by crowds of all sentiments and parties, such as the Churches will hardly contain, are those which apply the severest test to the popularity and influence of one commonly reputed a High Churchman, namely the great and populous towns of the country.

Although he is reputed a High Churchman, (I say reputed, because I do not profess to expound or to be responsible for the phrase,) there is no one who has laboured more, or with more success, to bring and keep together those portions of the Clergy and Laity, who respectively acknowledge and disclaim that appellation. I believe that a Bishop of the latter class, promoted by yourself, has only within the last few weeks been urgent with him to undertake a preaching tour in his Diocese for the sake of stirring up the people of the manufacturing towns.

As regards the government of a Diocese, in which he has [been] now for seventeen years, I say without hesitation that there is no Bishop in the whole country whose labours will bear a comparison with his for their sustained and successful energy. And those labours have been directed not to fostering in any form religious controversies and animosities, but to the union of clergy and laity in all good works, to the establishment of every institution adapted to promote the cause of religion, education, and charity, *most of all* to bringing the powerful instrument of preaching to bear, in a manner previously quite unknown, upon the moral and spiritual improvement of the people.

Nor should I be afraid to say that his government of his Diocese has on the whole been as much distinguished by prudence as by power. Though Oxford in our time has been the hot-bed of theological controversy, he has known how to moderate zeal, as well as to arouse it, and there has rarely been a case of imprudence among his very numerous Clergy, never I believe a single one in which he has himself given offence to the people of his Diocese.

It seems after all to be the opinion of the Diocese which affords the best test of the real merits of a Bishop : and I am confident that no Diocese in England would speak more unequivocally in favour of its Bishop, than the very trying one of Oxford. . . .

. . . People who view the Bishop of Oxford solely through the medium of Parliamentary and London life, have not the least idea of what he is. His rare and short relaxations amidst his unparalleled labours are sometimes denounced as worldly. He is on principle as well as by nature social : and he is one of not very many Bishops who have powers and qualities that maintain the hold and influence of religion upon the higher circles of civil life. But those who think he meddles too much in London would gladly see him removed from it to a spot where he would no longer be within an hour of the Metropolis.

Though it may be intruding into high matters, I cannot help saying that I have been told his promotion to the See of York would be very agreeable to the Queen. Of this you may easily know more than I.

Promoted or unpromoted, he is one of the great Bishops, necessarily few, who leave their mark upon their Church and upon the history of their time.

The exclusion of men of transcendant powers from places in proportion to them comes at length to bear the aspect and to produce the effect of proscription. There is no more grave feature in the condition of the Church of England at this moment than the indisposition of men of the highest intellect to take Holy Orders. My knowledge of Oxford assures me that this indisposition has been much increased by an impression which has gone abroad that mediocrity has under many circumstances a better prospect than great powers greatly used.

Though I have said much, I am far from having said all about him. I have said quite enough to enable you to judge whether there is or is not sufficient cause for *entertaining* the question. I am truly sorry to have detained you at such length but this is no common case, and having made up my mind to take what I admit to be a very great freedom, I have thought it best to show that it is not done hastily nor without reasons.

I am sure you will consider what I have said as much as it deserves : but I beg you will not think of troubling yourself to make any reply.

188 *Memorandum by Mr. Gladstone on the War in America*

Printed for the use of the Cabinet. October 25, 1862.
Secret.

I SUBMIT the following observations on the question raised by the Memorandum of Earl Russell (October 13), and that of Sir George Lewis (October 17).

The choice, I presume, lies between inaction on the one hand, and an interference limited to moral means on the other.

Under the name of interference I comprise all the various forms of proceeding that might be adopted, without for the present distinguishing among them ; as to armistice, good offices, mediation, or recognition.

Now, first, are we agreed as to the nature of the question itself ? Are we to decide respecting interference according to its expediency or inexpediency ; or are we stopped, *in limine*, by its being contrary to international law ?

I shall assume we are agreed in thinking that there is no barrier of international law in our way. Therefore the question simply is, shall we, by interference, do good or do harm ?

Could we see any likelihood of an early termination of the war by the exhaustion of either party, or by the willingness of the North to negotiate on the basis of separation, interference would be at the least gratuitous and needless. But there is plainly no such likelihood.

Again, if we desire the war to continue, either with a view to the possible success of the North, or to the extinction of slavery through a servile war or otherwise, or on any other ground, then of course all room for argument is gone. But I assume that we wish the war to end, and that we see no early probability of its ending if left to itself.

In answering, then, the main question, namely, whether interference will do good or harm, I think we must first know *who* are to interfere.

The sole interference of England would, in my opinion, be open to the charge of an unwarrantable assumption ; would be too weak to afford any hope of good ; and would too probably involve us, as Sir G. Lewis anticipates, in diplomatic, or even something more than diplomatic, difficulties.

I observe that the objections of Sir George Lewis to interference at the present time are applied, in most cases expressly, and throughout, I think, by implication, to an interference by England alone. With the removal of that supposition, the main part of the groundwork of those objections disappears.

The interference which the case requires is an expression of opinion, or a course of action, on the part of such a combination of the Powers as may virtually and constructively convey the prevailing judgment of the civilised world.

The union of England and France would not sufficiently answer to this definition, for France, by her Mexican policy, has in some degree compromised her impartial, above all her unsuspected, position in American affairs.

The union of England, France, and Russia, would

probably fulfil the definition. These are the three greatest Powers of Europe. These are three Powers which also represent the great rivalries of the Old World : and it is scarcely in the nature of things that the three should agree and co-operate, except for a good end. And not only by reason of their greatness may they fairly claim to represent Europe, especially in the absence of any contrary indication, but, in the particular case, Russia supplies in the largest measure the one vital element, otherwise deficient, of traditional and unquestioned friendliness to America. Besides, it may be assumed that if England, France, and Russia led, other Powers would be prepared to follow, if needful.

I wish to argue, in support of Lord Russell's proposal, that we should endeavour to promote a joint interference, supported by this vast weight of moral authority and force.

The change in the hypothesis from a sole to a joint, and to *such* a joint, interference, at once, as it appears to me, alters the whole force and bearing of the arguments.

All fear of insult to a particular Power, which would only have embraced a course taken by other Powers and in the common interests of humanity, disappears from the sphere of probable contingencies : so does all apprehension of attempt to embarrass it by throwing upon it the responsibilities of a task beyond its strength, or difficulties of detail which it would not have knowledge to surmount.

For a proposal having peace for its aim, and couched in just, considerate, and kindly language, when proceeding from such a source, we may anticipate, with something like certainty, on the part of the North, were it only with a view to her own interests, at least a serious and decent reception.

If this be so, then I think the apprehensions of evil connected with Lord Russell's proposal, if they do not totally vanish, dwindle into insignificance.

Sir G. Lewis anticipates that the Washington Cabinet,

even if well disposed, would be prevented from acting rightly by an overpowering popular agitation. But within the last two years we have seen that, under the professedly more popular forms of the American Constitution, public opinion, or opinion out of doors, acts much more tardily, and at a given time much more feebly, on the Government than it does with us. We have seen Mr. Buchanan proceed in defiance of the national sentiment, during his expiring term of office ; and we have seen Mr. Lincoln deliver up Mason and Slidell, contrary to expectation here, to all superficial signs, and to very serious and even authoritative indications of public sentiment. It seems little likely that the Government of the United States will be forced by popular agitation to do either right or wrong against its own convictions.

The fact should be remembered that it sits at Washington, and not in the great centres of popular feeling.

I urge, therefore, that on the suppositions before us, the question what evil we may do by interference should be put aside ; and the real question is, whether we may hope to effect such an amount of positive good, as is required in order to warrant so grave a step.

Now I feel no unhesitating confidence that the North would meet even the weightiest, wisest, and friendliest proposal with acceptance. But I do contend that we ought not to undervalue the amount and kind of force which belongs to the instrument that Lord Russell proposes to employ.

The nineteenth century has many boasts, some fictitious and some real. Among the most real, and also among the noblest of its distinctions, as I think, has been the gradual and sensible growth of what may be rudely called an international opinion, which carries in the main the authority of the mass of nations, and, whenever it is brought to bear, powerfully influences the conduct of each nation in particular ; acting in a manner more or less analogous to that in which public opinion, as we commonly term it, acts upon the institutions and policy of a well-ordered country. Moral force operated considerably in the Crimean war ; moral force destroyed the Treaty of Zurich ; and we have, I think, every reason to believe that America would feel the influence and weight of a general opinion on the part of civilized Europe that this horrible war ought to cease. The deliberate declaration of the principal States would be unimpeachable evidence of the existence of such an opinion.

The characteristic soreness and uneasiness of America under irregular criticism is in some degree a measure of the real weight she attaches to European sentiment. She may desire to hide from herself the fact of its existence ; she may very naturally resent the assumed expression of it by self-constituted and inadequate organs ; but it does not follow that she will add to her other follies the folly of denying that she is herself in some degree amenable to external opinion, and that there is force in what would virtually stand as the judgment, for the time at least, of the civilized world, on the great issue she has raised.

But other motives would co-operate with whatever deference America may feel for the opinion of Europe. Recognition, even when wisely accompanied with a declaration of continued neutrality, could hardly fail to awaken some apprehensions, perhaps the more salutary, under the circumstances, because somewhat remote. And America would not be slow, either in the North or the South, to calculate the great change in relative advantages, under which the war itself would be carried on after such a declaration from the principal Powers of Europe.

I therefore infer, that though we must not calculate too boldly upon the immediate acceptance by the North of any proposal, however excellent in form and substance, we may confidently reckon, provided justice be done to American honour and feelings, on a powerful effect to be produced on opinion and on the general course of affairs in favour of peace ; and on bringing greatly nearer, at least, the day of that happy release.

Next let us consider some reasons for proceeding on the proposal of Lord Russell at the present period, rather than adjourning a question which, by adjournment, we shall by no means escape :—

1. The period of the year is favourable, as being that when, for some months, there must be a great contraction of military operations.

2. The period of the war is favourable, when its fortunes have been placed for the moment *in equilibrio* by the failure of the main invasions on both sides, and the remarkable lessons administered by that failure.

It seems very improbable that another period of such balance should occur ; while, at the same time, the failure of invasion substantially means the general failure of the North in its aggressive purpose.

Sir G. Lewis says the sword has not yet traced the conditions of a Treaty ; but, surely, the sword has, at least, done much towards it, when the South has driven the North over the Potomac, and the North has driven back the South over that river in return.

3. Even those who are averse to present action would probably say, let us reserve ourselves with unbroken strength and authority for a future opportunity.

It appears to me that we may lose as well as gain in authority by waiting, and that loss is more probable than gain.

The terrible distress of Lancashire has thus far been borne with heroic patience and with perfect submission to the law. But, with all our confidence in the people, who can be certain that the positive suffering, the actual hunger which we have every reason to fear is endured there, may not at some time, at some place, perhaps from some apparently trivial incident, give rise to an outbreak ?

It appears to me that if once the public peace shall have been compromised in this country, we at least shall have lost much in the share of dignity and influence we have it in our power to contribute to any act of European inter-ference. And such an event, though uncertain, and, I hope, improbable, yet has not been thought unlikely by some serious observers on the spot, and should not, I think, be put wholly out of view in considering the case before us.

4. Another reason which seems to me to tell materially in favour of early action is this, that the people of England are being rapidly drawn into Southern sympathies.

It is one thing to anticipate an issue of the war favour-able in the main to the Southern view : it is quite another to sympathize with men whose cause is, as I think, seriously tainted by its connection with slavery. Yet the sight of a minority, heroically struggling against the effort of a much larger number to place them in a political connection that they abhor, probably with a withdrawal or limitation of their rights as freemen, has an irresistible tendency to arouse active sympathies in England on behalf of the weaker side, even apart from the disgraceful circumstances which have attended the forcible re-establishment of the Northern rule, particularly in New Orleans.

The more these positive Southern sympathies increase, the less shall we be able to maintain a friendly and im-partial aspect in any proceeding that may be taken.

But public opinion, not yet too widely committed for the South, appears to me to be in that state in which it would hail with cordial satisfaction any judicious effort for the termination of the war.

5. The increasing exasperation and deepening horrors of the war in America seem likely to counterbalance, or more than counterbalance, in warlike influences any tendencies towards peace that might be produced by a partial sense of exhaustion. But it is in vain to look to exhaustion. When did a war of this kind end by exhaustion ? It may remit

and flag from exhaustion, but end it hardly can ; and to expect that the severance of the American Union shall take place by the simple good-will of both parties, is to expect a course of things totally different from that which has commonly been found in like cases too familiar to quote.

Lastly, a few words on what we have to expect if inaction is preferred to interference.

In this part of the case it is impossible to put out of view the strange construction of American institutions, as well as the unfavourable action of other circumstances in the present condition of that country.

The suspension of all guarantees for freedom, and the expenditure by the Government of probably not less than £200,000,000 per annum, without control and without publicity, place the most formidable obstacles in the way of any movement of public opinion except in one direction.

But let us suppose these obstacles surmounted : let us even suppose the Democrats winners in the elections that are now going on. Even then, what means will they possess of influencing the Executive Government ? Will they have a majority in Congress ? and if they have, can they stop the career of the Cabinet ? Sir George Lewis says, " It may be doubted whether any reconstruction of the Federalist Cabinet can take place before the next Presidential election." I concur in this opinion. But the next President will assume office in the year 1865 ; and I, for one, am certainly unwilling to put aside the proposal to bring the moral influence of Europe to bear, in reliance upon a possible change of public opinion in America, which may not find regular and constitutional expression in the acts of the Government until after *three* winters shall have elapsed of the character of that which we have now before us.

We have in our view a war of which, according to our anticipations of its issue, we may now justly say, first, that, being the most gigantic, it has also become perhaps the most purposeless of all great civil wars that have ever been waged ; secondly, that it is certainly the one which has inflicted, beyond all comparison, the severest suffering on the other countries of the civilized world, and has given them the best title to be heard, if they shall think fit to speak, on the question of its continuance.

It may be said the war has only continued eighteen months : do not *yet* interfere. But months in war mean now almost what years meant a generation back. The cost, the bloodshed, the suffering, the disorganization, caused by our seven or eight years of war with our American Colonies were small in proportion to those of the last year and a half in America. Did the French Revolutionary war, from its first outbreak to the Peace of Amiens, arm a greater number of men than the 1,400,000 or 1,500,000 whom North and South between them have brought into the field ? or did it spend much more treasure ?

One concluding word on slavery. I cannot suppose that we are to refuse to cure, or to aim at curing, one enormous evil, because we cannot cure another along with it. But I feel it would be most desirable, in a process of interference by which the South would be ostensibly, though perhaps not really, the greatest gainer, to use every moral influence with a view to the mitigation, or, if possible, the removal of slavery. But if we are right in anticipating, as most of us seem to anticipate, that the course of the war from month to month, and year to year, will, on the whole, bring the South nearer and nearer to an independence achieved by its own daring and tenacity, then it is plain that the longer interference is delayed, the less favourable will be our position, and the less clear our title, for urging on the Government of the Southern Confederacy the just claims of the slave.

W. E. G.

October 24, 1862.

189   *Gladstone to Palmerston*

D[owning] S[treet]

Nov. 19, 62.

I quite agree—I think the considerations mentioned by Brand are material to keep in view when the proposal for the Prince of Wales shall be made. At the same time I do not suppose it will be practicable or even desirable, to omit all reference to the total income which we aim at securing for the Prince.

I suspect that in order to fulfil our pledge we may have to go a little beyond £30,000 a year.

190   *Gladstone to Palmerston*

Early and   Hawarden.

Most Private.   Jan. 1. 63.

The Revenue to Dec: 31, though not so good as the papers take it to be, is a good Revenue, and rather better on the whole than I had hoped for when we were in town.

The reductions already agreed upon for the Defence Estimates of 63-4 had led me to hope that it might be possible to provide in the Budget for

1. The reduction of the Sugar Duties to the *peace*-point,

2. The reduction of the Income Tax to 8d (from 9d its present amount).

3. Two minor remissions with which I need not now trouble you, costing together less than half a million. They have long ago been approved in principle by the Cabinet.

The two former ones would cost, together, nearly two millions.

It is impossible to move in the reduction of Income Tax without reducing either the Tea or Sugar Duties.

Still I cannot but see—I think you will agree in this—that if we could reduce the Income Tax to 7d its original amount, it would be not only an important remission, but a considerable political measure.

Now you are aware that all I write at this date is in a great degree guess-work—I may be wrong by half a million, or by more. But I am describing to you the outlines which I see before me dimly moving in the mist.

In order to take 2d off the Income Tax, even sacrificing one or both of the small remissions, we must still do what we can with the Estimates, and particularly apply a firm hand to the Civil Estimates.

Even independently of the consideration started in this letter, I should have written to you the letter which accompanies it : but I think they will materially serve to commend it to your attention, as part of a wider and very weighty subject.

I have marked both of them " Early " because this is the period of the year when the Estimates are in a state of fermentation, and every day is of value.

191   *Gladstone to Palmerston*

Early   Hawarden 1 Jan. 63.

You and the Cabinet will I think expect of me that, at a time when you have been considering the Defence Estimates with a view to Economy, I should make it my business, with the Treasury to examine the Civil Expenditure with a similar view.

My desire is to do what may be practicable in this province, and of course I have thought among others of the various Irish Estimates.

It is not enough to trust in a case of this kind to the detail of merely departmental correspondence. I naturally desire to get Lord Carlisle to apply himself with Sir Robert

Peel, to the work, and though my first thought was to write to him myself, I considered on reflection that I should do what was more fitting with reference both to him and to you, if I opened the matter to you, and requested that, supposing you concurred in opinion with me, you would yourself write to the Lord Lieutenant, making such use of this letter as you may think fit.

What I would ask is a careful and strict review of the Irish Votes in general : and I will now say a word on three branches of our civil expenditure in Ireland. . . .

192   *Gladstone to Palmerston*

Hawarden
Jan. 7. 63.

You remember the nature of our arrangement, as it is proposed, about the Prince of Wales Annuity.

The *first* step is to settle what his independent Income is to be taken at. I have had a correspondence with Sir Charles Phipps upon the various points of detail. Will you read it ? I doubt whether the Cabinet will—and it occurred to me that perhaps we might ask three or four colleagues to read it and thus spare all the rest. For instance

> Granville
> Lewis
> Wood
> Cardwell

What do you say to this ? It is I think only a question whether the Annuity to be given by Parliament should be £40,000, or whether there is a case for some trifle more.

I hope you received a letter from me about the Irish Estimates—which was pressing—we shall not go on with them at the Treasury until I know how the matter stands.

193   *Palmerston to Gladstone*

Downing St
7 Feby 1863

. . . The Cabinet have had under their Consideration this afternoon the Question about the Provision to be made for the Prince & Princess of Wales. One main Principle as it seemed to us to be borne in mind is that the allowance should be sufficient so as to avert that which would be a great Evil, the incurring of Debt, and to avoid what would be less bad, but still an Evil, the Impossibility of maintaining a Suitable Position, and of answering the Claims to which the Prince's Rank will constantly impose him. The Duke of Newcastle points out that if the £10 000 for the Princess is to be Part of the 100 000 for the Prince, a Sum of from 20 to £23 000 must be deducted from that 100 000 inasmuch as the Salaries to the officers of the Household will go far to make up that Amount. Besides this the Prince will have to contribute according to arrangements made with the Queen 20 000 towards the Expence of Monuments & Memorials to His Father. Upon a full view and Consideration of these Matters the Cabinet are inclined to think that the arrangement which we contemplated might fairly & usefully be modified, and that the £10 000 to be given to the Princess might be a separate Grant and in addition to the £40 000 for the Prince.

This would not make the Total greater numerically than what was given to George 4th and substantially it would, considering the altered value of Money be less than what was given on the two last similar occasions. Pray turn this over in your Mind. There is no Need for coming to an immediate Decision. The answer to the address will not be received till Tuesday, and we may well put off the Message about the Prince's Provision till Monday following.

If as we understand, the Prince is to keep up Marlborough House at his own Expence He will have a good yearly Crop of Bills of various Kinds.

194   *Gladstone to Palmerston*

Bowden Park

Chippenham

Feb. 10. 63.

. . . With respect to the question whether the £10,000 per annum for the Princess is to be in *addition* to the £100,000 we have contemplated, I shall cheerfully acquiesce in what the Cabinet may decide : but my own view is the opposite one. The Memorandum of last spring was very much considered : and I believe it is explicit in declaring (but I have not here the means of reference) that £100,000 is to be the total Income. It is true we reserved a discretion to meet change of circumstance : but no circumstance new or peculiar has occurred. I have been struck with finding many judicious persons give it almost spontaneously as their opinion, that £100,000 should be the Prince's Income when married : I do not feel sure that in carrying it farther we are free from the risk of exciting dissatisfaction. For these reasons and not because I think there is anything outrageous in fixing an Income of £110,000 per ann. I prefer the original arrangement, which will in practice lose all binding force if now disturbed.—It will be open to any Government to reduce its figures, when we its authors have on the very first occasion set an example of departure by increasing them.

Some little addition we might venture upon by a liberal view of items in deciding the question what sum is necessary to make up a *bonâ fide* £100,000 : but this could hardly go to the extent of £10,000.

When I saw the Queen at Windsor she appeared to me to understand and to be quite content that £100,000 should cover everything the Princess's allowance included.

195   *Palmerston to Gladstone*

1863
Downing S^t 11 Feby

We have put off the Decision about the allowance to the Prince & Princess till Saturday when you will be at the Cabinet.

If you will not be in the House on Friday let Brand know by Telegram tomorrow that he may arrange Notices accordingly

196   *Palmerston to Gladstone*

94 P[iccadill]^y. 17 March 63

This is the Letter I mentioned to you last Night : what shall I say to The Queen as to the Question of Time and amount ? Perhaps we should have less difficulty in the H^e of C^{ns} in proposing a vote without a Plan, than in getting People to agree to any specific Plan. I suspect that the whole Sum available including both the subscribed amount and a Grant of £30 000 would not be more than enough for a single Memorial on the Park Side of the Carriage Road and that the Hall and its appurtenances must necessarily be given up.

The Queen asked me some Time ago when I was at Windsor to look at the Plans, & to tell her what I thought of them ; and I wrote to her Word that if I was to pronounce an opinion I should say that unity is desirable for a Memorial that a Statue is the best Memorial of a Man, and that I should propose some arrangement on one side only of the Carriage Road, of which the main and principal object should be a suitable Statue of the Prince Consort.

197　　　　　　　　*Gladstone to Palmerston*

11 C[arlton] H[ouse] Terrace

17 March. 63.

General Grey's [1] letter does not refer to a consideration, which appears to me very important in considering what is fit and prudent, or otherwise in regard to a Parliamentary Vote for a Memorial to the Prince Consort.

I mean this, that such matters depend, in a very high degree, upon usage ; and that usage is altogether opposed with us to large votes from the public purse for such a purpose.

I confess I think the usage which prevails is a wise one. Parliamentary Votes may be governed, in a greater or less degree by secondary motives in one quarter or another ; and they present in but a small degree that spontaneousness of character which is the first and greatest element of value in a Memorial to the dead.

For my own part I should think it unwise and unsafe to propose to Parl[t]. a Vote of £50,000. Men would justly ask not only what were the precedents from the past, but what would be the effect upon the future, of such a change in the established methods of proceeding. They would I think ask with especial reason whether the recent Subscriptions did not take place under the belief that no such change in our usages was to occur : and likewise what would be the effect of such a change on the next proposal, in any case at all analogous, for a subscription by individuals.

I believe that if the Vote were carried by an arrangement between parties, this would not prevent serious dissatisfaction out of doors.

One party would resent the novelty, the other the amount ; or objection to the latter might be covered under the plea of questioning the former.

---

[1] Sir Charles Grey, Private Secretary to the Queen.

Next a Vote without a plan is what I for one should have desired. But are you in a condition *now* to propose a Vote, and remove from the mind of members the impression produced by the fact that the Committee appointed to consider the subject have a plan before the world? And that too a plan, which insofar as it embraced works partly in Hyde Park, and partly on the Kensington Estate beyond the road has not been received with favour?

I entirely agree (though this perhaps is beyond my province) in your observations on the plan, especially as regards the essential feature of unity. It appears to me that you would propose a Vote with greater advantage after it had become known (if so it is to be) that the *dual* plan, so to call it, had been abandoned.

I think you spoke the other day in Cabinet of £30,000. This would be much less unsafe than £50,000 : but I do not feel sure it would escape criticism, especially if intended for a merely personal Memorial. A larger sum would perhaps be given with cheerfulness for a Memorial embracing some auxiliary purpose, than for one which was to be a personal record only.

You will perceive from what I have said that I do not think the particular moment favourable. The same motives which lead us to postpone until after the Budget any proposal about the Museum or other Buildings, may I think deserve some consideration in this case also.

My own conviction is that the ground belonging to the Commissioners at Kensington is the true place for an effective Memorial to the Prince Consort. On that ground it will tell its own story, and tell it well : no one would have occasion to ask " why is it here". The Prince on that ground would be like Wren in St. Paul's.

But this again is somewhat beside the question.

198   *Palmerston to Gladstone*

94 P[iccadill]ʸ. 23 March 63

I wrote to The Queen on Saturday to say that the Cabinet thought all Things considered that thirty Thousand would be a better Sum to propose than fifty. I have had the accompanying answer & on talking the Matter over with Brand this Morning he has given his opinion that the House would be as likely to vote the 50, as the 30.

I own I am inclined under all Circumstances to give way to The Queen's Feelings & to propose the larger Sum, especially if we find that the Derbyites will support it I send you a Letter I have Just got from Derby. I have told him that I shall make no Statement tonight but only put a general Notice on the order Book.

199   *Gladstone to Palmerston*

11 C. H. Terrace,
March 23.

On my own part I cannot say more than that I am ready to abide by any decision at which you and your Government may arrive in the matter of the vote for the Prince's memorial. I confess however it appears to me that *on every account* it would be desirable, as matters now stand, to take a little time.

The Queen finds the opinions of all persons, except those officially responsible, one way, and those of the ministers who are officially responsible, the other way—The proposal of the Cabinet you will remember was not to propose a vote of £30,000, but a vote of £16,000 or £18,000, to be laid out on Wolsey's Chapel, as a Memorial of the Prince Consort. To the sum of £30,000, as I understand the matter, they have come in order to meet what they erroneously understood to be the Queen's wishes.

I by no means say that if the mind and wishes of H.M. continue unaltered after hearing all that is to be said the Cabinet should absolutely decline concurrence in them : but I think when we have thus appeared to thwart the Queen's wishes in a matter so near her heart, it would be well not to postpone the question indefinitely but to take time enough to make a statement of the facts and reasons drawn from usage and otherwise by which we have been governed, in order that whatever the upshot may be, it may not appear that we have been wanton or precipitate in our proceedings.

I offer this
for your
consideration.

200   *Gladstone to Palmerston*

24 March. 63.

I return the Queen's Note. It seems that yesterday the *intention* had oozed out : and what I heard of its reception greatly confirmed me in the belief that your decision to let the Cabinet hear again of the question had been a wise one. Nor do I see anything to be gained by proceeding at the present moment. The support of the two *D.s*[1] is quite certain at any time to any sum which they may think most agreeable to the Queen.

201   *Gladstone to Palmerston*

Private.   Downing Street
                              March 25. 63.

In reading the Queen's letter respecting the Prince's memorial to the Cabinet to-day, you made a good humoured reference to me. I do not know whether H.M.

---

[1] Derby and Disraeli.

R P

has been led to distinguish in any manner between one Minister and another with regard to the advice which we thought it our duty to tender ; but it would be rather a satisfaction to me than otherwise that H.M. should be aware that I was upon reflection and conviction a party to that advice : having originally urged the adoption of the plan for restoring Wolsey's Chapel as *the* State Memorial to the Prince ; having then only acceded to a Vote for £30,000 from understanding that it was desired by the Queen ; and having strongly urged to-day that in giving way to the Queen's further desire we should state fully and carefully the reasons upon which we have proceeded, as (I think) loyal subjects, servants, and advisers of the Crown, in recommending sums so much smaller than those which have appeared suitable to other persons, with less responsibility and, I must add, less opportunity of forming a judgment.

The question, in my view, has never been whether twenty or thirty thousand pounds, or a much larger sum, were to be put in the balance against the benefits conferred upon the country, by the Queen herself or by the Prince or against their virtues. I for one have acted in the belief that it was our duty to look in the first instance to the interests of the Throne as paramount in the question, and under the apprehension that those interests might be compromised by a measure, insignificant in a pecuniary sense, to a degree quite out of proportion to its apparent extent. —I have not felt or acted in the matter as Chancellor of the Exchequer, and I have on the other hand thought that if in giving way to the Queen's wishes we took steps to prove that our previous conduct had not been lightly considered, we might fail to produce any change, but we should show that we had done our duty to the best of our knowledge, and should perhaps have been in a better condition to fulfil the duty that still remains to us, namely that of meeting and overcoming objection from without should it arise.

202   *Palmerston to Gladstone*

94 P[iccadill]ʸ. 26 March

In the Communications which have passed between me and The Queen about the Memorial no mention has ever been made nor any allusion to any particular Members of the Cabinet. The Cabinet has always been mentioned as an aggregate Body, and therefore it would not do now to mention to The Queen the opinions of any one Member as separate from the Rest. My joking allusion to you was only the Expression of a Thought at the Moment passing through my Mind that the Minister more specially charged with Financial Matters was the one to whom Reference might in Thought have been made.

I find that some People think we are going to propose £80,000.

203   *Palmerston to Gladstone*

94 P[iccadill]ʸ. 24 March 63

I have just had the inclosed from The Queen. Would it not be well to strike the Iron while it is hot and give notice tonight for Thursday—we will talk of it in the House this Evening.

204   *Palmerston to Gladstone*

94 Piccadilly
21 May 1863

I was unable yesterday to answer your Letter of the 19ᵗʰ —as you do not send me Sir Rowland Hill's Complaint I cannot judge about it; but I had an Interview with him last year, and I clearly perceived from what he then said to me that he intirely misunderstands the relative Positions of a Secretary and the Head of the Department. He appeared to imagine that he ought to be vice Roy over his Chief, and the Substance of his Complaint was that Stanley acted upon his own opinions instead of being invariably governed by his, Sir Rowland Hill's, opinions.

I told Sir Rowland that I considered Stanley quite right in the Matter, & that I have always acted myself on the same principle. That I have been in several offices, and that in each I have always been willing to hear and to consider the opinions of my subordinate officers when they differed from my own, but that as I and not they, must be held responsible for what was to be done, I acted upon my own Decision when deliberately taken. Rowland Hill had no doubt the great merit of suggesting the Penny Postage, but he seemed to me to be the spoilt Child of the Post Office and he ought either to make his Mind up to be what he really is, a subordinate officer or to retire from a Post which his own Notions of his personal Importance make it unpleasant for him to hold—as to Leave of Absence, if I was Stanley I would give it him *sine Die*.

205   *Palmerston to Gladstone*

94 Piccadilly
31 May 1863

What shall I say in answer to this Letter of Chas. Grey —I certainly led The Queen some Time ago to think that some old Gun Metal might be supplied for the Memorial and that any levelling or other work on the Spot in Park to prepare it for the Memorial might fairly be done by the Board of Works which has Care of the Parks. I was not aware that any Alteration had been made as to the Disposal of the Multitude of old and useless Guns at Woolwich & elsewhere and I remembered that Russian Guns taken at Sebastopol had been liberally distributed to several Towns. I should think that this might somehow be managed, & that the H^e C^ns would not object to such a Transfer if within reasonable Limits.

I mean to see Scott and to impress upon him that he is bound in Honor as a Gentleman not to run the Queen into any Expence for the Memorial beyond the amount of the Subscriptions and the vote. Architects require the strongest Restraints to keep them within Limits.

206   *Gladstone to Palmerston*

11 Carlton House Terrace

June 1. 63.

As regards the gun-metal which Sir C. Phipps asked for Frogmore, you will observe that either a rule of public administration which is of great value—not to make grants in kind but to bring everything to account—must be broken, or else a Vote of money must be asked. Neither would I think be desirable, nor indeed do I understand that it is desired.

As respects the Memorial in Hyde Park, the question respecting the guns is exactly the same, and would assume the form of a further grant of money ; but as regards laying out the Park, that is no part of the Memorial though an incident of it, and I think all who have heard that the Memorial is to be erected in the Park will naturally have expected that this incidental charge shall come upon the Park vote, so far as it corresponds with the definition I have given and does not involve work that might be construed to be a part of the Memorial itself.

General Grey has evidently misapprehended one important point. The practice of giving guns for the material of military commemorations does not exist : it is *that* practice which has been abandoned ; for civil monuments it seems never to have existed.

207   *Palmerston to Gladstone*

94 P[iccadill]ʸ. 10 June 1863

I should like to have a short Memorandum stating generally the Grounds of our Proposal about the Purchase of the Kensington Building, and the uses to which it would be applicable. I think it would help us through, that I should say that we have no Intention of sending thither the learned Bodies nor the old Pictures in the National Gallery —this would disarm some objectors. The Men of Science would greatly dislike the Trouble and Expence of being sent to Kensington for their periodical Meetings and the general opinion about the National Gallery I take to be, that the best arrangement would be to erect an unpretending Building in Burlington Garden between the present House and Savile Row with no ornament except towards Savile Row, and lighted from the Roof, while the Building in Trafalgar Square might be sold to the Royal Academy whose Purposes it would intirely suit, and who I believe could give us £70000 for it which Sum would go a long way towards the Cost of a suitable Building in Burlington Garden.

208   *Palmerston to Gladstone*

94 P[iccadill]ʸ. 12 June 63

What are the answers to be given to the two Questions to be put to me today about the Kensington Buildings?

209   *Gladstone to Palmerston*

11 Carlton House Terrace
July 23. 63.

I have received the inclosed note from Cobden relating to business of today in the House of Commons.

(Enclosure)

27 Victoria St. Westminster

22 July 1863

MY DEAR MR. GLADSTONE

I have given notice of some remarks (if I can find an audience) on Thursday on the Memorial from Liverpool, complaining of the evasion of our foreign enlistment law, & I shall read an authoritative contradiction, by the U.S. Secretary of the Navy, of the statement made by Mr. Laird that the Federal government had authorised an application to be made to his house for the supply of war ships.

This is an opportunity which in the interest of future harmony between the two countries should be seized by the Government for offering some observations in a more conciliatory spirit than the utterances which fell from leading members of the House in March, which utterances led to the visit of Mr. Evarts to England & have sunk deep in the memory of the Americans.

It is too late to avert the mischief arising from the fitting out of Confederate cruisers in our ports. If you look at the amount of injury which they are inflicting on American commerce you may judge of the effect on the practical mind of that people. *The neutrality code is henceforth, so far as we may require its benefits, a dead letter.* It will only be felt when we become belligerents what a suicidal game we have been playing. But there is a far graver question involved in the iron-clad vessels of war now being built for the Confederate government. Without exception every American I see says if they go to sea & commence hostilities against the Federals, we shall have war at once. *Now* is the time for those whose voice can be heard to use their influence upon public opinion to put down this attempt to evade the law. If public opinion be not on the side of legality it is in vain to think of Acts of Parliament. It is in defence of the law—

the spirit as well as letter—that the Government should be heard before Parliament separates—as well as in denunciation of those individuals who by legal stratagem seek to compromise the interests of a nation.

Ever yours
R. COBDEN.

210   *Palmerston to Gladstone*

94 Piccadilly
12 August 1863

The Queen wishes me to settle which of Her Ministers are to be in attendance upon Her at Balmoral on her Return from Germany. Russell who is in Scotland will take the first Fortnight and I would propose to you and George Grey to take the second and third Fortnight in such order of Precedence as may best suit your mutual Conveniences —If you are not likely to be prevented by any other unavoidable Engagement I know the Queen would wish you to take your Turn, as you have not yet done Suit & Service at Balmoral. Communicate with George Grey and let me know the Result.

211   *Gladstone to Palmerston*

Private.

Balmoral
Oct. 8. 63.

It was settled on Tuesday that the Queen was to go to Aberdeen on Friday to attend the inauguration, as it is termed, of the Statue of the Prince, and to receive a County and City Address.

Last evening however, at dinner time, she had not returned home from a rather long expedition to a glen beyond Loch Muich, and at about half past nine we learned that together with the Princesses Louis of Hesse and Helena she had been overset in her sociable, and thrown out of the carriage upon the road, not a very hard one. The Princesses were not in any way injured. The Queen received a contusion on the temple, and sprained a thumb. She did not sleep very well. This morning she is up and in good spirits, and persists in her intention to go to Aberdeen : and indeed there will be much uneasiness, and a good deal of inconvenience, if she does not go. But Dr. Jenner is not well satisfied that she should. He considers the *tone* of her health low, though better than it was, and observes that persons in such a condition are more liable than others to an attack for example of erysipelas as the result of such a blow.

The matter is to be further considered this afternoon, and Dr. J. talks of sending for Mr. Syme from Edinburgh to give his sanction or withhold it, if it should appear desirable to take that measure.

On Tuesday evening when I received the notice of the Cabinet I immediately informed the Queen and added that I conjectured we were to meet on account of the Ironclads at Birkenhead—that I could not help regarding the question, according to my limited lights upon it, as a very thorny one indeed—and that I had no doubt we should all use our best endeavours to agree together upon a satisfactory course. She said in a very friendly manner that she hoped nothing would occur in regard to it of a nature to endanger the Government.

She did not appear to lean towards over-conciliation of the Federal Government.

She continues to be extremely anxious about the Schleswig Holstein question : and as far as I can gather, the special idea of it which she has is this, that gross injustice is done to the people especially of Schleswig in altering the terms of their succession and their relation to Denmark and to Holstein against their will or without their consent.

The Queen rode home on her pony last night from the place of the accident. It seems very undesirable that she should drive after dark in a country like this.

I write in haste for the Messenger at noon as I wished to give you the latest account and the clock is now near striking.

212   *Palmerston to Gladstone*

94 P[iccadill]ʸ. 9 Oct 63

On my arrival in London to-day to wait upon the King of Greece I received your Letter of yesterday. I am very sorry to hear of the Queens Accident, but I hope & trust it may have no serious Consequences. I shall however be anxious to get further accounts—The Aberdeen Ceremony, if she attended it today will have been a trying Exertion.

I conclude that the Cabinet on Tuesday will be mainly about the Mersey Iron Clads.[1] The History of their Birth and Parentage is curious and intricate. They were ordered for the Confederates and transferred after a Time by what is believed to have been a fictitious Transaction to Bravay. He offered them to the present Pasha of Egypt asserting that he had bespoke them by verbal orders of the late Pasha, or rather that having in Compliance with such verbal order applied to Laird for Two such Ships immediately, and Laird having said it would take a long time to build such, an arrangement was made by which Bravay bought them of the Confederate agent.

Then the Pasha refused them & referred Bravay to the Sultan, & the Sultan sent orders to buy them. In the mean Time I had suggested to Somerset to buy them for our Navy, or if not fit for that to sell them again to the Sultan, but when Somerset applied, he was told by Laird that they were not to be sold ; and a suspicious Circumstance is, that just before one of them was to make a Trial Trip which however has not been made, a Party of sailors from a Confederate Ship in a French Port arrived at Liverpool,

---

[1] Known as " the Laird rams ".

as if to carry her off, in spite of Laird's written assurance that she should only be used in the usual way and would be returned into Dock—Somerset did not trust to this assurance and ordered a Naval Detachment to go in her for her trial and thereupon it was discovered that her Engines could be tried in Dock as well as on the proposed Trip.

They are both provisionally detained, and as they are iron plated and furnished with projecting Beaks to act as Rams there can be no doubt that they are destined for Warlike Purposes—There can moreover be no moral Doubt that they are intended for Confederate Service, but we shall hear on Tuesday whether there is any such Proof of their intended Destination as would bear us out under the Act in seizing them.

213   *Gladstone to Palmerston*

Edinburgh.
Oct. 12. 63.

Many thanks for your letter. At the moment when I left Balmoral on Friday in great haste, I arranged with General Grey that he should by telegraph refer it to you to consider whether Sir G. Grey should come to Aberdeen for the ceremonial of tomorrow, or whether you would arrange with some other Minister to attend it.

I could not prevail on myself to offer to go back, at the cost of being absent from the Cabinet.

I saw the Queen before coming away. She declared herself quite well. She rowed me good-humouredly for writing to you about the accident. I will describe to you, when we meet, exactly what took place.

I have another word to say, from H.M., which I should like to tell you before the Cabinet, if you will send word to me to come either to Cambridge House, or to your official room in D. St. just before the meeting.

214   *Gladstone to Palmerston*

Hawarden
Nov. 8. 63.

I have learned to-day, from head quarters, that Dr. Stanley is to be Dean of Westminster. This being so, you will have to fill his Professorship : and as the turn of mind, and the kind of knowledge, which it requires, are not very common gifts, I make no scruples of submitting for your consideration the names of two of my constituents, whom I know to be eminently qualified to discharge its duties with honour and advantage.

One of them is the Rev. James Mozley (brother of the well known writer in the Times, but a person of pursuits wholly clerical) of Shoreham. Mr. Mozley is well known by his theological works : I may add that he wrote in defence of the famous ' Gorham Judgment ' and he has a marked capacity for questions of history.

The other is the Rev. Richard Church, Rector of Whatley—Somerset. I can speak of his character and his capacity for this particular office in the highest terms. He has given a sample of them to the world in the shape of a volume of Essays displaying remarkable ability. I rather think (but I do not take time to verify my recollection by inquiry) I have heard Dr. Stanley speak of him in very high terms. But both these gentlemen are men of real mark and force, and such as ought to be put when occasion offers into teaching offices of the nature of that now vacant.

I see my last sentence is a little peremptory : what I mean is they are too strong for their present places, and would do credit to the one vacant.

215   *Gladstone to Palmerston*

Early   D[owning] St[reet].
                    12 Nov. 1863.

Having troubled you by reference to more names than one with a view to the Chair at Oxford, I am anxious (so far as depends on me) to simplify the matter by saying that after having received very many letters, and seen many excellent witnesses, of divers colours, I am convinced that with a view

1. to presumable efficiency,

2. to general satisfaction, in the first place Mr. Lake is not the man, and that his claims on the Government should be met in some other way : 2 that Mr. Church is preferable to all other candidates. I believe he has not himself lifted a finger in the matter : but among the last witnesses to him stands Mr. Montagu Bernard, Sec. to the Public Schools Commission, a man of the highest ability and authority.

216   *Gladstone to Palmerston*

Private.   C[arlton] H[ouse] Terrace
                                    Nov. 20. 63.

You asked yesterday in Cabinet about the Revenue.

I have an account and Estimate from the Departments : up to the 30 of September as account, and as estimate for the six months to follow.

The *new* Estimate of Revenue exceeds the *April* Estimate by £1,261,000
The Estimate of Expenditure falls below
           the April Estimate by . . 230,000
                                                  ─────────
                                                  1,491,000
My Estimated Surplus was . . 473,000
                                                  ─────────

Thus the probable Surplus will stand at £1,964,000

This Surplus will create a great *expectation of* reduction of taxes.

But if we look onwards to the coming year, nearly a million of its revenue is already disposed of by that part of the remissions of the present year which does not take full effect within the year.

Nor can I expect an Excise Revenue for 64-65 equal to that of the present year, which, as I explained yesterday, will in the article of Malt duty exhibit a portion of the revenue of *two* years.

If our expenditure were to remain stationary, I could not make sure even of reducing the Sugar Duties. But with a moderate reduction, such as I trust we shall have, of a million on the Estimates (which would leave our Estimates for Army and Navy at twenty four millions and three quarters) we should be sure of the Sugar Duties : and if things went well in the interim we might do something more.

Brand mentioned to you a sketch which I made for him containing a programme of financial possibilities with some reference to the great event of next year but one. With that sketch what I have here stated would fall in.

217   *Palmerston to Gladstone*

94 P[iccadill]ʸ. 21 Novʳ 1863

Your Statement of the Condition of our Finance is very satisfactory, and proves that your Estimates last year were formed on the safe Side, which is a great Merit—I should be very glad to find that we could save on Army and Navy for next year the Sum you mention, but the present Aspect of Things in America in Europe in Asia is very discouraging as to the Prudence of making any material Reduction in our Naval or Military Forces and I suspect that there is not much left to be cut off from Stores and Things of that Kind. We have no Doubt spent a great Deal, of late years in Military and Naval Defence ; but not more than other Nations whose Preparations might bear an offensive as well as a defensive character ; and it may fairly be said that we have got our Money's worth in present Freedom from Molestation, and in probable Security for the Future.

I think the Nation understands this Matter, and would not be well pleased with any material Diminution of our defensive means even though accompanied by some Diminution of Burthens. Clap Trap Reductions are sure to be followed by a Recoil of public opinion, and by a necessity for increased Expenditure. These Matters however should be well considered—as to Brand's Notion of what might be done on the Eve of a Dissolution, that Scheme is a very natural one for the Secretary to the Treasury who has to attend to Elections, but it may be doubted whether Such a *Coup de Finance* would answer as well as Napoleon's *Coup d'État*.

I wish you the Joy of the avalanche of *Irish Eloquence* with which John of Tuam has tried to overwhelm you.

218   *Gladstone to Palmerston*

Carlton H[ouse] Terrace
Nov. 24. 63.

With reference to my letter on Expenditure and Estimates, I would further say that, on account of the uncertain aspect of Foreign questions at some points, it seems to me desirable to postpone any actual decision on the amount of force for 1864–5 until the time when it will become necessary to fix it with a view to the Session. But I confess I do not see how, except in the time of war, or near danger of it, we could be justified in asking for a vote of 75,000 seamen when we have a reserve which exceeds 15,000, and which may at any time I believe be raised to above 20,000.

219   *Palmerston to Gladstone*

94 P[iccadill]y. 26 Novr. 1863

Here is a Letter from Phipps about the Gun Metal required for the Prince Consort's Memorial. The Demand is large, in as much as the value of the Brass Guns is £100 a Ton. 71 Ton would therefore £7100. The H^e of C^{ns} might probably agree to allot Gun Metal to that amount of value for the Memorial considering that they would not be voting the application of any Part of the sum raised by Taxation within the Year, but simply sanctioning the application of so much Material now lying profitless in the public Stores. The vote if proposed would I apprehend be Part of the Civil Service Estimates.

There seems to arise a Question connected with this and that is whether there is not at Woolwich and elsewhere a large Quantity of Things which are of no possible use to the Service and which might realize some amount worth having if they were sold—I cautioned Scott last Summer not to exceed the sum available for his Work, but I fear he is an incorrigible Encroacher and thinks of nothing but what he calls his own Fame as an architect.

220   *Gladstone to Palmerston*

11, Downing Street,
Whitehall.
Nov. 27. 63.

I return your inclosures relating to the Bronze in the Prince's Monument.

I think we have much reason to complain of Mr. Scott who seems to have treated your representations and injunctions as so much waste paper, or waste vapour.

I do not however look on this as a Chancellor of the Exchequer's question—the sum is of no great significance—the real point lies between the gratification of the Queen's desire (if it really is hers—I would not give 1 /- to Mr. Scott, after the warning he has had, on the ground of his fame) on the one side, and the risk that the House of Commons will take the matter ill on the other. It might pass in silence or with approval : but I confess I think that if complaint did arise, it would not be easily got rid of.

I should strongly recommend mentioning the matter in Cabinet.

As to your second suggestion, with respect to old stores generally, it seems to me a very valuable one both for arsenals and for dockyards and if you would move the Duke of Somerset and Lord de Grey the question would be started in the best manner. *Next* best will be, if I do it under your authority and sanction.

(Enclosures)

Private.

Windsor Castle,
Novr. 24. 1863.

MY DEAR LORD PALMERSTON,

Immediately after seeing you at Windsor I wrote to Mr. Scott desiring him to send me an account of the quantity of Bronze that might be required for the National Memorial to the Prince Consort under three conditions.

1st. The quantity that he would consider it desirable to have, if all the works were executed in Bronze which might be advisable both for the perfection of the Structure and for the purpose of economising in other material.

2ndly. The quantity that he would desire to have for the perfection of the design only.

And 3rdly. The least quantity with which the design could be carried out, as originally approved by the Queen.

I enclose you his Answer.

Believe me, faithfully yours,
C. B. PHIPPS.

20, Spring Gardens,
November 23rd 1863.

MY DEAR SIR,

I have had careful calculations made by an experienced practical founder who is accustomed to casting bronze

SP

statues etc., of the quantity of metal which would be required for all the figures in my design for the National Memorial to the Prince Consort. I had some time back by Lord Palmerston's request written to him on the same subject. The quantity I then made it amount to was one hundred tons. That now arrived at is somewhat greater: I suppose from the circumstance of the founder having now had the small models to help his calculations.

The amounts are as follows,

	Tons.	cwt.	
The four Great Groups at the outer angles of steps	34	0	0
The four smaller groups at the angles of the Monument itself	22	8	0
The Bas relief round the Podium	26	0	0
The Principal Figure	4	12	0
Eight single figures round the lower part of the Monut. ..	10	0	0
Four large figures above ..	7	0	0
Twelve smaller ones	12	0	0
Total	116	0	0

The above, as you will see, is for Sculpture *alone*. We shall, however, need a certain quantity for architectural purposes. That for foliage to be attached to Granite cornices and capitals seems to amount to about 14 tons while there would probably be about an equal quantity needed for the decorations of the tabernacle work and roofs above.

The above quantities, taken together, will furnish my reply to your first question. The others are less readily answered. The means of getting at the replies to these is, I suppose, to consider what portions of the above work *could* be advantageously, or without serious detriment, executed in other materials.

I am not, as a matter of taste, very favourable to the use

of Bronze for the Relief round the Podium. I think its dark colour would be unfavourable in its effect for that part ; and that, if white marble is hardly to be considered trustworthy, some very fine and durable description of stone would look better than Bronze. The only saving beyond this would be by using the electro-deposits for the figures in the tabernacle work above. This would reduce the metal wanted for *Sculpture proper* to the following items :

		Tons	
The four great groups	.. ..	34	
The four smaller groups	.. ..	22	8
The Principal figure	.. ..	4	12
The eight single figures round the Monument itself	.. .. ..	10	
		71	

To this, however, should be added a certain quantity for Architectural purposes ; still leaving a result of about 100 tons. I would, therefore, state the three quantities at : 71 tons as the lowest, 100 tons as the next, and 144 tons as the greatest ; and would recommend that the amount applied for should not fall short of the medium quantity, while something between that and the highest—or

(Total)   (Relief)   Tons
144   —   26   =   118   is that which is
desirable.

                I have the honour to be
                    My dear Sir
                        Your very faithful Servant
                            GEO : GILBERT SCOTT

To Colonel
    The Hono¹
        Sir Charles B. Phipps, K.C.B.

221　　　　　*Palmerston to Russell*

94 Piccadilly. 4 Dec. /63

MY DEAR RUSSELL

I will talk to Gladstone about what you propose as to Cobden. Gladstone mentioned to me more than a year ago the wish of Cobden's friends that a Parliamentary Pension might be obtained for him, as he was very poor, having sadly mismanaged his own affairs, just as he would, if he could, the affairs of the nation. Gladstone felt at that time that it was too soon to make any such proposal, because the fruits of the French Treaty were not then ripe ; and I therefore offered Cobden his choice of being made a Privy Councillor or a Baronet. But in the true spirit of a Republican Radical he refused any Honour that was to come from that hated Being, a Sovereign ; and so the matter rested. I daresay he would gladly accept a House of Commons Pension, and I for my part should have no objection to propose it to Parliament, if the Cabinet should think fit. Cobden had certainly great merit in the conception of the Treaty, and in working it out ; and the Treaty has no doubt proved advantageous to both countries. Nothing can be worse, with the single exception of Bright, than the line which Cobden has taken and the language he has held both in and out of Parliament during the last two years, and he has set against him the vast majority of honest men in the country ; and many men in the House of Commons would find it very difficult to vote him anything but a censure. Still his merits and services about the Treaty are a matter quite separate from and independent of his political conduct, but there are still a certain number of men, though not a large one, in the House of Commons who consider the French Treaty as an evil.

The Proposal certainly could not with any justice be represented as springing from Party Favour, for with the

exception of Bright and Disraeli we have not a bitterer
enemy than Cobden on any bench in the House of Commons.

222   *Palmerston to Gladstone*

Broadlands
21 Decr. 1863

I send you some Papers which I have received from
Sir W^m. Gibson Craig about the proposed Junction of
the Botanical and Horticultural Gardens at Edinburgh.

I went to look at them when I was at Edinburgh last
Easter and I must say that the Proposal appeared to me
to be reasonable. The Botanical garden is far too small and
the accommodation it affords for Study is far too limited
but if the Horticultural Garden were added to it all Requirements would be Satisfied. Edinburgh as you know is a
great School for Botany and Medicine and it is unnecessary to enlarge upon the public Importance of those
Branches of Science. The Cost of a Compliance with this
Request would be moderate, and would chiefly consist in a
Payment made once for all, the after yearly charges would
be very small. The People of Edinburgh take a great
Interest in this Matter and as their wishes and Feelings
coincide with the Interests of Science they may be allowed
to be an element in the Consideration of the Matter.
Unless there is some strong Reason, of which I am not
aware, against this Proposal it would seem to me to be
one which it would be right to agree to.

223   *Palmerston to Gladstone*

94 P[iccadill]^y. 16 March 1864

I understood the Cabinet to have determined on Saturday that if the accounts to be received from New Zealand

justified a Deduction from the Sum estimated for the Extraordinary Expences of the War in that Colony, we might apply a Portion of such Saving to the calling out of the Yeomanry on permanent Duty ; and it appears that Ld. Grey can Strike off £50000 from those charges and thus fully cover the £46000 required for the permanent Duty of the Yeomanry—

I have just had a very large Deputation of Yeomanry officers of both Sides in Politics urging that we should allow them to go out. I felt that Time is of Importance for their arrangements, as their permanent Duty is most conveniently performed in the Month of May and I thought that on the Principle of *Bis dat qui cito dat* as well as in Deference to those who had come to me it was better to tell them at once the Decision of the Government rather than send them away with an evasive or dilatory answer.

I therefore told them that our Decision not to train the Yeomanry this year had been made for the Purpose of making a Saving on that Head, in order to Meet in some Degree the extraordinary Expences of the New Zealand War, and that as we have by the last Mail received accounts which justify us in striking £50000 off from the Estimate for that War we mean to apply that Saving to the Training of the Yeomanry this Year.

I have had also a monster Deputation of Paper Makers who after a long and diffuse Statement of their grievances have left the inclosed Paper with me. Their proposed Remedies are three. The Imposition of an Import Duty on Foreign Paper which they seemed to admit would under our Treaties be difficult. The Payment to them out of the public Revenue of a Sum equal to the Export Duty levied by Foreign Countries on their Rags, This they thought an excellent and easy Remedy though they observed that I smiled upon hearing it proposed ; and lastly the appointment of a Committee of the House of Commons to inquire into their Case. Upon this I gave no answer or opinion.

224   *Gladstone to Palmerston*

[Quoted in *Glad.* II. 109]

11 Carlton H[ouse] Terrace
March 27. 1864

... It would seem that Garibaldi is coming. The Duke of Sutherland had some idea of inviting him to Stafford House : I do not know whether he will act upon it. I do not know what persons in office are to do with him : but you will lead, & we shall follow suit.

225   *Gladstone to Palmerston*

11, Carlton House Terrace, S.W.
May 10. 64.

1. I think Sir C. Phipps' recollection may be in error. At any rate mine is as follows. You mentioned in the Cabinet the request for a grant of Metal in aid of the Monument. It appeared that this must be a grant of *money* ; the Cabinet thought it was not expedient to propose such a grant ; you concurred ; since then I think the Cabinet has heard no more of the matter. Doubtless they would give way in such a matter if it is insisted upon, but I think they considered it an unwise proceeding and wished to stop it accordingly. . . .

226   *Palmerston to Gladstone*

94 P[iccadill]y. 11 May 64

I hope that in what you may say upon Baines's Bill you will not commit yourself and the Government as to any particular amount of Borough Franchise—

The Six Pound Franchise may I think be considered as gone to the Bottom and *if* at any future Time our Government should have to bring in a Reform Bill which the present State of public opinion does not appear to favor, it is of great Importance that we should be free to look at the Question without any fresh Pledges—No doubt many working men are as fit to vote as many of the Ten Pounders, but if we open the Door to the Class the Number who may come in may be excessive, and may swamp the Classes above them.

This Result would arise not merely from the Number let in, but also from the Fact that the Influx discourages the Classes above them from voting at all ; and then these working men are unfortunately under the Control of Trades Unions, which unions are directed by a small Number of directing Agitators.

227   *Gladstone to Palmerston*

11 Carlton H[ouse] Terrace
11 May 1864.

Your note reached me in the House of Commons. Others will give a better account of any impression left by what I said than myself. But as to the intention and the words, while I am warmly in favour of an extension of the Borough Franchise, I hope I did not commit the Government to *any*thing : nor myself to a particular form of franchise. I stated that I wished to leave the form and figure open ; that I was for a sensible and considerable, but not excessive enlargement : and that I meant by these words such an enlargement as *we contended* would have been produced by our proposal in 1860. I underline the word contended, because while our final estimate in 1860 of the numbers to be admitted was under 200,000, I believe the opponents ascribed to our measure a different effect. I could not honestly say less than this : but I do not think I could be understood to say it for any one but myself.

I showed your letter to the two Ministers present, Grey and Gibson.

228   *Palmerston to Gladstone*

[Partly printed in *Glad.* II. 128]

94 P[iccadill]ʸ. 12 May 1864

I received yesterday your Letter in answer to mine of the Morning. I have read your speech and I must frankly say, with much regret as there is little in it that I can agree with, and much from which I differ. You lay down broadly the Doctrine of Universal Suffrage which I can never accept. I intirely deny that every sane and not disqualified man has a moral right to a vote—I use that Expression instead of " the Pale of the Constitution ", because I hold that all who enjoy the Security and civil Rights which the Constitution provides are within its Pale—What every Man and Woman too have a Right to, is to be well governed and under just Laws, and they who propose a change ought to shew that the present organization does not accomplish those objects. If every Man has a Right to have his Share in chusing those who make Laws, why should he not have a Right to express his own opinion on Laws to be made. You did not pronounce an opinion in Favor of a specified Franchise, but is there any essential Difference between naming a Six Pound Franchise, and naming the additional numbers which a Six Pound Franchise was calculated to admit. I am not going to perform the Duty which Whiteside . . . ingly assigned to me, of answering your Speech but if you will not take it amiss, I would say, that it was more like the Sort of Speech with which Bright would have introduced the Reform Bill which he would like to propose than the Sort of Speech which might have been expected from the Treasury Bench in the present State of Things. Your Speech may win Lancashire for you, though that is doubtful but I fear it will tend to lose England for you. It is to be regretted that you should, as you stated, have taken the opportunity of your receiving a Deputation of working men, to exhort them to set on Foot an Agitation for

Parliamentary Reform—The Function of a Government is to calm rather than to excite Agitation.

229   *Gladstone to Palmerston*
[Partly printed in *Glad*. II. 129]
11 C[arlton] H[ouse] T[errace].
May 13th 64.

It is not easy to take ill anything that proceeds from you : and moreover frankness between all men, and especially between those who are politically associated, removes as I believe many more difficulties than it causes. In this spirit I will endeavour to write.

I agree in your denial " That every sane and not dis-qualified man has a moral right to vote ". But I am at a loss to know how as you have read my speech you can ascribe this opinion to me. My declaration was, taken generally, that all persons ought to be admitted to the franchise, who can be admitted to it with safety. Or as I see my words quoted this morning (and I dare say the report is not far from the mark) " Every man who is not incapaci-tated by personal unfitness, or whose admission would not be attended by political danger, is morally entitled to come within the pale of the constitution ", or in other words as I meant it to the franchise. I hold by this proposition. It seemed to me neither strange nor new nor extreme. It re-quires I admit to be construed ; but I contend that the interpretation is amply given in the speech, where I have declared (for example) that the admission I desire is of the same character or rather extent as we proposed in 1860, and that if the effect of any proposal were to give the working clubs a preponderating instead of an inferior share in the borough representation, then the case would be re-versed, and that promoters of such a change might justly be called upon to shew cause against the obvious objec-tions to such a proposal.

THE FALSE START

PAM (The Starter). "Hi! Gladstone! Democracy! Too soon, Too soon! You
mustn't go yet!"

I have never exhorted the working men to agitate for the franchise, and I am at a loss to conceive what report of my speech can have been construed by you in such a sense.

Having said thus much to bring down to its true limits the difference between us, I do not deny that difference. I regret it and I should regret it much more if it were one likely to have (at least as far as I can see) an early bearing upon practice. In the Cabinet I argued as strongly as I could against the withdrawal of the bill in 1860, and in favour of taking the opinion of the House of Commons upon that bill. I think the party which supports your Government has suffered and is suffering and will much more seriously suffer from the part which as a party it has played within these recent years, in regard to the franchise. I have no desire to force the question forward. I hope no Government or (in Scotch phrase) intending Government will ever again take it up except with the full knowledge of its own mind and a reasonable probability of carrying it. But such influence as argument and statement without profession of political intentions can exercise upon the public mind, I heartily desire to see exercised in favour of an extension of the franchise, that the question may if possible be disposed of for another generation to come, while it remains manageable and before it runs the risk of becoming formidable.

I have written under more pressure for time than I could have desired : but as the matter is one of interest to the other members of the Government, I shall be glad with you concurrence that they should see this letter.

230   *Palmerston to Gladstone*

94 P[iccadill]ʸ. 13 May 64

I have marked in the accompanying Number of the Times that Part of your Speech to which I alluded as an Exhortation to the working men to agitate for Parliamentary Reform.

231   *Gladstone to Palmerston*

11 Carlton H[ouse] Terrace

My. 14. 64.

I do not see in the passages marked anything in the nature of an exhortation, or any thing which goes beyond the nature of a simple recital of what I take to be beyond doubt viz. that among the reasons for the recent inaction of Parliament respecting the franchise has been the allegation, and the belief, that the working classes themselves were indifferent about it.

Mr. Cave who preceded me in debate had taken up the strain, and contended, that ' nobody desired it '.

232   *Palmerston to Gladstone*

[Quoted in *Glad.* II. 130]

94 Piccadilly

14 May 1864

The Deputation said, according to your Speech, that they were dissatisfied with Parliament with Regard to its Conduct about the Extension of the Suffrage, and you said to them in Reply that the Conduct of Parliament in that Respect has been connected with the apparent Inaction, and alleged Indifference of the Working Classes with Respect to the Suffrage. It is quite true that you did not use words directly exhorting them to agitate but what you said seems to me to have no other meaning. The Case is shortly this, the Deputation say they want an Extention of the Suffrage, and are dissatisfied with Parliament for not taking Steps to give it them, you say in answer the Reason Parliament has done nothing about it is that you have been inactive and are therefore believed to be indifferent. The Conclusion obviously is that if they the working Classes are not indifferent about the Suffrage they ought to cast off that Inactivity which has led to their being thought to be indifferent.

I have no Doubt that you have yourself heard a great
Deal about the bad effect of your Speech but I can assure
you that I hear from many Quarters the unfortunate
Impression it has produced even upon many of the Liberal
Party and upon all Persons who value the Maintenance of
our Institutions.

233   *Palmerston to Gladstone*

94 P[iccadill]ʸ 21 May 1864

I am told that you are thinking of publishing as a Pam-
phlet with a Preface or Introduction your Speech upon
Baines's Motion and I wish to submit for your considera-
tion whether such a Course may not be attended with
Inconvenience as recording in a more formal and deliberate
Manner that which you Said on that occasion.

The Government may at some future Time have to consider the Question of changes in our representation arrangements, though I for one feel well satisfied with Things as
they are ; but if every Member of the Government were
now and before hand to pledge himself by premature
Publication to his own particular views upon a Subject
with regard to which it is well known that Differences of
opinion exist, any Thing like agreement which could only
be arrived at by Mutual Modifications would be rendered
impossible, and the Day when the Subject may be taken
up by the Government would be the Day fixed for the
Breaking up of the Administration.

234   *Gladstone to Palmerston*

11, Carlton House Terrace,
S.W.

May 21. 64.

I have endeavoured to consider carefully your suggestion : but I come to this result that I think the difficulty you
mention will be diminished and not increased by the

publication of my speech on the franchise. It is certainly in the nature of a justification of what I said ; I wish to point out to you that its more evident and its principal purpose is to get rid of the strange misconstructions of which it has been the subject. They now prevail on both sides : for after the articles in the Times, though not upon the first appearance of the speech in the papers, I have found newspapers hailing from the radical side my accession to the doctrine of manhood suffrage. I am not willing however to be bound altogether by newspaper reports, knowing as I do the tendency of all reporters, especially in the case of a speaker difficult to follow, to omit qualifications, which are sometimes in themselves material and which always affect the general colour of a speech. The applause which I do not deserve vexes me at least as much as the criticism : it seems almost a duty to give an authentic text when there is so much comment : and I am persuaded that people who read will see that what I had in view was in thorough conformity as to its spirit, without undue restriction as to the ʿorm, with the proposals of two Cabinets to which I have belonged. It seems better they should see this than that I should make no protest either by word or deed against the absurd rumours which have taken possession of the minds of many worthy men. I do not say publication will relieve me from any inconvenience which may be attendant upon repeating my adhesion to the proceedings of 1854 and 1860 : but I think it will get rid of much further inconvenience with which the case is now incumbered.

235   *Palmerston to Gladstone*

94 Piccadilly
23 May 1864

I have received your note of the 21st. You are of Course the best judge as to your own Line ; but with Reference to your proposed Declaration of Adhesion to what the

OUT OF THE RACE

GLADSTONE. " Permit me to explain—Democracy—"
PAM. " Oh, bother your explanation ! You've blown your horse, and you're out of the race."

Cabinet proposed in 1854 and 1860, I would observe that it was the low Rate of Franchise and the great Transfer of seats which produced the Failure of those Schemes of Change a Failure which I and some other Members of the Cabinet foresaw & foretold from the Beginning. The Fate of those two Proposals and the well known Fact that if Parliamentary and public opinion with regard to them have altered since, the alteration has been unfavourable to those proposed Measures, would seem to lead to the Conclusion that any Man or any Government who really desired to pass a Reform Measure would abstain from presenting to Parliament a third Time an arrangement which had been so decidedly objected to upon two former occasions. If that is so, can it be useful to any political Man to tie himself by an uncalled for Pledge to a Scheme which in all human Probability he would never be able to carry into Effect.

236   *Gladstone to Palmerston*

11 Carlton H[ouse] Terrace

May 23. 64.

My meaning was this. The Speech cannot I admit be taken for less than a declaration that, when a favourable state of opinion and circumstances shall arise, the working class ought to be enfranchised to some such extent as was contemplated in the Bill of 1860. But it has been, and is, taken to mean much more.

This accretion it seems to me material to get rid of : first for the sake of truth, secondly, to narrow, not to widen, any apparent difference between others and myself.

My speech has been talked into importance : and will be quoted : it is desirable I think that this should not be from a text loosely and roughly framed.

In any words I may prefix, I shall derive benefit from what you have written, and will bear it in mind.

237   *Palmerston to Gladstone*

94 P^y. 16 June 1864

Brand has just read to me the Note he wrote to you about your proposed answer to the York address and he has in that note stated shortly the Substance of my observations to him yesterday Morning—

My view of the general Matter is, that a Member of the Government when he takes office necessarily divests himself of that perfect Freedom of individual action which belongs to a private and independent Member of Parliament and the Reason is this, that what a Member of the Government does and says upon public Matters must to a certain Degree commit his colleagues, and the Body to which he belongs if they by their Silence appear to acquiesce : and if any of them follow his Example and express as publicly, opposite opinions, which in particular Cases they might feel obliged to do, Differences of opinion between Members of the same Government are unnecessarily brought out into Prominence and the Strength of the Government is thereby impaired.

Upon a similar Principle it is undesirable that a Member of the Government should advise the House of Commons to object to, or try to reduce Estimates which the Government have proposed ; or that he should Endeavour to excite Agitation out of Doors for the Purpose of forcing upon the Government, Measures which the Parliament may not be disposed to adopt, & which the Government upon a Review of the State of Things, may not think it advisable to propose.

238   *Gladstone to Palmerston*

11 C[arlton] H[ouse] T[errace].

June 17.

Before receiving your letter, I had with pleasure complied with the wish you expressed to me through Brand, that the latter part of the draft which I had prepared by way of answer to the York working men, should be omitted.

My desire was simply to frame that answer so as to discourage a repetition of like addresses elsewhere, and I was very glad and thankful for your advice in doing it.

In your letter however, you state that " it is undesirable that a member of the Government should advise the House of Commons to object to, or try to reduce estimates which the Government have proposed ". I confess myself at a loss to understand your introduction of this subject unless it is intended to convey your opinion that I have done the thing, which you described as undesirable.

I do not in the least degree complain of your expressing that opinion if you entertain it. But I should deceive you if I allowed you to remain under the impression that I acquiesced in its justice. I have gone great lengths in the matter of expenditure to meet your views and those of others : and while studiously avoiding either direct or indirect manifestations of difference, have contented myself with pointing to future retrenchment. If such a course is unadvisable in your judgement, I only wish I could better meet your views, but I cannot reproach myself with want of effort to do it. Nay more I can give no pledge of indefinitely prolonged acquiescence in the present scale of expenditure.

It is unnecessary to say more, but with the expressions in your letter before me, it would scarcely have been honest to say less.

239   *Palmerston to Gladstone*

[Quoted in *Glad.* II. 119]

94 P[iccadill]y. 28 June 1864

They have had their Meeting and have agreed upon a vote of Censure[1] to be proposed probably on Thursday— We shall want a great Gun to reply to Disraeli. Would you be ready to follow him? . . .

[1] On the Government's Schleswig-Holstein policy.

Tp

240   *Palmerston to Gladstone*

29 June 64

If you have not taken the Trouble to look at the blue Book about the Danish Negotiations in 1851–52 which was laid on Table at the Beginning of the Session it would be worth your while to do so.

241   *Palmerston to Gladstone*

94 P[iccadill]ʸ. 3 July 64

It would be well not to be too hard upon the Danes. It is true that they were wrong in the Beginning and have been wrong in the End, but they have been most unjustly used by the Germans and the sympathies in the Majority of the House and in the Nation are Danish.

242   *Palmerston to Gladstone*

94 Piccadilly 6 July 1864

What is your opinion upon the Matter to which this Letter from Phipps relates. It would seem that there would be no more Reason for pulling down Claremont than for demolishing and alloting for Villas any other Palace and Park belonging to the Crown and Claremont might be useful as a Residence for some Member of the Royal Family, Prince Alfred for Instance when he is older and has left the Navy. The matter does not press in Point of Time, because King Leopold has at present no Intention of bringing the Question to a practical Issue by the Extinction of the surviving Holders of the Property.

243   *Palmerston to Gladstone*

94 P[iccadill]ʸ. 15 July 64

It may be from unacquaintance with the Details of these Matters, but I do not understand the Distinction which is

drawn between Houses and Palaces which formed Part of
the Crown Domains before the Transfer of those Domains
to the Public in Exchange for the Civil List, and Claremont
which it seems was bought out of Land Revenue Capital,
and is on the Termination of the present Interest in it, to
become Part of the Crown Property. Are not the Houses
and Palaces mentioned by me Part of that Crown Property
which was given during this Reign, in Exchange for the
Civil List, and why should Claremont when it becomes
Part of the Crown Land Property be dealt with in a
Manner different from that in which those other Houses
and Palaces, forming equally Parts of the Crown Property
are dealt with and if Hampton Court & Bushy Lodge and
the others are not pulled down in order to sell the Sites or
to let them on Building Leases, why should a different
System of Treatment be applied to Claremont ?

244   *Gladstone to Palmerston*

Balmoral

Oct. 3. 64.

. . . 2. A man named Galt [1] has recently written a book, in
which he recommends the purchase of the Railways by the
State, with a view not to State Management but to a large
reduction of charges and an *approach* to uniformity in the
rates throughout the country, on principles partially
approximating to those of the Post Office Reform. Roebuck
has taken up this matter with great enthusiasm ; and
writes to me proposing to move for a Committee at the
commencement of the Session, and asking the support of
the Government. I have not given him any binding reply,
but have promised him one at a future date. I am by no
means sure that the question does not contain materials
for a very great and fruitful measure, and indeed I have for
some time been considering whether a good arrangement
might not be made with respect to the taxes on locomotion

[1] Sir A. T. Galt, M.P.

(including the Railway tax) which might secure a reversion of the Railways to the state. . . . On this, and matter akin to it, I will shortly write again : at present I only mention the particular subject on account of its magnitude, as one offering a promise of good, but requiring much care and caution.

245   *Gladstone to Palmerston*

Balmoral
Oct. 6. 64.

In my last letter I glanced at the probability that next Session, as the last one of a long-lived Parliament, would be distinguished by considerable vivacity on the part of independent members with regard to taxation and expenditure. It is possible that next week, when I have several public engagements to discharge in Lancashire, I may see some indications of the state of feeling on these subjects. In anything I may have to say, I shall endeavour to observe caution. But as among ourselves, this seems to be the proper time, before the Estimates are framed, for considering our position. Whatever the Session may do, the Election, which must come next year, is pretty sure to lead to the overhauling of the entire subject, both by independent supporters, and not less (I think) by a large part at least of the Opposition.

The question of taxation need not now be particularly touched : but there are two points of view from which I will take a summary view of our Expenditure. Neither of them, it may be said, is the really essential one : still it cannot be questioned that they are important, and possibly they may tend to assimilate the views of those who might not precisely concur as to the absolute needs of the public service.

One of them is the state of our Expenditure now, as compared with what it was under the Derby Government of 1858-9. The other is the movement of our Expenditure since the China war, and since the Vote of the House of Commons for retrenchment in the Session of 1862.

With regard, however, to that portion of the public charge which is for civil purposes, it may be briefly dealt with, and then put aside. It may be shown that, on the whole, we have succeeded in arresting the upward growth which, until you came into power in 1859, had been for a long series of years both rapid and pretty constant : which was no doubt in great part justified by the real exigencies of the country, but which was felt to be reaching an inconvenient height, and to admit the operation of the pruning knife. In one very important point, the economy effected has been accompanied with a great and salutary reform, I mean the Administration of the Vote for Education in Great Britain. I am far from thinking that all, which is desirable and practicable, has been effected : but it is something to say that we have checked what was almost an inveterate tendency to rapid expansion of charge, without the smallest decline (but the contrary) in the efficiency of the expenditure : and further, for the present year in particular, that the three heads of miscellaneous estimates, Revenue Departments, and packet Service, taken conjointly, for which last year we voted £13,476,000, have this year only required us to vote £13,190,000. There is probably no very broad ground of attack in connection with this part of the Expenditure of the country.

Now in turning to the Military and Naval charges, I should observe that I include the outlay on Fortifications as a portion of the aggregate. Some attempt was made, in the Act of 1860, to separate this from the regular annual expenditure : but by law it appears, four times a year, in the balance sheet of the country, though as a distinct item, apart from the rest ; and I accordingly take it into view. I may add my opinion, that when the works provided for in 1860 shall have been completed, Parliament will require any further works which may be contemplated, to be put upon the annual Votes : unless some great change in opinion or in circumstances shall have occurred in the interval. Although it may be said that the charge is not a permanent one, yet on the other hand it must, even for the works already sanctioned above, continue for several years. To prevent however any confusion I may mention that the sums issued last year under this head amounted to £800,000. The same amount is taken for 1864–5.

I suppose that members of Opposition will incline to hold that the Expenditure of 1858 is the only one for which their Government is responsible. The Estimates of 1859 were, I think, prepared by them : but, perhaps, they would say, augmented by us. The Expenditure, however, for Military and Naval purposes, as it now stands, is I apprehend greater than that of *either* of the years I have named.

I will now look more particularly at the movement downwards, which has occurred since 1860 and 1861.

In 1860–1, the Naval and Military charge of the country was £30,330,000. If we deduct four millions of this sum for the China War, we have remaining £26,330,000. Now the Naval and Military charge of 1863–4 was £26,345,000 and that *voted* for 1864–5 is £26,352,000. Notwithstanding however the apparent approach to equality among these figures, there has been a reduction in the Expenditure, of which the precise amount may be open to dispute. First of all, there is the unquestionable item of a large amount of charge for India which is now borne upon the Estimates, and covered by repayments to the Exchequer, over and above what was so borne in 1860–1. This could be ascertained with precision : we may take it at £900,000. We may next claim some allowance for the War in New Zealand : I cannot give the extra charge there exactly, but perhaps we might put it at half a million. Thirdly, the expenditure under the Fortifications Act, which was no more than £50,000 in 1860–1, was £800,000 in 1863–4, and stands at a similar amount in the estimate of charge for 1864–5 ;

showing a difference of three-quarters of a million. The deduction of this difference might be contested. But if it were conceded, and conceded in full, then the total diminution in our charge for Defence since 1860–1 would stand at something beyond two millions. And the period, with which we compare, was one when all the operations of reconstruction, rearmament, and sanitary improvements, were at their height ; and when there was a wide spread belief in imminent danger from France, which disposed Parliament to an extraordinary freedom in defensive expenditure.

It may be asked, first, whether the statement I have given is fair, and secondly whether, with reference to the present and coming state of things, it is altogether satisfactory. As to details, it is subject to correction ; but in the main I believe it to be fair as a comparison, and perhaps even something more than fair. Can we however say it is wholly satisfactory, in the view either of party or of national interests ? Can we maintain that a sum, approaching to twenty-six millions and a half, if we include the Fortifications, and exceeding twenty-five millions and a half, if we exclude them, is really necessary to maintain the peace establishments of this country in a state of efficiency ? On the whole, I am persuaded, this is the form in which the question will be put to the nation next year. If we plead, and plead with truth, that some portions of our expenses are temporary, it will be answered with equal truth, that various postponed charges are hanging over our heads, that no one can answer for our having arrived at the end of our series of reconstructions and that the tendency of the time is to heighten the value of labour and thus in various branches to raise the scale of charge. On the whole therefore I think the question will be, whether the present standard can be defended as a fair and reasonable one for our peace expenditure on defences. I confess that I think necessity does not exact so large an outlay.

It may be well, however, to consider how the question stands with reference to the Resolution of the House of Commons in 1862. That Resolution was followed by an ostensible reduction of two millions in the Estimates for the year immediately succeeding. And in the careful Speech which you made in moving the Resolution, I think you deprecated the idea of rapid and sweeping action, but indicated a course of gradual retrenchment as the interests and circumstances of the country might permit. The reduction however of two millions, which came there and then, appears to have been, if I comprehend the case aright, about the whole reduction effected up to the present time, since we were at the high water mark of 1860.

I need hardly say the purpose of this letter is to place before you, and to obtain your favourable and timely consideration for, the necessity (such it seems to me) of our resuming the process begun in the Estimates of 1863-4, and operating again on the total figures of the Estimates. I will not attempt to point out reductions in detail. My opinions upon such a subject are of little value. The proceedings of last winter were disappointing : the small reduction in the Estimates, which was chiefly valuable as a pledge for the future, seems to have disappeared. The coming season is likely to be one of a more critical character as regards the whole subject. I feel that, for the totals of these Defence Estimates, I have, next to, or together with, you and the heads of the particular Departments, a special responsibility. And the state of public opinion, especially the inclination of the public mind with respect to foreign policy, appears to me to concur with the general interests of the nation, and the narrower but equally clear interests of the Government and its party, in requiring a diminution of our Military and Naval expenditure.

I have not made known my intention of writing this letter to any of our Colleagues.

246   *Gladstone to Palmerston*

Worsley Hall.
Oct. 16. 64.

Let me correct an error in my letter of the 16 :

The *retrenchment* of Defence Expenditure was I think rightly stated : but in reckoning the *absolute* amount I inadvertently omitted to deduct the million (in round numbers) paid by the War Department on Indian account. I should not because of this error wish to alter any part of the context : but I was desirous on its happening to occur to my mind that it should not escape your attention.

247   *Palmerston to Gladstone*

Broadlands 19 Oct 1864

I duly received you Letter of the 6th. but I have delayed answering it till you had finished your severe but successful Labour in Lancashire. I agree with you that we must before Parliament meets, consider well the Subjects to which your Letter relates but I am not able to concur in the Conclusions to which your Statements seem to lead.

It is likely that, as you say, the next Session being generally understood to be the last before a Dissolution, we shall have a certain Number, of what I should call, Clap Trap Motions, of various kinds made by men who will imagine by such means to serve their personal Interests with the Constituents they represent, and no Doubt Economy & Retrenchment will figure away among the Number. Now as you very justly say, no great Diminution of our annual Expenditure can be made except by a considerable Reduction of army and Navy ; and I think that any Body who looks carefully at the Signs of the Times Must see that there are at present two strong Feelings in the National Mind, the one a Disinclination to organic Changes in our representative System ; the other a steady Determination that the Country shall be placed and kept in an efficient Condition of Defence.

The first of these Feelings is shown by the Fact that in Spite of many Endeavours made in the Course of the Year to get up agitation for Parliamentary Reform, the Nation has not stirred and the various appeals made have produced very little Effect even upon the Classes on whose Behalf they were made, and have been disapproved by others— The second opinion is shewn by the Readiness with which the House of Commons has voted the great Bulk of the Army & Navy Estimates, with the full approval of the Nation at large ; but above all by the zealous and persevering Devotion of Time and Money by 170,000 Men of all Classes, and in every Part of this Island, who have formed themselves into Volunteer Corps, for the Purpose of obtaining Instruction in Military Discipline, in order to be ready to take part if needed in the Defence of the Country— The Motives which impel this Mass of Men cannot be mistaken. They are not as vain and childish seeking for amusement ; they are not a mere Fancy for a Military Dress ; the Motives which influence these Men from John o'Groats House to the Land's End, are a deeply rooted Conviction that in the present State of the World, Events may at any Time happen, which would expose this Country to Danger ; together with a strong opinion that our Naval & Military Establishments, though as efficient and large, as in Time of Peace, it would suit the Finances of the Country to make them, are nevertheless insufficient of themselves to repel and avert those sudden Dangers to which we might be exposed. It seems to me that this Conclusion is as demonstrable as any Proposition in Euclid.

But you say that in your opinion our Military and Naval Establishments are too large and too costly ; and you give two Reasons for that opinion. First that those Establishments cost more now, than they did in 1858–59 ; and secondly that you think twenty five million and a half, too large a Sum for the yearly Cost of our Peace Establishment of Army and Navy.

Now with Regard to your first Reason namely, that the aggregate Charge was less in 1858–59 than it is now, I would observe that that is the Statement of an historical Fact, but is not a political argument. In order to prove that the Establishments of the present year are too great, merely because they happen to be greater than those of some given former Year, it is necessary to shew, first, that the Establishments of that year were fully sufficient for all the Risks and Chances of that Time, which is a retrospective Proof very difficult to make out ; and secondly that all the Circumstances of the present Year with Reference to which, Naval and Military Establishments require to be fixed, are identically the same as those of the former Year, which is to be taken as a Standard ; and this, is as I conceive from the very Nature of Things, impossible.

Such a Mode of arguing, if argument it can be called, has no Limit in its application. Why stop at 1858–59? Why not go back to 1835 ? or as old Joseph Hume used to do to 1792 ? The only rational, and statesmanlike way of dealing with these Matters, is to look carefully at the Posture of affairs in the World at the present Time, to calculate possible Dangers great & small, to which our widely extended Interests at Home and abroad may be exposed ; to reckon up the amount of Force, which those various Interests and the Services connected with them may seem to require, and then to fix accordingly, our Naval and Military Establishments for the year, leaving the Past out of the Comparison, and the Future to take Care of itself

With Regard to your Second observation that 25½ Million is too large an annual Cost for our Peace Establishments, I would ask what is the necessary and inherent Connexion between any arithmetical Sum, and the wants of the various Services of a great Nation ? What abstract Fitness is there in any arithmetical Number to represent the yearly cost of the Establishments of a great Country either in Peace or in War ? The arbitrary assertion that $25\frac{1}{2}$ Millions are too much, might just as easily be applied to any other Sum which might be substituted for it, and we come back to the Fallacy of Joseph Hume who always maintained that the Financial Concerns of a Nation were similar in their nature to those of a private Individual, whose Income being a fixed & definite Sum, his Expenditure ought to be regulated by it : whereas in Fact the Cases are just opposite to each other, and with Regard to a Nation the proper and necessary yearly Expenditure is the fixed Sum, and the Income ought to be adapted to meet that Expenditure.

Now I will frankly own, that in the present State of Things in the various Parts of the world, I do not see our way to any National Reduction of Army or Navy—

With Regard to the Army, it is possible though I am not able to give an opinion about it without sufficient Information, but it is possible that the Termination of the War in New Zealand and some Diminution in the amount of Force in India, if it is true that Sir John Lawrence thinks that Force might be safely diminished would give us some Reduction in the amount of our army, though it seems to me that our Home Garrison is not larger than it ought to be. With Regard to the Navy the Duke of Somerset will tell us how we stand as to the Number of Men, but in the uncertain State of our future Relations with the Federal Government of North America, as well as with Reference to various Circumstances in other Parts of the world, I greatly doubt the Prudence of any Material Reduction.

With Regard however to both army and Navy it ought to be borne in mind that the Inventions of Science and the Progress of Improvement have much increased those

Branches of Expenditure which do not consist of Pay and Food & Clothing. The Comforts and general Condition of the Men in both Services have of late years been much attended to ; and though the Improvements which have been effected have caused an additional yearly outgoing, yet I believe, that by conducing to the Health of the Men, and by rendering the two Services more popular, they have been consistent with sound Policy and well understood Economy.

The Fact that as civilization advances, one Generation is not content with the arrangements which satisfied their Forefathers. Gentlemen's Houses are better and more extensively provided than was formerly the Case. Tenant Farmers are not disposed to live in the Houses which were held good enough for their Predecessors ; and the Labourers have had provided for them Habitations which would have satisfied the Smock Frock Farmer of former Times. In the same way our new Barracks are immense Improvements upon the old ones ; much to the advantage of the Soldier, but at the same Time with a certain Increase of Expence ; and I am sorry to say that I believe much remains to be done to provide healthy and sufficient accommodation for our Home Garrison even on our present Establishment, while on some of our colonial Stations many of the Barracks are extremely injurious to Health.

Then with Respect to our Navy, a total & sweeping Change is taking Place in every maritime Country as to the Construction of Ships of War, & this change is accompanied by a great Increase in the Cost of Each Ship. In former Times the Cost of a Ship fit for Sea and ready for action was reckoned at a Thousand Pounds a Gun, a Three Decker of 100 or 120 Guns would cost therefore so many Thousand pounds. Then came steam as auxiliary to Sails, and the Steam Engine & its apparatus added about Fifty Thousand to the 120—But now no large Ship of War is good for any thing unless it is armour Plated, and the arrangements connected with that last Change have I believe added nearly a Hundred Thousand, or something not much short of that Sum, to the Cost of a first Class Ship of War.

The Result is, that as other Naval Powers are multiplying their Iron Clads, and as we cannot without Danger be left behind, we are obliged to add more to the Building Charges of each Year, for the present, than would have been required, if the world had chosen to go on content with the wooden Ships of former Times. We shall however soon come to the Length of our Tether, because we never shall see such numerous War Fleets as those which met each other in the great war with France, but we must keep Pace with France America & Russia, & we must not forget that the Fleets numerically smaller of the larger Maritime Powers will tell more effectively than in the olden Time, because of their modern Construction.

Then again both Services require Cannon and Muskets of improved Kinds.

Whatever may be the Number of men in our Army & Navy, it is absolutely necessary that they should be armed with the best weapons which the Ingenuity of the Day has been able to invent. But this is attended with much additional Expence ; and the Process involves continual & costly Changes—The old Smooth Bore Musket nicknamed Brown Bess, has long been discarded for the more expensive but far more efficient Enfield Rifle. The Enfield is found now to be much inferior to the Whitworth ; and both require alteration to make them Breach Loaders, in order to put our Troops on a Par with those of other nations. Then as to Cannon the Changes & consequent Increase of Expence are much greater. As to Field Pieces, I believe Sir William Armstrong has given us as good a Gun as any other Nation possesses ; and I fancy we have a sufficient store of Cannon of that Kind—We are also pretty well off as to the Kind, though not as to the number of heavy Guns, for Land Batteries at Home and abroad ; with the Exception of Batteries to Seaward against Ships. With Respect to such Batteries, and our Ships of War, as both are destined to act against ships Iron Clad, we are as yet unprovided with Cannon of Sufficient Power. There is little use in firing at an Iron Clad Ship, unless you can send a Shot through Iron Plates. We have risen from 24 Pounders, to 32 Pounders, & now have got 68 Pounders on Board our Ship, but the Smooth Bore 68 Pounder will not send a Shot through $4\frac{1}{2}$ Inch Iron Plates. We have had Guns tried at Shoeburyness which have smashed to atoms the strongest Iron Plates, but those Guns were single Specimens, and to supply any great number of them will cost a good Deal ; and yet, efficient guns it is evident, we must have.

You say that you include in your Statement of our yearly Expenditure the Sums applied to the Construction of our Dock Yard & other Defences. In one Sense that mode of reckoning is right, because that money has been spent in each Year ; But as regards the Burthen to be borne by the Nation in the Shape of Taxation for our yearly wants, that mode of stating the Matter is not correct, because the only Addition which the Cost of those works makes to the yearly Demand on the Taxation of the Country, is the amount payable in each Year for the terminable annuities granted in Exchange for the Loan, and this is a comparatively small Sum. You say that you think that Parliament will require that the Expence of any further Portion of the defensive works recommended by the Commissioners, beyond those Parts which have been begun, should be defrayed out of annual Votes, and not by a further Issue of terminable annuities.

I should hope that Parliament would not on this Point reverse a Decision deliberately made, and overset the fundamental Principle on which the whole Scheme was framed ; and indeed the Proposal of such a Change would only be tantamount to an indirect Invitation to Parliament to stop the Completion of the Works ; and as that is true of Fortifications, which is true of Mechanics, that nothing is stronger than its weakest Part, it would be very unwise to leave incomplete a System of Defence recommended as an Intirety. We are often told by financial Critics that the Concerns of a Nation ought to be managed on the same Principles as those of private Persons ; it is often impossible to do this, but with Regard to these defensive works we have strictly done so.

When a Landowner wants to make some great & expensive Improvement on his Property, by draining or building Farm Houses, or the like if it does not suit him to throw the Burthen upon his yearly Income, which would perhaps much distress him, he borrows the Money by an arrangement, under which he repays the Principal with Interest in a stated number of years by annual Payments ; and this is reckoned and admitted to be good Management. In the same way if a Coal Mine is to be opened, a Harbour Made, or any great and expensive Work undertaken, the Individual, the Joint Stock Company, or the Corporate Body concerned, raise the amount by Loan, to be repaid by annual Instalments, & Improvements are thus made, which otherwise could not be accomplished. This system has been adopted as the Foundation of the Scheme for our Dockyard & Arsenal Defences, and by means of it, we shall have been enabled to add greatly to our National Security, without any great Addition to the Demands on the Taxation of the Country.

The Conclusion then to which I would come is that when the Cabinet meets we ought to consider our Naval & Military Establishments, and to fix this amount with Reference to the wants of the Service and the general Interests of the Country and not with Reference to any preconceived adoption of any particular arithmetical numbers.

248   *Gladstone to Palmerston*

Hawarden

Oct. 22. 64.

I thank you for the very full statement contained in your letter of the 19., although I regret that I should have given you the trouble of writing at such length, and I am still more concerned to find there is not so much agreement between us, as I had hoped to find. Indeed I fear I have not conveyed clearly to your mind the gravity of the situation in which I stand.

I will not touch upon the subject of the franchise ; nor on the opinion I have given with respect to any future loan for the purpose of erecting fortifications, since neither of them are essential to the matter in hand.

My belief is that our expenditure for defence is larger than the reasonable wants of the country require. Collaterally with this it appears to me that it is your own personal popularity, and not the public conviction or desire, that would alone keep the Estimates at their present high level : that their amount will be injurious to the Government and the party when the Dissolution arises : and that the Finance Minister is, after the Prime Minister, specially responsible for the sum total of these estimates taken together.

A few months ago, you remarked (and I do not in the least complain of it) upon my having at various times referred to the hope and the possibility of prospective reduction in these estimates. But that which you probably took for a sign of restlessness was in point of fact the only condition upon which consistently with my sense of duty I could be a party to the proposals we have made. I have been able to become responsible for them partly in consideration of the wants, partly (besides other grounds) of the opinions and feelings of the nation : but not as proper to form at their present height, the standard for our peace establishment. I do not now see either in the public mind

Up

that alarm, or in the state of affairs that ground for apprehension, which could alone justify their continuance unabated.

You state that the expenditure of a country must be governed by its wants, and not tied to a sum chosen in the abstract. I quite agree that no such reference to an abstract standard should be forced upon the Executive Government : but I do not think it unreasonable that the Government itself should look at totals as well as items.

To illustrate my meaning, I will refer to what took place in 1861 and 1862. Sir George Lewis, on becoming Secretary of State for War, proposed an increase in the Army Estimates. This would have required an increase in taxation ; and after a debate it was abandoned : but Sir George Lewis said that the reductions would have to be considered as postponements, and that the Estimates would have to be increased in the following year. However, in the summer of 1862, the House of Commons passed a Resolution in favour of retrenchment : and in the autumn of that year, without Debate, the War Department and the Cabinet, instead of increasing the Estimates as the ' wants ' of the country required, reduced them by a million.

The truth is, I believe, that the measure taken of these wants in detail, being of necessity vaguely dependent upon opinion, is also very elastic, and yields to the pressure of circumstances one way or the other.

And that considerations of finance enter into the determination of the sufficiency of this or that amount of provision, is very plain from your letter ; for you state that " our naval and military establishments " are " as efficient and large as, in time of peace, it would suit the finances of the country to make them ". For " as large as " I simply substitute " larger than " : and I add, that the wants of the country admit of their being abated.

Your conclusion is, that when the Cabinet meets we ought to consider our establishments and fix them with reference to the wants, and the general interests of the country. But I demur to the assumption that the usual process of going over the heads of service and the names of stations is one adequate to the occasion. The state of information in a Cabinet never allows this operation to be a searching one. No serious reductions are ever effected by it. They are effected so far as I have seen, by the Departments, in obedience to a general sense of the Government, the country, or both, that retrenchment ought to be effected. Especially, in such a debate, the person holding my office is powerless. To be able to do any kind of justice to his case, he ought to have all the aptitude and knowledge of an experienced War Minister, and an experienced First Lord of the Admiralty ; which never has happened, and hardly can. Simply to abide therefore the issue of a discussion of this kind, begun without a foregone purpose of retrenchment, would be the direct abandonment of the aim with which I have written to you. Nor, though I do not look for sweeping changes, should I thus have troubled you for slight cause.

While, however, I deprecate taking issue upon each head of expenditure in particular, I will refer to one, and at once avow my belief that a vote of 70,000 seamen, with a reserve of 15,000 men which I understand is susceptible of easy, early, and considerable increase, is decidedly beyond the measure of the wants of the country for its peace establishment : especially at a period when the transition to more costly armament promises a large reduction in the number of men requisite to supply a given amount of destructive power. I am not aware of having used the words that there ought to be a considerable reduction of Army and Navy : but it appears to me that the Vote to which I refer ought not to be nominally but sensibly lessened.

To revert to the subject of my declarations respecting prospective retrenchment. I assure you that all along the question for me has lain not between saying what I have said, and saying less, but between saying it and saying, or doing, more. The arguments in your letter, as I fear I must interpret them, (glad as I should be to find myself in error,) point to some twenty five millions a year as about the proper charge for the defence of this country in time of peace, such peace as this latter half of the nineteenth century affords. Unfortunately, this would be the very proposition, to which I could not honourably subscribe ; nor could I, without disloyalty to you and our Colleagues, conceal my belief (be it shared by others, or be it not, a point of which as yet I know, and have sought to know, nothing) that the next Session cannot arrive without bringing the matter to a point. At the same time, what I ask is simply a step in a downward movement : and nobody is, by taking one such step, committed to any other.

249   *Palmerston to Gladstone*

Bds. 28 Oct 64

You mentioned in a Letter some Time ago, a Scheme which has been suggested according to which the Government would buy up all the Railways, but not with a view to work them by any Department of the State but in order to arrive at a large Reduction of the present Charges. This seems to be a large Question, seeing that the Capital laid out in our Railways amounts to about Four Hundred Millions and that the working Expences are about Sixteen Millions a Year. We should like however to hear the Nature of the contemplated arrangement. Supposing however that all existing Railways could be acquired by the Public, how would you deal with Railways to be henceforward made ; for we may be pretty sure that we have not yet come to a *Ne plus Ultra* in the Construction of Railways.

250 *Gladstone to Palmerston*
Hawarden
Nov. 2. 1864.

In reply to your question about the mode of dealing with new Railways, I will not attempt to be very specific, because the whole subject is in too crude a state for it. But I may venture to say that if once the matter were to be settled for the old ones, the question of the new would raise little or no difficulty. Indeed we have *now* an Act known as 'Gladstone's Act' which authorises the State to buy at 25 years purchase of the nett receipts, 21 years after opening, any Railway authorised *in or since 1844*. This Act would not be *easy* to apply to all the lines of the last twenty years, but simply because it has not been attended to in the private Bills of the Companies or by the Committees. Were its policy formally adopted, there would be no difficulty in choosing the form of application. The surrender or sale of the railway tax is an engine of considerable power which we have in our hands.

A more serious difficulty I think would have to be encountered in making provision for extension of stations and other permanent improvements in the lines while under lease. But I suppose this might be dealt with in a manner resembling that which prevails with regard to agricultural holdings where the landlord furnished the capital and the tenant pays a full interest. Or again they might be done by the lessees with consent, and valued over to the landlord at the expiry of the term.

The question is indeed as you say a large one, and will require a great deal of sifting before an opinion can be formed.

I think it looks a hopeful one, but I would not say more. Sometime ago I wrote a letter to Mr. Glyn containing a rough outline : if you think it will not try your patience too much to peruse I will send it you. Of course it was written 'without prejudice' and without pledge. I think Mr. Glyn, with his long head, thinks well of the subject generally.

251   *Palmerston to Gladstone*

[Quoted in *Glad.* II. 139]

Broadlands 7 Novr 1864

I ought sooner to have answered your Letter of the 22nd of last Month which I am sorry to see does not tend to bring us nearer to an agreement upon the theoretical Matter to which it relates. I say theoretical because it can hardly be said that you stated any practical Question for Consideration.

It is not unnatural that our abstract Ideas as to National Expenditure should not be quite in Accordance ; because Chancellors of the Exchequer are apt to form their Conclusions from Considerations connected peculiarly with the Concerns of their own Department, while those who from Time to Time are at the Head of the Government must feel it their Duty to form their Conclusions upon a general view of the Interests of the Country at Home and abroad to look to its Security at Home, and to the maintenance of its proper Position among the nations of the world. A most important Element in these Considerations is the amount of naval and military Stores and other means which in any given year the Circumstances of the Country may appear to require. No satisfactory Result upon such Matters can be arrived at without a careful Investigation of the Details out of which aggregate Totals, and proper Conclusions are to be formed ; and such Results must grow out of the Deliberations of a responsible Cabinet, all the Members of which must share in Common the Blame of any Mischance which Default on their Part may bring about. But if I rightly understand the Drift and Statements of your Letter, you are disposed to propound a Theory which would hardly be consistent with the Position of the Constitution ; that is to say that a Chancellor of the Exchequer, who according to your Statement cannot have the aptitude and knowledge of a War Minister, or of a First Lord of the Admiralty, is nevertheless to be entitled, without that knowledge, to come to an arbitrary Conclusion as to the proper amount of our Naval and Military Establishments : and to impose his Will upon the Government of which he is a Member, upon the Plea that his Honor requires that his opinions whatever they may be, should be blindly adopted, under Pain of those Consequences which his Colleagues would of Course deeply regret, and would be very sorry to be compelled to accept. To justify such a Theory the Chancellor of the Exchequer ought to add to a Supreme Control at Home a Command over all those Transactions and Schemes of Policy of the other Nations and Governments of the World upon which our Course must from Time to Time necessarily depend.

Your general Position is, that the Government ought without any Examination of Details, to decide that great Reductions must be made ; and that the Heads of the Army and Navy should be told to find the means of making such Reductions ; and that the Cabinet ought not to listen to any Statement of national wants, and alleged Requirements of the public Service ; as an Example you say that you are justified in declaring that the Number of our Seamen and Marines is too great, and ought to be reduced. My answer is that neither you nor I can properly affirm or deny that Proposition, until we have heard from the first Lord of the Admiralty a Statement of his views on this Matter, and from the Minister for Foreign Affairs what are likely to be our Relations with foreign Powers. But the Navy Estimates furnish an Example of the Fallacy of your System for arriving at Conclusions. There was no Point in our Naval Expenditure, upon which theoretical Reformers who were above going into Details, had a more positive and dogmatical opinion than on the Dockyard Expences, which they all pronounced to be abuseively excessive. Well, a vacancy having happened among the Lords of the Admiralty I filled it up by appointing Stanfield, a declared Economist, and the Mover of the Retrenchment Resolution, and he was turned loose into the Dockyards, and devoted several Months to a diligent Investigation of all the Details connected with their Management. The Result, as I have been informed was that although he introduced many useful and important Improvements into the System of Management & Account, he was prepared to state that he did not find the aggregate amount of Money spent on the Dock Yards greater than the public Interest required it to be. When Stanfeld was unfortunately obliged to resign, I appointed as his Successor Childers, a Man likely to scan with a rigid Eye the civil Expences of the Naval Service.

I quote these appointments as a Proof that I have no Desire to maintain Expenditure which can be shewn to be unnecessary.

You say that my arguments tend to point to some 25 Millions a Year as the proper Peace charge for the Defence of the Country in Time of Peace, at least of such Peace as we have had in this latter Half of the nineteenth Century.

What I meant to say is, that there is no fixed amount of Charge nor of Army and Navy which for this Country can be stereotyped as permanently fit to be abided by when we are actually engaged in some great war. My Position is, that from year to year those Circumstances may change, upon which the Decision as to those amounts ought to depend ; and I certainly expressed my Impression that in the present State of Things in various Parts of the world, we are not likely upon Examination to find that any great Reductions in the Charge of our Establishments can safely be made. If the Contrary could be shewn I should be as glad as any Body Else.

You say that you think that it has been my personal Popularity, and not the Conviction or Desire of the Nation that has kept up the Estimates at their present Amount. In this it appears to me that you misplace Cause and Effect. This British Nation is not one that would be disposed to bear unnecessary Burthens out of Regard for any individual Man ; and if I have in any Degree been fortunate enough to have obtained some Share of the Good will and Confidence of my Fellow-Countrymen, it has been because I have rightly understood the Feelings and Opinions of the Nation, and because they think that I have, as far as any Scope of Action of Mine was concerned, endeavoured to maintain the Dignity and to uphold the Interests of the Country abroad, and to provide for its security at Home. You may depend upon it that any Degree of Popularity that is worth having can be obtained only by such means and of that Popularity I sincerely wish you the most ample share.

Somebody whom I do not know sent me the other Day the inclosed Extract from a newspaper. I do not want to have it again. The Evidence of the French Admiral quoted in it is of old Date, but you may rely upon it that the Spirit which it breathes lies at the Bottom of every Frenchman's Heart, and that nothing but sufficient defensive Strength on our Part can render our Relations with France satisfactory and secure. The Nile Trafalgar, the Peninsula, Waterloo and St. Helena are Records which Frenchmen would gladly seize fair opportunity of counterbalancing.

(*Enclosure*)

Nothing is to us more certain than that, if the aristocracy of this country means to remain so, it must show that it *is* so, in the original sense of the word. Its members must show themselves our best leaders, wherever we require leadership. And we do require it, at this moment, in the art of war, applied to the sacred duty of national defence. We require that it shall be rendered impossible for any man, without incurring the derision of Europe, to repeat such language as Vice-Admiral Dupetit-Thouars applied to this country in the following passage of his evidence before the Committee of the French National Assembly appointed in 1849 to investigate the whole question of naval organisation and government :—

" In my opinion, though England may have erected fortifications, a disembarkation is always possible there, and for it we should not require line-of-battle ships. We should only require seventy corvettes, and some avisos of auxiliary steam power. *With these means, without the English having power to resist, we could throw 70,000 men on the coast of England,* who could never have resisted an invasion. All invasions of England have been crowned with success. She is not prepared for a land war, as we could make it. THE ENGLISH HAVE NOT THE WARRIOR SPIRIT, and if we have war with them, we should have but one thing to do, that is, *a landing.*"

Englishmen !—this has been said of England, before a select and grave committee of French legislators—and before the epoch some persons regard as the origin of all menace towards us—that of the restored empire. Since that epoch, there is no question France is infinitely more able, should her Ruler be willing, to plan and execute the invasion of England.

There is increased reason therefore for preparation as against increased power, handled with increased secrecy and decision ; though there is hitherto no reason to ascribe hostile intentions to the present Ruler of France against this country. M. De Montalembert has described him as steadily adhering to the *unpopular* English alliance. But to have steady allies, or friendly neighbours in France, we must not depend on the good will, or good judgment, of her Emperor. To be respected where nothing but force is so, we must in force render ourselves respectable.

252   *Gladstone to Palmerston*

11 C[arlton] H[ouse] T[errace]. N. 9/64.

I join in your regret that this correspondence has failed to attain its object : but you will I am sure forgive me if I decline to be bound by your statement of the theory which you have construed out of my letters.

I have not referred to the aggregate of military and naval expenditure as more than an item among others in the case for consideration, and a very important one, and that particular one on which the person holding my office embodies a judgment more highly responsible than on the details of distribution and such as to warrant my expression of opinion.

Having thought that last year there might have been a further reduction, and considering as I do that the circumstances which have happened this year tend towards diminution and not increase of charge, I am guilty I think of no disrespect to my Colleagues of the War Department or the Admiralty if I have formed an opinion, subject of course to correction from new occurrences or from disclosures if such were to be made, that charge ought to be reduced in the forthcoming estimates.

You speak of a Chancellor of the Exchequer imposing his will upon his colleagues : but it has been my desire to avoid the renewal of struggles in the Cabinet such as might wear that unseemly aspect, which in great part led me to make this appeal to you, and to apprise you at so early a date of the drift of my convictions, and views.

In order to make them acquainted with what has passed I would suggest your circulating this correspondence.

It will now ` ith your permission remain to see what are the figures when they are prepared and produced. The two lines *may* be found to coincide ; your letter, though it does not encourage, yet does not require me to abandon the hope that those figures may be such as to satisfy my moderate and reasonable expectations, having a full regard as you say to the real events of the country, and not forgetting I would add the topics named in my first letter and especially the manner in which the Resolution and declarations of 1862 encouraged the House of Commons and the public to estimate one view of the probable necessities of the State.

253   *Gladstone to Palmerston*

Hawarden Dec. 19. 64.

You lately asked me what arrangements would be made, in the event of the purchase of the Railways by the State, to regulate the making of new lines from time to time.

I will now try to answer that question : but only in the general manner suitable to the early stage which the subject at large has as yet reached. We do not yet know that there are reasons sufficiently cogent to make it right for Government to address itself to what would certainly be a great undertaking, even *presuming* the absence of insurmountable working difficulties. All therefore that seems requisite at present is that there should be no such difficulty staring us in the face, and thus cutting short all consideration of the question.

The case to which your inquiry refers is as follows. We suppose the Railways

1. To have been purchased and taken into possession by the State.

2. To be worked by Commercial firms or companies as lessees from the State, in conveniently divided groups. And probably

3. To be superintended, as far as the State is concerned, by a Board or Department having a qualified independence of the Executive Government.

And of course we speak of Railroads such as are now commonly understood by the term.

I do not see any system perfect in the abstract for regulating the construction of new Railroads after the supposed change.

But I think it plain at the outset that there would be a great mitigation of the present evils.

The chief, or among the chief, of those evils are

1. The existence of powerful bodies, fighting for what they call territory against one another and against all new comers.

2. The temptation to start and carry new schemes, not with a *bonâ fide* prospect of commercial success, but in order to be bought up by the powerful bodies in possession.

The bodies in possession have vast interests, dependent on the investment of their large capitals in perpetuity.

But these bodies would altogether disappear from the field. In lieu of them would be found small and manageable bodies, strictly traders, having only short terms of interest and not concerned in competition which was only to take place after the expiry of their leases.

The rapid growth and development of traffic is I think conclusive to this point, that the leases [to] be given, in the state of things I suppose, would commonly be very short leases, not for more than five or seven years, perhaps for less.

Under these circumstances the causes, the *irritamenta*, of the two great evils I have stated in connection with the question of new lines, would of themselves be greatly mitigated, or would in many cases wholly disappear.

Perhaps I have understated the case : for I do not see why the Working Companies should be allowed to appear at all as opponents of new lines : and it would be ill worth their while to adopt the circuitous and uncertain course of working through third parties.

All new lines would be proposed in good faith and not in order to be bought up. On the one hand they would not be subject to the present Railway Tax, and so far the inducement would be increased to the extent of about ten per cent on the nett return *per annum*. But on the other hand, of course, they would take only a long lease, instead of a perpetuity.

Usually, no Company would start on this basis, with the burdensome obligation of finding all its capital in order to compete with Companies that found only a working capital, unless there was a good prospect of return.

If this be so, it would be right not to permit the State to oppose the line before the Committees of Parliament on the ground of injury to its property.

In the greatly easier task, they would then have to perform, it appears to me that the Committees would be fully competent ; and they might have the aid of a Report from the Railway Board, founded on the merits, and not on the consideration of competition.

Considering all this, and considering that the day of new trunk lines, properly so called, has almost gone by, it seems to me that the practical upshot of the arrangement as regards new lines would to some extent be this ; that new loops, branches, and so forth, would fall into the category of *new works* ; for which at the instance commonly of the Lessees, the State would find the capital when they were approved, and charge a remunerative interest upon it.

Perhaps it may suggest itself, that the property of the State invested in the Railways would under the rather open system I have in view be seriously damaged by new lines. But I would reply 1. Parties would have little inducement to spend their money on *bad* schemes. 2. Committees would protect the State property against wanton and needless damage. But 3, which I regard as by much the most important, experience seems to have shown that if the old companies had had the wisdom to sit still and be content, with their own ground, and to let competition take its chance, they would in general have judged most wisely for their own interests. And that is what the State should incline to do.

I will only add that I am endeavouring to obtain materials which will enable you and the Cabinet to judge whether we ought to institute any inquiry with a view to clearing the ground for this question.

I am sorry your inquiry has brought upon you so long a story.

254   *Palmerston to Gladstone*

Broadlands 23 Decr 64

I have received your Railway Scheme Letter of the 14th. It is impossible to form a Judgement of your Plan till the Details are made out, but I own it appears on the first Blush a wild and more than doubtful Project.

To buy up existing Railways would I apprehend require an outlay of Two or Three Hundred Millions, striking off liberally from the Four Hundred Millions invested in them all that belongs to Litigations and other Expences not represented by any existing value. This would be a permanent addition to the National Debt and would be tantamount to a loan of that amount, and a Creation of such much additional Stock.

What would be the Effect of such an operation upon the value of existing Stock?

But then the Interest of this new Debt would be provided for by leasing the Railways to Companies for short Periods of 5 or 7 years. The Debt would therefore be permanent, the sources from whence Interest would arise would be precarious and temporary, and those sources might fail. Would Companies incur the Expence of creating all the requisite Plant for a Railway, of which they had only a 5 or 7 years Lease?

You may be prepared to answer all such objections and to clear away all such Doubts, and therefore I await your Development of your Scheme.

255 *Gladstone to Palmerston*

Hawarden
Dec. 24. 64.

My letter of the 19th was directed to answering a question which you had put upon the assumption of a certain state of things, not to showing that that state of things ought to exist. If you refer to it you will see that this is its effect. I mentioned short leases as an obvious means of dealing with the difficulties of apprehended competition, when that offers a formidable prospect to lessees for a long term. There is no difficulty as regards rolling stock. It can be hired even now : and in the supposed state of things it is probable that it would be often, perhaps generally, hired.

The question whether the present system and scale of railway charges would admit of great reductions with a loss comparatively small, and if so under what circumstances, is one which has great claims to examination, on account of the vast benefits that such a reduction would offer to the community. If this question were answered in the affirmative, then the benefits might be had by purchase of the railways ; I will not say it is impossible they might be had without it.

Perhaps I was wrong in taking hold of the subject at the wrong end, instead of waiting until I could have stated the general reasons which seem to recommend, and which may perhaps be found to compel, our looking at it at all. But I did it in order to answer your inquiry.

The question of purchasing the mass of railway property is a vast and staggering one ; and there is much between looking at it and adopting it. The mode in which I was myself disposed to contemplate it was one which would have created no debt in lieu of stock, and which only looked to a distant reversion. But the other plan may very likely be forced into discussion.

Wishing you a happy Christmas and New Year.

256   *Gladstone to Palmerston*

11 C[arlton] H[ouse] Terrace
Jan. 28. 65

The differences of opinion among us to-day in regard to Naval Establishments, especially as to force, were considerable : but the feeling was generally against me : and I freely allow that the concessions made, inadequate as I think them, were made in a spirit of conciliation, for which I am sincerely thankful, and which I desire to meet in a corresponding spirit. I therefore, although reluctantly, agree to the Navy Estimate.

257   *Palmerston to Gladstone*

Brocket 31 Jany 1865

You must have had a disagreeable journey & voyage to and from Osborne, but I hope you found The Queen in good Trim.

I am glad you acquiesce in the Navy Estimates as proposed at the Meeting of the Committee of Cabinet, I do not think that the House of Commons or the Country will expect any greater Reduction of Force than that which is thus agreed upon.

With Regard to the Income Tax about which something was said, it seems to me that a Reduction of that Tax to Five Pence, would imply no Decision as to its continued Retention or intended abolition but that a Reduction of it to Four Pence would generally, and inevitably be looked upon as the Result of a Decision come to by the Cabinet to abolish it altogether as fast as that can be done. Now no such Decision has been come to by the Cabinet ; and there are several Members of the Cabinet, among whom I may mention Russell, Somerset, Charles Wood and myself, who think that there are other Taxes which it would be better to reduce or to abolish whenever a farther Remission of Taxation may be advisable. Objections have been raised to the Income Tax, but which is the Tax against which some Objection or other cannot be raised. It is said that the Income Tax is unequal in its Bearing ; but quite as much so, if not more, are the Taxes on the Consumption of articles in general use. The Taxes on Tea, Sugar, Coffee Beer & Spirits take away a far larger Proportion of the Spendable Means of the Poorer Classes than of the richer Classes, and in this Point of view they may be said to bear unequally on those who contribute to pay them. The Income Tax bears exclusively upon the upper and middle Classes, that is to say upon those who have an Income contradistinguished from daily or weekly Wages, and the labouring Classes, the most numerous Part of the Nation are intirely exempt from its operation.

> When Gladstone gleans from each Man's Yearly Hoard
> How much more free the workman than the Lord
> Safe Skulk the Poor beneath the taxing Power
> And leave the wealthier Grumbler to look sour.

One advantage of the Income Tax is that it has a Tendency to become more productive every year by Reason of the progressively increasing Wealth of the Country, without

WP

any addition to its Pressure upon those who pay it, whereas some of the Taxes on consumable articles are liable to Fluctuations from Cause beyond Controul and which evade Calculation before Hand. I should say therefore that when we have got the Income Tax down to Five pence, it would be best whenever a further Remission of Taxation can be made, to lighten by a diminution of Taxes on articles consumed by the lower Classes the Pressure of Taxation upon that Portion of the Community.

258   *Gladstone to Palmerston*

11 C[arlton] H[ouse] T[errace]
Feb. 2. 65.

I am sure we shall be agreed in thinking that the time has not yet come for the definitive discussion of the financial proposals of the year. What I shall now therefore say is fragmentary and without prejudice. It will be said without foregone conclusions upon my own views, and with a due sense of the importance that would attach to yours : yet I must express the hope that you will not allow yourself to arrive at positive conclusions without being in full possession of all the facts that bear upon the case.

I admit to you, in the fullest manner, that no step ought to be taken, in the present state of opinion within the Cabinet, which would in any manner involve, as a matter virtually decided on, the ultimate extinction of the Income Tax. And this is a large admission, when it is recollected that about half of us were members of a Government, which formally submitted a plan for that purpose, every such plan bearing more or [less] resemblance to a promise ; and which at the time took great, I might perhaps say vital benefit from that plan. I must add that during this Parliament the undivided responsibility of abandoning that plan, or, as men say, of breaking that promise, has been borne by me ; of which I make no complaint.

Together with this admission, I will ask leave to contest strongly the proposition on that the reduction of the Income Tax to 4d in the £ would imply a decision to abolish it : but that leaving it at 5d would be leaving the question open. Now to reduce a tax to a very low point *may* under certain circumstances be to mark it for abolition : but to keep it up to a certain magnitude absolutely precludes abolition or keeps it out of view. Let us see which of these propositions applies. The Income Tax at 4d would yield more than £5,120,000 : a larger sum than the seven penny Income Tax of Sir R. Peel. How can it be said that in levying *such* a sum we should become pledged to the abolition of the Tax ?

Now look at the other side. The Income Tax at 5d would yield near £6,200,000. Such a sum would be an unmanageable sum. I venture to lay it down positively that the tax *must* be brought down below that level ; before its abolition can become the subject of a financial measure. Therefore to leave it at that point is not to leave its abolition an open question, but to keep it absolutely *out of reach*. In proof of this I claim the authority of the Budget and Act of 1853, adopted by Parliament on our proposal. By that Act, as a necessary preliminary to the abolition, it was provided that the Tax should first be brought down to a yield of between four millions and a half.

I think there is very great force in what you say as to indirect Taxes. But the pinch of this part of the case is serious. It would be possible to give away (in round numbers) a million with admirable effect, by repealing the duties on corn, wood, and pepper. But I have not ventured to suppose that the Cabinet would at this moment look in the face the repeal of the duty upon corn, which is a purely protective though small duty, and quite indefensible. If I am wrong in this, I admit that it materially affects the argument. Another difficulty is this ; that, by force of agitation and otherwise, the special wish of the House of Commons is set upon making a serious sacrifice of revenue to repeal

the Fire Insurance Duty : which, as Buildings and Furniture, is much more strictly a tax upon property than the
Income Tax. We could not hope to encounter this successfully (I fear) by acting boldly on the Income Tax. And a
further point is this. Our indirect taxes on articles of consumption, except those I have mentioned, are now balanced
and adjusted with reference to one another in such a manner as to make partial interference at the best difficult, and,
in the face of a Malt Tax Repeal agitation, very hazardous.

Now this is not a statement of a case : it is rather a sample
of reasons why no case should be stated. A Budget could
not, even at the proper time, be given in a letter.

On one point however I must, as a matter of individual
feeling and honour, reserve my freedom : I must remain
free to consider for myself whether, and up to what point
and in what circumstances, I at least am bound, whatever
view others may take, to use the first opportunity, offered
by a legitimate and full consideration of the public interests,
for placing Parliament in the condition, in which we told
them that they actually *were* in 1853 : a condition of freedom to determine whether they will, or whether they will
not, part with the Income Tax.

259   *Gladstone to Palmerston*

Feb. 6. 65.

I would suggest that these papers might be printed for
the Cabinet : & that Capt. Hore might be asked to explain
what the *infanterie de la marine* really are : & that the guns,
tonnages, or both, of the English and French Navies, &
tonnage of the U.S. Navy, might be added.

260   *Palmerston to Gladstone*

94 Piccadilly
1 March 65

General Knollys[1] came to me yesterday to speak about
the Prince of Wales's affairs & to ask how he could be
_____
[1] General Sir W. T. Knollys.

assisted to defray the Expence of his intended visit to Ireland to open the Exhibition in the name and on Behalf of the Queen. I asked Genl. Knollys how much would probably be required, he said about a Thousand Pounds ; and I inclose a Note confirming that Calculation. This Sum is too small I conceive for a vote of Parliament, because it would give Rise to Discussions, and from what General Knollys said, I fear that we may by & by have an application for more extensive assistance ; on the other Hand as this Expence will be incurred, for what may be termed a public object, not sought for by the Prince, and not Part of his own Natural Expenditure might we not when the Expence has been incurred and the amount has been ascertained, pay that amount out of Civil Contingencies ?

261   *Palmerston to Gladstone*

These Letters of Mr. Cobden's are like his Speeches Illustrations of the Saying that shallow Streams run with the most violence and the most Noise. The Letters are full of Inconsistencies Contradictions and Forgetfulness of Facts. He compares the British Navy with the Federal one, forgetting that England on his own admission ought to have a Navy superior to that of any other naval Power in Consequence of her smaller Condition and her beyond sea Possessions, whereas the United States are purely Continental with no Possessions beyond Sea, and they are now at War with an adversary without a Fleet that could put to Sea and thus all that the U.S. want are Ships to blockade and attack certain Confederate Sea Ports.

Then he says that to take Steps for putting Canada in a State of Defence is irritating to the United States & provoking a war, but he would have us build Iron Clads and make cannon to defend ourselves against France, not thinking it must be presumed, that such steps would irritate France & provoke a war.

He thinks the being stronger on the Lakes would give Canada to the Federals, but the Lakes are not Canada. They are only a Road to Canada, and a less convenient Road than if they were so much Dry Land. To land in Canada is not necessarily equivalent to conquering it. He is always railing at the aristocracy & alleging that our Institutions are maintained for and exclusively filled by them. This is very snobbish, and fitter for a Shop apprentice in a Back Alley in the City, than for a Man engaged in public Life and with a Knowledge of the practical working of our Constitution. What was the aristocratical Parentage of Nelson of Clyde,[1] of Lyndhurst,[2] of Campbell[3] of Thompson[4] of Longley,[5] of Peel ?

It is worthy of Remark that in the two Nights Discussion of Navy Estimates the Complaints made were not that we have too many Sailors, but that we have injudiciously reduced the Number of Sailors Boys and Marines, and that we have not Iron Clads, Guns, and Docks Sufficient for our wants.

12/3-65   P.

262   *Palmerston to Gladstone*

94 P[iccadill]y 27 March 1865

I understand that you propose to state Tomorrow on Dillwyn's Motion about the Irish Church your personal views upon that Matter, as an Individual but not as a Member of the Government—I do not know what your personal views on that matter are, but is it possible for a Member of a Government speaking from the Treasury Bench so to sever himself from the Body Corporate to which he belongs, as to be able to express decided opinions as an Individual, and leave himself free to act upon

[1] Field-Marshal Sir Colin Campbell, afterwards Lord Clyde.
[2] John Singleton Copley, Lord Lyndhurst, Lord Chancellor, 1827–30, 1834–5, 1841–6.
[3] John, first Lord Campbell, Lord Chancellor, 1859–61.
[4] Archbishop of York, 1867–90.   [5] Archbishop of Canterbury, 1862–8.

THE OLD SENTINEL

PAM. " Don't you meddle with things you don't understand, young feller."

different opinions, or to abstain from acting upon those opinions when required to act as a Member of the Government taking Part in the Decisions of the Body ? And if the personal opinions so expressed by him should not accord with the personal opinions of any Colleague sitting on the same Bench, would not such Colleague be placed in the Dilemma of either being understood by his Silence to acquiesce in the opinions so expressed, or of stating in what Respect his own personal opinion might differ from yours, and thus bringing unnecessarily and prematurely before the Public Differences of opinion between Members of the Government, before those Differences had been made known to, and considered by the Cabinet, and before any attempt had been made to find any Means of bridging the Difference over, supposing it to be practicable to do so.

263   *Palmerston to Gladstone*

94 Piccadilly
27 March 1865

We shall adjourn Parliament on Friday 7 April to Monday the 24 April and I believe you have fixed your Budget Statement for some Day very soon after the End of the Easter Holy Days. Several Members of the Cabinet would much like to hear from you before the adjournment the general outline of your intended financial arrangements, as there would scarcely be Time for Consideration and if necessary Discussion as to any Part of them during the short Interval between our Meeting after Easter Holy days, and the Time when you have fixed for your Statement to the House of Commons.

I do not know what Surplus you may reckon upon nor how you propose to apply it, but it seems to me that if you should have the Means of giving a Part of the Surplus to a Reduction of some Portion of the Malt Tax, it would be well taken by a large Portion of the House of Commons, would give much Satisfaction to the rural Producers, and to the working Class Consumer and would relieve our Candidates in many Places from injurious Embarrassment at the General Election.

264   *Palmerston to Gladstone*

94 P[iccadill]ʸ. 29 March 1865 [1]

The accompanying Paper was given me a few Days ago by the Ghost of Poland as Zamoysky calls himself.

He said he hoped that we might be willing to make some addition to our annual Polish Grant. I do not think his Expectations run very high.

265   *Gladstone to Palmerston*

Carlton H. Terrace

March 29. 65.

You may remember the experiment made at the Admiralty in January of submitting the *abbozzo* of a Budget —Nothing could succeed worse.

For the last three years, the financial proposals have been, in the main, of a simple character and the facts once given, neither I nor the Cabinet have had much difficulty in determining upon them.

This year I presume that we shall all be disposed to adhere to the general basis which we adopted in 1863 and 1864, and to make as fair a division of relief as we can between direct and indirect taxation, or between taxation on property and taxation on consumption.

But when we come to apply the principle it involves for the present year, two questions of difficulty arise : one the Malt Tax the other the Fire Insurance Duty.

As regards the latter we shall not have before the recess the results of the experimental measure of last year relating to Insurance against Fire on Stock in Trade : and without this I could hardly venture on framing a proposal to the

[1] Possibly 1863.

Government with regard to this question, which is one involving very important public interests. But again, until I know what are the facts, and the bearings of them, with respect to Fire Insurance, I do not know what I ought to propose to the Cabinet about Income Tax.

With regard, however, to the Malt Tax, the case is different. I am engaged in collecting the facts, and I hope to be in possession of them next week, in time for the Cabinet to determine before the recess, if you think that convenient, the very important question, whether anything should be attempted (in conformity with your apparent leaning) as to Malt, or whether we should give a reduction of duty on some other important article of consumption. For, though I do not yet know the surplus, I have little doubt it will be such as to admit of a considerable operation upon indirect taxes ; while I am not able to say it will be such as to admit of our dealing with Malt compatibly with the principle of equitable division which I have assumed.

My own opinion is that *all* would be best judged at once ; and that if there is not sufficient time between our reassembling and the 27th, then we had better postpone the Budget to the 31st : but I am quite willing to yield, and bring forward the question as to Malt, immediately before we separate, if you think it best. In any case I have no doubt I could get the *whole* ready so as to write it to you before you come up again.

Please to let me know your wishes.

266　　　　　　*Palmerston to Gladstone*

[In Lady Palmerston's writing]

Brocket Hall

18th. April

I have got the Gout in my Right Hand and cannot write —I scarcely expect to be able to go to London on Saturday for the Cabinet—I wish you would send me confidentially an Outline of your financial Scheme—We settled last week not to attempt Malt but Brand told me some time ago that you had a vague Notion of laying a tax on the Owners of Houses. This I think would be highly objectionable. It would bear grievously hard on the Duke of Bedford on the Duke of Portland Sir John Sutton on Sir John Ramsden and a great many other House Owners, who pay Income Tax on the Rent they receive from their House Property. It would impose a double Tax upon them which would be most unjust. If the Tax was to be imposed on the occupiers of Houses it would be equally unjust and would set all the 10 Pound Householders against us. I am very much against any shifting of Taxation.

267   *Gladstone to Palmerston*

Secret.   Brighton
                                    April 19. 65.
I can now give you an outline, but still in round numbers, of the plan I propose to lay before the Cabinet on Saturday.

The knot of the case lies in the Fire Insurance Duty. There is an improvident mode of proceeding, and a provident one ; the former in some respects the simpler and more attractive : I shall propose to pursue the latter.

The Surplus may be taken at £3,750,000. We have agreed not to propose a reduction of the Malt Duty. I should lay down as the bases of the plan these two rules.

1. We will as heretofore make as fair a division as we can of relief between direct and indirect taxation.

2. Whatever relief we give to direct taxation, or taxation upon property, we will give through the medium of Income Tax.

1. Because it is most widely felt.

2. Because the surrender is not final but can in case of need be retracted.

I take then

1. Taxes on Commodities
   a. Tea, reduced from 1 /– per lb to 8d
      will cost for the year 1865–6 .   £1,200,000
   b. Duty on Pepper, repealed . ⎫
   c. Duty on Wood   do . . ⎬   355,000
                                                          ⎭

                                              £1,555,000

2. Income Tax.

Reduction of 2d (the second penny subject
to the condition that the House shall adopt
a *provident* plan with regard to Fire Insurance) will cost in all £2,600,000, but in
1865–6 only £1,650,000
         Add Customs remissions .   1,555,000

                  Together . £3,205,000
and, as you will see, very equally divided.
     The Surplus was . . £3,750,000
But we have given away . 3,205,000

          There remains .   545,000

and now we come to Fire Insurance.

It happens that in the case of this duty we have a considerable sum to take up in *arrears* : and also the change in
duty cannot well take effect before July 1. Our danger
therefore is not for the *present* year, since our remission will
only operate during *half* of it, when we reckon the arrears :
but for *next* year, which will have to bear the brunt of the
whole remission.

The plan more or less indicated by the proceedings of
the House of Commons on Fire Insurance, which I call the
improvident plan, is to place the duty uniformly at the rate
of 1 /6. In figures, it would work probably as follows.

Present Estimate of receipt
from this duty £1,450,000
Nearly one half years
revenue would be re-
ceivable say .   .   .   £700,000
One half at the reduced rate
with an allowance of 10
per Cent for increase   .   450,000   1,150,000

Loss   £300,000

1. This would leave us with an exceeding small surplus of only £245,000.

2. It would not effectually enlarge the practice of Insurance—nor permanently settle the question.

3. It would still leave the anomaly of the agricultural exemption still a very gross one.

4. It would not induce those, who now ' insure themselves ' to abandon the practice.

5. It would still leave us liable to the present system of paying a heavy percentage to the Companies for collection.

6. It would not extensively let in new Companies so as to increase competition and reduce premiums.

7. But especially, it would cast a serious burden on the year 1866–7. To see the importance of this, it is necessary to consider the prospects of that year as they are *already* affected.

a. The 2^d off Income Tax will cast on it a
loss of £950,000
b. The changes in Customs Duty a further
loss of   130,000
c. The China Indemnity will fall off by   .   200,000
d. Fire Insurance instead of £300,000 as this
year, would cause a loss of £550,000   .   550,000

Loss in 1866–7   .   .   £1,830,000
Hardly any of it recoverable.

Now if we adopt a plan of this kind, not only should we have no margin for any possible increase in expenditure which the public service might require, but, unless the harvest be a good one, of which at present we know nothing, the new Parliament would probably have to begin its work with fresh taxation.

The only mode of rescuing ourselves under *this* plan, from the first charge of improvidence, would be to reduce only 1d instead of 2d on the Income Tax. Such a course would be very unsatisfactory to the country : and besides the plan would still be an extremely bad one.

I now proceed to explain what I have termed the provident plan. It would be to proceed by way of *commutation*.

Of the £1,460,000 of revenue from Fire Insurance, near £1,200,000 is derived from property, viz. buildings and furniture ; and the House in condemning the *medium* through which this tax is levied as a bad one should not be understood to condemn the substance of the tax as a tax, especially on buildings, which have of late years received immense relief.

I propose

1. To reduce the Fire Insurance Duty from 3/- to 4d : and thus effectually set insurance free—escaping *all* the objections (as I could easily explain in detail) to the 1/6 plan.

2. To levy a rate of 4d in the £ upon all rateable buildings—payable by the landlord, since insurance is a landlords charge, except in cases where by agreement it has devolved upon the tenant.

The present insurance duty is equal to an Income Tax of 7d in the £. This will be reduced to less than 1d. Also there will be 2d in the £ off the Income Tax. That will be a relief of between 8d and 9d. Against this we should impose 4d.

If we took the 1/6d plan, we should reduce 7d to $3\frac{1}{2}$d and (probably) take 1d off the Income Tax : so that the relief would be nearly equal in both cases to the owner of *house* property when insured. It would not be very unequal even with 2d off the Income Tax.

The Financial effect would be as follows :

Revenue as now computed (= supra) .	.	£1,460,000	
Six months receipts as before	£700,000		
Fire Insurance at 4d say	.	200,000	
Buildings Tax at 4d for half a year	500,000	£1,400,000	
	Loss	£60,000	

For 1865–6 this would leave us a surplus of near half a million, instead of one under a quarter of a million.

But the principal difference would be in the effect next year.

The eighteen penny plan would as I have said throw a burden of £550,000 on 1866–7 in respect of Fire Insurance.

Under the commutation plan, that account would stand as follows.

Fire Insurance Revenue, unreduced .	.	£1,460,000	
1866–7 Fire Insurance at 4d probably . . }	£225,000		
Buildings Tax	100,000	1,225,000	
	Loss	£235,000	
Instead of a loss of		£550,000	

In short, we should thus get out of this very troublesome and critical question, with Fire Insurance effectually liberated from every serious burden, without any sacrifice of a valuable tax upon property, and without too much clipping the moderate surplus of this year, or throwing so very large a burden on the next.

This statement is of course a very abrupt one : but I hope you will find it intelligible in the main points.

I shall be at your command on Saturday morning should you desire any explanations.

268   *Gladstone to Palmerston*

Brighton

Ap. 20. 65.

I am very sorry to hear you are suffering from gout.

Your letter reached me last night after mine was gone.

I agree in your objection to the shifting of taxation but I am sorry that my proposal reached you in a form, in which it *could* not be understood. From my letter of yesterday you will see that the plan does not shift taxation, as respects all who insure their houses and buildings ; but only retains under another name, and saves, a portion of what we now receive from them. The man who now insures, whether he be landlord or tenant, would under the plan pay a tax of under 5d on his house or work or factory, receiving at the same time a relief of above £9.

Landlords such as those whom you name I apprehend bind the tenant to insure. In the cases of annual, short, and very small tenancies, the landlord I believe commonly insures.

Few have to insure who are not payers of Income Tax : even those few would pay less than 5d instead of paying 7d.

I hope this may make the matter clear to you. Although however I think the Government is bound, in dealing with this important revenue, to propose a plan really effectual for the purpose in view, and to avoid one which would make a needless and final surrender of a part of our taxation upon property, I would not ask you or the Government to *force* this plan upon the House of Commons by the *ultima ratio*. We might I think proceed in this order :

propose

       1. The Customs remissions

       2. The 4d rate on Buildings

       3. The remission on Fire Insurance

       4. The Income Tax.

We should then keep it in our own power, if the House refused the 4d rate, to regulate the reduction of Fire Insurance and the Income Tax accordingly.

But I never was more clear in any financial question, than as to the goodness of the one plan, and the badness of the other.

Our fiscal system already levies much less off Buildings than (I believe) any other : and they have no claim whatever to relief, except as regards the *Income Tax* which works hardly in regard to them.

I use the word Buildings because a large fraction are not inhabited Houses but Works, factories, Warehouses and the like.

If you would like to see me I would run down for an hour tomorrow. Otherwise I shall hope to hear from you on Saturday morning ; unless, best of all, you are able to come up.

269   *Gladstone to Palmerston*

Private   Downing Street
                                        Ap. 22. 65

I have nothing from you today. The Cabinet has discussed pretty fully the various plans for the Budget. The difficulties really inherent in the question before us are serious : but we have I think now pretty well got them in view.

I will tell you very briefly the different views

1. Income Tax 2d off—Tea duty 4d off—some minor changes—Fire Insurance uniform 1/6d instead of as now 3/- and 1/6. Rejected unanimously on account of the unsatisfactory and ineffectual nature of the reduction on Fire Insurance

2. Income Tax 2d off—Fire Insurance Duty to 1/- —Tea duty to 8d (i.e. 4d off) The effect of this would be (while £5 out of every £7 is raised in this country off trade or consumption) to give £5 out of every £7 of our surplus not to trade and consumption but to property. I objected to it strongly. Grey and some others the same. No one *presses* for it.

THE ELECTION BUDGET

GLADSTONE. " I think, Mr. Bull, we may now reckon on *your* support ! "

3. Income Tax 1d off—Fire Insurances to 1/- —*Tea* to 6d, and some minor changes of the same kind. This plan I am willing to propose, without thinking it the right one.

The Cabinet *generally* are very desirous to have 2d off the Income Tax.

4. Income Tax 2d off, Tea to 8d and some minor changes. Fire Insurance reduced to 4d (Cardwell's amendment is, to abolish it, or reduce it to 1d) a charge of 3d in the £ laid on all rateable buildings.

This plan I think the best and soundest on the whole.

We have decided nothing and there are various shades of opinion. We propose that if you think fit you should call a Cabinet on Tuesday at such hour as you think fit and I suppose at your house. Of course I do not attempt to state arguments.

I hope you are making progress.

270   *Palmerston to Gladstone*

Brocket Hall
April 23ᵈ

I am much obliged to you for your Letters. I mean to go to town tomorrow afternoon and will have a Cabinet at my house Tuesday Morning—I abstain from discussing at present the various plans mentioned in your letters,—but on one point I have the clearest possible Opinion and that is that having a Surplus of 3 Millions & a half to dispose of, it would never do to attempt to impose a new Tax upon persons or Property.—If you will allow me to say so some of your best financial arrangements lost much of their deserved popularity, by the ingenious Complications with which they were accompanied.—It will be well on this occasion not to fall into the similar mistake—As to direct & indirect Taxation our remission ought to be fairly divided between them but we are not bound to make that division on Algebraical Equation.

Xᴘ

271   *Gladstone to Palmerston*
                              11 Carlton House Terrace
                                       June 17. 65.

Allow me to recommend to you for careful consideration, with reference to the see of Chester now vacant, the name of Dr. Jacobson, Regius Professor of Divinity at Oxford.

He is at the moment the Chairman of my Election Committee, but it is on other grounds that I place his claim before you, and grounds which I think you will fully appreciate. . . . He has long been known as a man of earnest piety, enjoying universal respect. He has never been a party man : in his general opinions he may be described as mildly liberal. . . .

272   *Palmerston to Gladstone*
                              94 Piccadilly
                                 22 June 1865

I have written to The Queen to recommend the Son of Jacob for the vacant Bishopric of Chester and as soon as I hear from her I will let you know, in order that you may yourself inform Dr. Jacobson of his intended Promotion.

By Rights it is the Turn of Cambridge to furnish a Bishop, and the more so as the vacancy happens by the Death of a Cambridge Man,—but I thought that the appointment of Jacobson would be useful to you with Reference to your oncoming Election and so Cambridge may well wait for next vacancy.

273   *Gladstone to Palmerston*
                              11 Carlton House Terrace
                                       June 22. 65

I must not lose a moment in thanking you for your most kind and handsome note. I am sure that this appointment will do you no dishonour ; rely upon it, the children of Abraham and Isaac, and the children of all the tribes of this

many-coloured world will be well pleased, but by the manner
of doing the act, you confer upon me a great obligation.

Of course I keep the secret.

274   *Palmerston to Gladstone*

94 P[iccadill]y. 24 June 65

I have this from Jacobson ; he has probably written to
you also to the same Effect.

I have no Doubt that he will make a very good Bishop,
& win general approval.

(*Enclosure*)

Christ Church, Oxford,
June 23, 1865.

My Lord,

The Chancellor of the Exchequer informs me that you
have, with the approval of Her Majesty, desired him to
offer me, in your name, the See of Chester.

I beg leave to request that your Lordship will accept my best
Thanks, and allow me to assure you that, with God's Help
and Blessing, I hope to do my best to justify the Selection.

I have the honour to remain
Your Lordship's faithful & obliged Servant
WILLIAM JACOBSON

The Viscount Palmerston
&c   &c   &c

275   *Palmerston to Gladstone*

94 P[iccadill]y 17 July 65

Granville has just been here & has read me your Letter.
I should like to put off a Decision as to an increased allowance to Princess Mary[1] till the Cabinet meets but the
Gentleman[2] has proposed and the Lady must give an
answer & that answer depends on our Decision. It seems
to me that to raise Princess Mary's Income from £3000 as a

---

[1] Princess Mary of Cambridge.   [2] Francis. Duke of Teck.

Spinster to 6000 as a Matron is so reasonable and moderate a Proposal that I am quite prepared to undertake it on my own Responsibility. Derby & Disraeli would of Course support the Proposal.

It is said that Princess Sophia of Gloucester had £6000 a year as an unmarried Lady advancing in the Vale of Years. The real Fact is that £6000 a year is a very narrow Income for any Body who has the Misfortune of having Royal Highness attached to their name. But I believe the Duchess of Cambridge would be able by her will to leave something to her Daughter which would add to her future Means.

We cannot keep this matter open till we have searched for Precedents which would probably not be found.

276   *Gladstone to Palmerston*

I am much concerned to learn that you think it necessary to decide the question as to Princess Mary's Allowance without waiting for the Cabinet or having the precedents —I can only recollect that (I think) her sister has, given upon her marriage, *three* thousand a year. I apprehend it is, at least it may be, an entire novelty to fix a life Income for a Princess, and then to double or augment it on her marriage.

I hope that, if you take this step, you will endeavour to put it on some special grounds, to prevent its being drawn into a precedent.

With what you say as to the narrowness of an Income of £6,000 per ann. I quite agree.

What are we to say hereafter to the Queen's daughters? Surely you should not go to the figures of Princess Alice.

I write in extreme haste, just setting out, after my defeat at Oxford, for a short but sharp Lancashire campaign.

Hawarden
  July 18. 1865.

PEGASUS UNHARNESSED

277   *Palmerston to Gladstone*

94 P[iccadill]^y 24 July 65

I congratulate you on your Success in Lancashire though many Friends would have preferred seeing you still for Oxford.

I find I was going rather too fast ahead about Princess Mary. Six Thousand would be rather out of Proportion to other Grants and I believe that five that is to say an addition of two to what she now has would better preserve the alignment but we will talk of this when we all meet this afternoon.

278   *Gladstone to Palmerston*

Hawarden

Aug. 19. 65

I have read Mr. Hamilton's Report of the proceedings relating to the proposal of a general half holiday on Saturdays for the Civil Service, and I very much agree with him. . . . It may, I suppose, be altered in detail here and there at the discretion of the heads of departments, and as the state of business will permit : but it would be impossible I think to justify a general deduction from the time of work in the Civil Service to be followed (whether avowedly or not) by an increased charge upon the public.

In the Post Office you will observe while the half holiday is given (to certain classes) the annual vacation is less.

It occurs to me that it might be well to have some inquiry made as to the comparative amount of time given by the Civil Service to the public, & by the clerks & others in great non-public establishments to their employers—such as the Bank, & some of the great private Banks, Companies, & Houses of business.

279   *Palmerston to Gladstone*

Brocket 23 aug 1865

These Reports are just what might have been expected ; no Employers of Labour like to give up any Portion however small of the Time of those who work under them ; and nothing is easier than to prove arithmetically that considerable Loss would be incurred by any Relaxation. This was the Line taken by Master Manufacturers against the Ten Hours Bill. If men were mere Machines which would regularly do a given Quantity of Work in a given Time like a Steam Engine such Calculations would be unanswerably decisive, but in considering such Matters we ought to bear in Mind that men are moral and intellectual agents, and that the work performed by them in a given Time, depends much on the cheerfulness & good will with which it is done, and that both Cheerfulness & Goodwill very much depend upon the Belief that those who superintend and direct have some Sympathy for the Employed, and a Desire to lighten their work as far as can be done, without Injury to Interests concerned.

I quite agree that it would not do in most of the Government offices to shut up at two every Saturday, but it seems to me that the Naval Principle of watch & watch might be adopted in most cases. That is to say that the Clerks should be divided into two, or into three Portions, one of which should successively, have the Saturday half Holiday unless urgent Pressure of Business should prevent it. This arrangement might be adopted experimentally from this Time till the Meeting of Parliament. Of course the Business of the office should not be allowed to get into arrear & such an arrangement could not form any Reason whatever for an increased Establishment.

280   *Gladstone to Palmerston*

Haw[n].

Aug : 28 : 65

The manner which you suggest for trying an experiment of the Sat[y]. half holiday seems to me the most hopeful. But I presume you would not think it wise to try such an experiment, until doing the thing in one form or other had been finally decided on, for it would be very difficult, to say the least, after making the concession to retract. And such decision I also presume you would not arrive at until after having consulted the heads of the political offices. I would therefore propose to turn to account the interval before the Cabinet meets by ascertaining the actual practice as to vacations and hours of work and holiday, and as to leave of absence, in the Bank and a few great offices of the class most nearly approaching to the public offices, and I write to Mr. Hamilton requesting him to cause this inquiry to be made unless he hears from you that you think it better not.

I wish I could feel with you that the half holiday is not likely to lead to increase of establishment. It might not do so, if the present hours of work are excessive : and reference to the practice of some other great employers would tend to show whether they are so or not.

281   *Palmerston to Gladstone*

Brocket 21 Sept. 1865

I send you a Letter which I have received from the Duke of Somerset, and which he has written in accordance with a Conversation he had with me here a few Days ago. There seems to me to be a great Deal of Reason in his Proposal and in the Grounds on which he rests it. The office of Civil Lord of the admiralty as he has now arranged its Duties, has become a very important one. To investigate & controul the Dockyard Expenditure is a Duty requiring not only much Labour & Devotion of Time but also much sagacity in its Performance and some Parliamentary ability to enable the officer to satisfy the House of Commons in Discussions upon Naval Expenditure which are, every Session becoming more frequent. We require therefore for this office a Man of ability, and we must offer something like an adequate Price for that Commodity. In former Times the Sea Lord of the Admiralty had nearly a Sinecure, his Duties being confined to passing a couple of Hours a Day in the Board Room doing little or nothing but sign Papers on Matters of Form. I hope you will make no objection to Somerset's Proposal, so that we may go into the Market with an offer which may be accepted. Childers though the best appointment we could have made to the Treasury, is a great loss to the Admiralty, and our Choice of Men to succeed him there is very limited. I have been in Communication with Brand and Somerset upon this. The Men we think the most likely to fill the office well are Goschen[1] Enfield and Fenwick of Sunderland. As to Goschen I fear he would not accept a subordinate office like the Lordship of the Admiralty even with the proposed Improvement, and it may admit of Doubt whether he would consider the offer as a Compliment. I imagine that he is largely engaged in commercial Pursuits which he would not give up for office, unless it were an office of some prominent political character. As to Enfield it may be feared that he would not be strong enough and might not carry sufficient weight with the House although one would not hastily come to that Conclusion. Fenwick I do not personally know but he is said to be a Man of good fair Capacity has an independent Fortune, and some acquaintance with Business, and he sits below the Gangway Do you know anything of him, and can you suggest any other good Candidate ?

282   *Gladstone to Palmerston*

Inverary
Sept. 29. 65.

Your letter reached me on Tuesday ; but I postponed my reply in order to inform myself on a particular point about the emoluments of the Civil Lordship of the Admiralty.

---

[1] G. J. (afterwards Viscount) Goschen, M.P.

I hear from Mr. Hamilton that down to 1852 the Civil Lord received an allowance, probably £200 per ann. for a house. I am rather doubtful whether this had been very long enjoyed.

It appears to me that if anything is to be done to improve the position, the best way wd. be to restore this allowance. But I confess my doubts whether even this measure is necessary, or wd. be prudent.

I understand that allowances for House Rent, taken away in 1852, were restored to the Naval Lords in 1854, on the ground of the difficulty which was found in obtaining the services of Naval Lords without such allowances. But you certainly cannot plead the difficulty of obtaining good service in an office, which, on the 3 last vacancies has been taken by 3 such men as Mr. Stansfield Lord Hartington and Mr. Childers.

Neither can it be said that the ordinary provision for representing the Admiralty in the H. of C. is defective. The Admiralty has often been represented by no less than 4 M.Ps.; rarely by less than 3 : and it has I think been a most unfortunate relaxation wh. has (quite recently I believe) allowed a body of Naval Officers to sit at & form the bulk of the board of Admiralty, no one of them having Parliamentary experience or responsibility. It has probably been due to accident : and when again a Naval Lord takes his place in Parliament, the Admiralty will be represented, even with a first Lord in the House of Lords by the Secretary, the Civil, & the Naval Lord. Sometimes I think 2 Naval Lords sit in Parliament.

I do not think an argument cd. be made for giving a Civil Lord a salary equal to that of our Under Secretary of State. It would I think be justly objected to such a proposition that our Under S. of State is not a mere Secretary of a Board, subordinate in 3 different ways, first to his Chief, secondly to the Board, thirdly to the representative of the Dep^t. in the H. of C., but that he often represents his

Dept. and that his salary has reference to this position and responsibility.

It seems to me probable that a proposition to raise the Salary of the Civil Lord to the level of an Under Secretary of State, wd provoke a motion fm the other side for a Committee to consider the numbers duties and emoluments of the offices of the Govt., held by the M.Ps and that such a motion wd be carried agst the Govt. A smaller proposal might have a chance of escape, but would not be free from risk. It wd be said with some plausibility, that, looking to the large provision already made (tho' by Choice we do not use the whole of it) for the representation of the Admiralty in Parliament any proposal of increase in that Dept., indicated an intention to make other proposals of a similar kind.

The office of the Civil Lord is evidently in excellent credit. Men accept it *because* of its serious duties, who wd not look at any one of those four very unsatisfactory offices, the Junior Lordships of the Treasury, and the Secretaryship to the Poor Law Board. The truth is, as it seems to me, that we want *more* offices of this kind, which represent the first step of the ladder in a creditable form : and men put their foot on the first step not so much considering what it is in itself as what it leads to. You have had at different times Lords of the Treasury who thought themselves aggrieved by being kept for several yrs in that position. The office affords them no adequate opportunity of proving their fitness for higher office : and this I think is the kind of mischief that calls for a remedy when the time comes to set about it. We want in the Ty. few hands, and stronger ones.

I admit that if the Govt. offices in the H. of C. were under review generally in order to bring about a closer adjustment of duty and emolument, it wd be found that various offices, with less duty than the Civil Lord's had greater pay. But I doubt the wisdom so long as we can see the office well filled of touching this inequality alone, in the sense of

increasing the charge upon the public, while we leave un-
touched other cases where the change wd be in the opposite
direction. The advantage seems to me very small, and the
risk not inconsiderable.

With regard to *men* for the office, I mentioned to you that
Hugesson was anxious for a change : and I think his
abilities are good : perhaps you wd think it worth while
to ask Brand about him. His office has given me no opportunity of judging what he is : and I take it that the Civil
Lordship requires more at this moment than it might do
at other times. I hear young Trevelyan[1] very highly spoken
of, and I shd think he was a man of energy as well as talent.
Enfield is certainly fit for a better place than the one he
holds : but I shd suppose the work of the Civil Lord to be
rather *rough* for him. To Goschen I suppose you will hardly
offer it. One man I can name to you with considble confidence at least for inquiry : Mr. Edwd Hamilton, the new
member for Salisbury, a distinguished Cambridge Mathe-
matn, a practical Australian planter, and a very able and
active man of high character. I feel sure he is worth in-
quiring about : I think he wd probably make a first rate
appt. I shd. suppose he cannot be less than 54 : but with
a ready capacity for business. I am sorry this is such a
long story. Of Fenwick I know nothing : beyond having
heard him speak like a man of business.

283   *Palmerston to Gladstone*

[Partly printed in *Ash.* II. 274-5]

Brocket 3 Oct 1865

I have this Morning received the inclosed from an
eminent Physician of Southampton.

The Report he makes of the Health of Helps[2] and of the
State of the Council office Establishment seems to me to
require immediate and effective action—I have therefore

[1] George Otto Trevelyan, M.P., just elected for Tynemouth.
[2] Sir Arthur Helps, Clerk of the Privy Council.

written to Helps positively to forbid his going to Balmoral and as it seems that his Second in Command Harrison is also knocked down by excessive work and as the limited Establishment of the Council office is clearly too small & weak for the daily work pouring in upon it, by Reason of these Cattle, Sheep & Pig Diseases together with a threatening of Extension to Horses, I have written to Waddington to request him to send some Home Office clerk to Balmoral to Officiate at the Council—For the way in which the Queen now holds these Councils a Stuffed Figure would do almost as well as a Man for Clerk of Council

I have also told Helps that as Head of the Government I authorize him to take without any Delay such Steps as may be necessary to procure additional assistance for his Office while this great Influx of daily Business continues to press upon it, and I have desired him to write officially to the Treasury to state the Case and ask for the proper Authority but not to delay getting the assistance. I have told him that I will write to you to ask you to give the necessary Directions for giving Helps an official sanction for the arrangement which he will propose but I have said that he ought not to delay taking the necessary steps for obtaining Relief by additional assistance.

284   *Palmerston to Gladstone*

Brocket 5 Oct 1865

Helps tells me that he has made arrangements which will enable him to abstain from any application to the Treasury.

I send you a Letter I have received from Baring of Home Office

285   *Palmerston to Gladstone*

Brocket 7 Oct 65

I do not foresee any Reason for calling the Cabinet together till the 10th of November.

APPENDICES

APPENDIX A

TEXT OF THE CORRESPONDENCE

In the case of letters from Palmerston to Gladstone, ' H ' signifies that the original is in the Hawarden Papers, ' B ' that a draft or copy is in the Broadlands Papers.

In the case of letters from Gladstone to Palmerston, ' B ' signifies that the original is in the Broadlands Papers, ' H ' that a draft or copy is in the Hawarden Papers.

1		B
2	H	
3	H	
4	H	
5	H	
6	H	
7	H	
8	H	
9	H	
10	H	
11	H	
12	H	
13	H	B
14	H	
15	H	
16	H	
17	H	
18	H	
18 (Enclosure)		B
19		B
20	H	
21		B
22	H	
23	H	
24	H	
25	H	
26	H	
27	H	

28	H	
29	H	
30	H	
31	H	B
32	H	
33	H	
34	H	
35	H	
36	H	
37	H	
38	H	
39	H	
40		B
41	H	
42	H	
43	H	B
44	H	
45	H	B
46	H	B
47	H	
48	H	
49	H	B
50	H	
51	H	
52	H	
53	H	B
54	H	
55	H	
56	H	
57	H	
58	H	
59	H	
60	H	
61	H	
62	H	B
63	H	
64		B
65	H	
66	H	B
67	H	
68		B
69	H	
70	H	
71	H	
72	H	
73	H	
74	H	

75	H	B
76	H	
77	H	
78	H	
79	H	
80	H	B
81	H	
82	H	
83	H	B
84	H	
85	H	
86		B
87	H	
88	H	B
89	H	B
90	H	B
91	H	
92	H	
93	H	
94	H	
95	H	
96	H	
97	H	
98	H	B
99	H	
100	H	
101	H	B
102	H	
103	H	
104	H	
105	H	B
106	H	
107	H	
108	H	
109	H	
110	H	B
111		B
112	H	
113	H	
114	H	
115		B
116	H	
117	H	B
117 (Enclosure)		B
118	H	B
119	H	
120	H	

Yp

121	H	B
122	H	
123	H	
124	H	
125	H	
126	H	
127	H	
128	H	
129	H	
130	H	
131	H	
132	H	
133		B
134	H	
135	H	
136	H	B
137	H	B
138	H	B
139	H	
140	H	B
141	H	B
142	H	
143		B
144	H	
145	H	
146	H	B
147	H	
148	H	
149	H	
150	H	
151	H	
152		B
153	H	
154	H	
155	H	
156	H	
157	H	B
158	H	
159	H	
160		B
161		B
162	H	
162 (Enclosure)		B
163		B
164	H	B
165	H	B
166	H	B

167	H	B
168	H	B
169	H	B
170	H	B
171	H	
172	H	
173	H	
174	H	B
175	H	B
176	H	
177	H	
178	H	B
179	H	
180	H	
181	H	
182	H	
183		B
184	H	B
185	H	
186	H	B
187	H	B
188		B
189	H	B
190	H	B
191	H	B
192	H	B
193	H	
194	H	B
195	H	
196	H	
197	H	
198	H	
199	H	B
200	H	B
201	H	B
202	H	
203	H	
204	H	B
205	H	
206		B
207	H	
208	H	
209		B
210	H	
211	H	B
212	H	
213	H	B

214	H	B
215	H	B
216	H	B
217	H	B
218	H	B
219	H	
220		B
221	H	
222	H	
223	H	
224		B
225		B
226	H	
227	H	B
228	H	
229	H	
230	H	
231	H	B
232	H	B
233	H	B
234	H	B
235	H	B
236	H	B
237	H	B
238	H	B
239	H	
240	H	
241	H	
242	H	
243	H	
244		B
245	H	B
246	H	
247	H	B
248	H	B
249	H	
250	H	B
251	H	
252	H	B
253	H	B
254	H	B
255	H	B
256	H	
257	H	B
258	H	B
259		B
260	H	

261	H	
262	H	B
263	H	B
264	H	
265	H	B
266	H	
267	H	B
268	H	B
269	H	B
270	H	
271		B
272	H	
273		B
274	H	
275	H	
276	H	
277	H	
278		B
279	H	
280	H	
281	H	B
282	H	
283	H	
284	H	
285	H	

APPENDIX B

LIST OF MINISTERS

Members of the Cabinet marked *	LORD ABERDEEN'S GOVERNMENT.	LORD PALMERSTON'S FIRST GOVERNMENT.	LORD PALMERSTON'S SECOND GOVERNMENT.
FIRST LORD OF THE TREASURY	*Earl of Aberdeen	*Viscount Palmerston	*Viscount Palmerston
LORD CHANCELLOR	*Lord Cranworth	*Lord Cranworth	*Lord Campbell (succeeded by Lord Westbury, 1861)
CHANCELLOR OF THE EXCHEQUER	*W. E. Gladstone	*W. E. Gladstone (succeeded by Sir G. C. Lewis, 1855)	*W. E. Gladstone
PRESIDENT OF THE COUNCIL	*Earl Granville (succeeded by Lord J. Russell, 1854)	*Earl Granville	*Earl Granville
PRIVY SEAL	*Duke of Argyll	*Duke of Argyll	*Duke of Argyll
HOME SECRETARY ..	*Viscount Palmerston	*Sir George Grey	*Sir George Cornewall Lewis (succeeded by Sir G. Grey, 1861)
FOREIGN SECRETARY	*Lord John Russell (succeeded by Earl of Clarendon, 1853)	*Earl of Clarendon	*Lord John Russell

359

	LORD ABERDEEN'S GOVERNMENT.	LORD PALMERSTON'S FIRST GOVERNMENT.	LORD PALMERSTON'S SECOND GOVERNMENT.
COLONIAL AND WAR SECRETARY	*Duke of Newcastle (succeeded by Sir G. Grey, Colonial Sec., 1854)	*Sidney Herbert (succeeded by Lord J. Russell, Sir W. Molesworth, Mr. H. Labouchere, 1855)	*Duke of Newcastle (succeeded by Mr. Cardwell, 1864)
FIRST LORD OF THE ADMIRALTY	*Sir J. R. G. Graham	*Sir J. R. G. Graham (succeeded by Sir C. Wood, 1855)	*Duke of Somerset
PRESIDENT OF THE BOARD OF CONTROL	*Sir Charles Wood	*Sir Charles Wood (succeeded by Sir Vernon Smith, 1855)	
SECRETARY FOR WAR	Duke of Newcastle	*Lord Panmure	*Sidney Herbert
SECRETARY AT WAR	*Sidney Herbert		
FIRST COMMISSIONER OF WORKS AND PUBLIC BUILDINGS	*Sir William Molesworth	*Sir William Molesworth (succeeded by Sir B. Hull, 1855)	
CHIEF COMMISSIONER			Henry Fitzroy
[NO OFFICE] ..	*Marquess of Lansdowne	*Marquess of Lansdowne	
SECRETARY FOR INDIA			*Sir Charles Wood
PRESIDENT OF THE BOARD OF TRADE	Edward Cardwell	Edward Cardwell	*T. Milner Gibson

	LORD ABERDEEN'S GOVERNMENT.	LORD PALMERSTON'S FIRST GOVERNMENT.	LORD PALMERSTON'S SECOND GOVERNMENT.
POSTMASTER GENERAL	Viscount Canning	Viscount Canning (succeeded by Duke of Argyll, 1855)	*Earl of Elgin (succeeded by Lord Stanley, 1860)
COMMANDER IN CHIEF	Viscount Hardinge	Viscount Hardinge	Duke of Cambridge
MASTER GENERAL OF ORDNANCE ..	Lord Raglan	Lord Raglan	
PAYMASTER OF THE FORCES AND VICE-PRESIDENT OF THE BOARD OF TRADE	Lord Stanley of Alderley	Lord Stanley of Alderley	James Wilson
CHANCELLOR OF THE DUCHY OF LANCS.	Edward Strutt	[Vacant]	
LORDS OF THE TREASURY	Lord Alfred Hervey F. W. Charteris John Sadleir	Lord Alfred Hervey Lord Elcho C. S. Fortescue	*Sir George Grey E. H. Knatchbull Sir Wm. Dunbar John Bagwell
LORDS OF THE ADMIRALTY	Vice-Ad. Hyde Parker Rear-Ad. M. F. F. Berkeley Capt. R. S. Dundas Capt. Alexander Milne W. F. Cowper	Rear-Ad. M. F. F. Berkeley Rear-Ad. R. S. Dundas Capt. Peter Richards Capt. Alexander Milne W. F. Cowper	Vice-Ad. Sir R. S. Dundas Rear-Ad. F. T. Pelham Capt. Charles Eden Capt. Charles Frederick Samuel Whitbread
UNDER SECRETARY FOR WAR	Frederick Peel	Frederick Peel	Earl of Ripon

	LORD ABERDEEN'S GOVERNMENT.	LORD PALMERSTON'S FIRST GOVERNMENT.	LORD PALMERSTON'S SECOND GOVERNMENT.
VICE PRESIDENT OF THE COMMITTEE OF PRIVY COUNCIL FOR EDUCATION ..			Robert Lowe
UNDER SECRETARY FOR INDIA ..			Thomas George Baring
UNDER SECRETARY FOR THE HOME DEPARTMENT	Henry Fitzroy	Henry Fitzroy	George Clive
UNDER SECRETARY FOR FOREIGN AFFAIRS ..	Lord Wodehouse	Lord Wodehouse	Lord Wodehouse
UNDER SECRETARY FOR THE COLONIES ..	Frederick Peel	[Vacant]	C. S. Fortescue
JOINT SECRETARIES OF THE TREASURY ..	Wm. Goodenough Hayter / James Wilson	Wm. Goodenough Hayter / James Wilson	H. B. W. Brand / Samuel Laing
SECRETARY OF THE ADMIRALTY ..	R. B. Osborne	R. B. Osborne	Rear-Ad. Lord Clarence Edward Paget
JOINT SECRETARIES OF THE BOARD OF CONTROL ..	Sir T. N. Redington / Robert Lowe	Sir T. N. Redington / Robert Lowe	
SURVEYOR GENERAL OF THE ORDNANCE	Lt.-Col. Lauderdale Maule		
CLERK OF THE ORDNANCE ..	William Monsell	William Monsell	

	LORD ABERDEEN'S GOVERNMENT.	LORD PALMERSTON'S FIRST GOVERNMENT.	LORD PALMERSTON'S SECOND GOVERNMENT.
ATTORNEY GENERAL	Sir A. J. E. Cockburn	Sir A. J. E. Cockburn	Sir Richard Bethell
SOLICITOR GENERAL	Richard Bethell	Sir Richard Bethell	Sir H. S. Keating
JUDGE-ADVOCATE GENERAL	Charles Pelham Villiers	Charles Pelham Villiers	Thomas Emerson Headlam
CHIEF POOR LAW COMMISSIONER	M. T. Baines	M. T. Baines	*C. P. Villiers
SECRETARY TO THE POOR LAW COMMISSIONERS	C. L. G. Berkeley	C. L. G. Berkeley	Charles Gilpin
Scotland—			
LORD ADVOCATE	James Moncrieff	James Moncrieff	James Moncrieff
SOLICITOR GENERAL	Robert Handyside	E. F. Maitland	E. F. Maitland
Ireland—			
LORD LIEUTENANT	Earl of St. Germans	Earl of St. Germans	Earl of Carlisle
LORD CHANCELLOR	Maziere Brady	Maziere Brady	Maziere Brady
CHIEF SECRETARY	Sir John Young	Sir John Young	*Edward Cardwell
ATTORNEY GENERAL	Abraham Brewster	Abraham Brewster	J. D. Fitzgerald
SOLICITOR GENERAL	William Keogh	William Keogh	Rickard Deasy
Queen's Household—			
LORD STEWARD	Duke of Norfolk	Earl Spencer	Earl of St. Germans
LORD CHAMBERLAIN	Marquess of Breadalbane	Marquess of Breadalbane	Viscount Sydney
MASTER OF THE HORSE	Duke of Wellington	Duke of Wellington	Marquess of Ailesbury

	LORD ABERDEEN'S GOVERNMENT.	LORD PALMERSTON'S FIRST GOVERNMENT.	LORD PALMERSTON'S SECOND GOVERNMENT.
MASTER OF THE BUCK-HOUNDS	Earl of Bessborough	Earl of Bessborough	Earl of Bessborough
VICE-CHAMBERLAIN	Lord E. A. C. B. Bruce	Lord E. A. C. B. Bruce	Viscount Castlerosse
TREASURER OF THE HOUSEHOLD ..	Earl of Mulgrave	Earl of Mulgrave	Viscount Bury
COMPTROLLER OF THE HOUSEHOLD ..	Viscount Drumlanrig	Viscount Drumlanrig	Lord Proby
CAPTAIN OF THE YEO-MEN OF THE GUARD	Viscount Sydney	Viscount Sydney	Earl of Ducie
CAPTAIN OF THE CORPS OF GENTLEMEN AT ARMS	Lord Foley	Lord Foley	Lord Foley
CHIEF EQUERRY AND CLERK MARSHAL	Lord Alfred Henry Paget	Lord Alfred Henry Paget	Lord Alfred Henry Paget
MISTRESS OF THE ROBES	Duchess of Sutherland	Duchess of Sutherland	Duchess of Sutherland

INDEX

Italic numerals—e.g. *2*—indicate references in Commentary.
Plain numerals—e.g. 2—indicate references in Correspondence.

365